A Game for Rough Girls?

The result of several years of original research, the book traces the continuities in women's participation since the beginnings of the game, and highlights the significant moments that have influenced current practice. The text provides:

- insight into the communities and individual experiences of players, fans, investors, administrators and coaches,
- examination of the attitudes and role of national and international associations,
- analysis of the development of the professional game,
- comparisons with women's football in mainland Europe, the USA and Africa.

A Game for Rough Girls? is the first text to theorise properly the development of the game. Examining recreational and elite levels, the author provides a thorough critique, placing women's experience in the context of broader cultural and sports studies debates on social change, gender, power and global economics.

Jean Williams is a Senior Lecturer in Education in the School of History and International Studies at De Montfort University, Leicester. She is a consultant to media and sports organisations including FIFA, and is currently involved in a major cross-national research project into women's football.

A Game for Rough Girls?

A History of Women's Football in Britain

Jean Williams

LONDON AND NEW YORK

First published 2003
by Routledge
11 New Fetter Lane, London EC4P 4EE

Simultaneously published in the USA and Canada
by Routledge
29 West 35th Street, New York, NY 10001

Routledge is an imprint of the Taylor & Francis Group

Typeset in Times New Roman by
Florence Production Ltd, Stoodleigh, Devon
Printed and bound in Great Britain by
Biddles Ltd, Guildford and King's Lynn

British Library Cataloguing in Publication Data
A catalogue record for this book is available from the British Library

Library of Congress Cataloging in Publication Data
A catalog record for this book has been requested

ISBN 0–415–26337–9 (hbk)
ISBN 0–415–26338–7 (pbk)

Contents

Plates

The following plates are between pages 106–7:

Tables

Acknowledgements

A number of individuals have assisted me in the course of the completion of this book. The research would not have started without the interest and enthusiasm of Wray Vamplew and has been sustained by colleagues Pierre Lanfranchi and Matt Taylor. Their contrasting personalities meant that I had access to advice, criticism, encouragement and inspiration by turns. My indebtedness to them is self-evident as I am neither a historian by nature or by nurture, however constructive the training may have been at the International Centre for Sports History and Culture at De Montfort University. While we agree that I do not think like a historian, we have agreed to differ about whether this is, in itself, a bad thing.

My largest obligation is to the women, men, girls and boys who participated in the research. They gave up their free time and welcomed me into their homes, clubs and social circles principally to celebrate their love of football and I have tried to capture some of their altruism and animation here. Collectors of women's football memorabilia to whom I am indebted include Gail Newsham, Jane Ebbage, Dr Colin Aldis, Sheila Rollinson, Peter Bridgett, Angela Henson, Elsie Cook, Winnifred Bourke, Nancy Thompson, Ali Melling, Clare Illand and Ruth Shuttleworth to name but a few. Obviously, though agreeing to help me, they do not necessarily share my opinions, so their generosity is all the more kind.

On a personal level my coach mentor, Jim Kelman, provided steadfast guidance, many an anecdote and generous advice. Jim is very much of the 'train hard and win easy' school and takes coach-education to the level of art form; typically with sayings oblique enough to make Eric Cantona and Sven Goran Erikkson envious, including: 'You can make a rabbit into a hard rabbit, but you can't make it into a fox.' Janet Sharman, entirely beyond the call of duty, helped with the layout and format of an early vision of the typescript. I am thankful for Janet's expertise and goodwill.

I would not have developed an interest in writing about football had I not had a considerable interest in the subject and though 'your friend in football' is a cliché, I have many acquaintances who I know purely through playing sport. Those individuals are too numerous to list so I prefer simply to express my appreciation and look forward to seeing them again soon.

I would, however, like to make special mention of those close to me who either actively dislike, or are not interested in football, particularly Lorna, Daryl, Deborah and Margaret, as they have lived through this project with me and now know rather more about the subject than they would like.

Finally, I would like to thank my family; particularly my parents for taking the trouble to provide me with four co-competitors (and my brothers and sister for expanding the squad). I could not have completed this project without the backing of my mother in the early stages; as one of my favourite later memories is of her riding a bike across a rickety bridge whilst almost in her seventies it is easy to see where I got my interest in physical activity from. In the circumstances it is hardly surprising that I grew up kicking a ball, racing go-karts, riding ponies, trying to be Olga Korbut and practising spin bowling. Though at the time we very much had the attitude that it was the winning, not the taking part, that counted, I have remained involved as an average amateur, rather than a successful specialist, ever since. In the period of writing up I also lost a close friend and team-mate, who, to the untutored eye, looked like the archetypal South American striker. However, Karl Lathbury's love of life was much more honed than his football skills and his generosity of spirit is missed to the extent that we now talk nostalgically of his scything tackles. My biggest personal debt, however, is to Simon who has provided patient and practical encouragement and support in this project, as in everything else, and it is to him that I dedicate this book.

Abbreviations

AIAW	Association for Intercollegiate Athletics for Women
BUSA	British University Sports Association
CAAWS	Canadian Association for the Advancement of Women in Sport
CAF	Confédération Africaine de Football
ESFA	English Schools Football Association
FACA	Football Association Coaches' Association
FA	Football Association [English]
FAI	Football Association of Ireland
FAW	Football Association of Wales
FAWPL	Football Association Women's Premier League
FIFA	Fédération Internationale de Football
IAPESGW	International Association of Physical Education and Sport for Girls and Women
IOC	International Olympic Committee
LFAI	Ladies' Football Association of Ireland
LTA	Lawn Tennis Association
MLS	Major League Soccer
NAIA	National Association of Intercollegiate Athletics
NCAA	National Collegiate Athletic Association
NIWFA	Northern Ireland Women's Football Association
NSSU	Namibian Schools Sports Union
PFA	Professional Footballers' Association
SFA	Scottish Football Association
SWFA	Scottish Women's Football Association
UAU	University Athletic Union
UEFA	Union of European Football Associations
USSF	United States Soccer Federation [abbreviation also used to denote US Soccer Foundation]
WCA	Women's Cricket Association
WFA	Women's Football Association

WFAI	Women's Football Association of Ireland
WNBA	Women's National Basketball Association
WRFU	Women's Rugby Football Union
WUSA	Women's United Soccer Association

Introduction

'The future is feminine', declared Joseph Blatter, the General Secretary of the Fédération Internationale de Football Association (FIFA), the international governing body of football, in 1995. This pronouncement in *FIFA News*, the official publication of the association, effectively included women players in the family of football on behalf of the worldwide community. At the same time, Blatter, arguably the most powerful man in world football at the time, was careful to distinguish their place within that family. Female players contributed 'a distinctive style of play, characterised by a certain elegance which has prevailed over a more robust impersonation of the man's game' (Blatter, 1995).[1] If the place of the announcement was significant, so too was the timing. There had already been two Women's World Cups (China in 1991 and Sweden in 1995) and the inaugural Olympic women's competition was scheduled for the Atlanta Games in 1996. Blatter's epigram captured women's football as successfully established and with tremendous potential for growth but was otherwise, and perhaps deliberately, vague.

Football as a sport, business and cultural trend is a highly visible aspect of popular culture in 'New Britain' and against this background a feminine bias appears highly unlikely. The competing rights of fans, professionals and investors are widely debated in the academic and popular press. In contrast, the entitlements of women players and administrators are not generally discussed. Most British people could name a male football star whether or not they consider themselves to be enthusiasts of the sport. The majority of self-confessed football fans could not name a female player. Such differences clearly pose a challenge to any assumption about football being either England's national game, or the world's most popular sport. What we have instead are various communities of players, fans, investors, administrators and so on with significant points of reference. Some of these groups work professionally in football, others volunteer their time and interest and, of course, affiliation and alliance network across this divide. The starting point for this project was to explain how communities of women football players are embedded within, and interact across, a surrounding cultural context over and above football as a sport or a business. Any analysis of women's football has to go beyond attempts by FIFA and national associations to engineer female participation. Indeed, one of the challenges for the apparently confused bureaucracies is that dealing with women as players proposes a series of working relationships across different football entities. Should women be fully integrated across the current structures or should they be treated as a distinct branch of the family tree?

The discussion in Part I begins by looking at the production of women's football culture. Women's participation at local, regional and national level is explored in terms of football's development, women's sport and social change to ask how we have arrived at this moment of obvious inequality in Britain. If the invention of tradition has been used to create communities and these practices transmitted by memory, then how can the production of culture in women's football be characterised? Chapter 1 outlines the construction of tradition in women's football before moving on in Chapter 2 to discuss community and, finally, in Chapter 3, memory. Part I as a whole argues that structural and organisational constraints shaping women's access to football are only a part of the picture and there is much more work to do in uncovering the meanings and values that women bring to playing the game in a culture of production.

Part II opens out the discussion to look outside football as a sport and a business in order to consider what is going on within it. By looking at the meanings that are given to football in equal opportunities legislation and in segregated employment opportunities for men I'm suggesting a shift towards wider questions about British culture. The marginalisation of women in football has yet to be contested in any sustained and systematic way, even by players themselves. The recent apparent increase of interest on behalf of women is embedded in a context of national, regional, ethnic, religious and linguistic affiliation and the expression of identity through forms of football. Women who choose to play the game are always in the process of translating and mediating these identities in addition to gender. How do the male/female and heterosexual/homosexual 'roles' and stereotypes that can be found in football translate into other, broader patterns of practice? What aspects will affect the potential professionalisation of football for women and how will gender, sexuality and the taboos around mixed contact sport create patterns which shape the presentation of women players to a potential audience?

Part II also questions the extent to which women's football can be understood to be a globally popular game. For the minority of women who choose to play, and for the majority who do not, football is more than a sport or recreation. FIFA and the Olympic movement, as professional and occupational communities, have given women's football a specific form through working practices that have been changed little by the incorporation of women into those systems. The resilience of the structures to change and to accommodating women as decision-makers is therefore another facet of the construction of women's football.

The discussion includes women making football cultures in other countries in order to highlight the typical and the unusual elements of the

English case. The aim is, first, to move away from the idea that women's football can be understood by the engineered and corporate perspective of national and international sports associations and second, to see what areas of continuity thread through the different case studies. How are the practices of various kinds of football for women shaped by these large sporting bureaucracies?

In summary, to comprehend the place of women's football in contemporary society it is necessary to consider the broader patterns that intersect with it. So the focus of this work is specifically about the construction of a women's football culture, but it is also about women's football within English culture. The 'politics' of football have been discussed as a struggle of consumption and production both inside and outside the corporate entertainment industry. In analysing both the past and the potential for women's football in the future, then the consequences of increased bureaucratic monitoring and intervention has to be set alongside the large degree of independence that the majority of players and administrators have enjoyed because this interference is so very recent. Women's football has been experienced in various ways: as a form of collective leisure, as a sports community and as an administrative category to name but a few. Women players have invented and defined football in specific forms, spaces and places. The distance between these sites and the interests and agendas of the bureaucrats is an issue that the book begins to address and one that future researchers will refine.

What are the components of women's football that the researcher should compile at any given period? In terms of methodology, I have tried to capture what is evident at women's matches, be they tournaments and league fixtures or impromptu games. It is very clear on these occasions that there are diverse aspects of women's football created across complex amalgams of identity including the way that people dress, behave, talk and interact. It is not, therefore, appropriate to use concepts and methodologies that in any way collapse differences or to introduce players via a series of labels as, say, 35 years of age, married with two children and living in the south. This will frustrate readers keen to draw conclusions about the social background of players but the intention is to allow simultaneously the participants to speak for themselves and in doing so, to criticise simplistic attempts to characterise the women's football community.

Oral history and ethnographic methods helped to compare the world of the participants with depictions of women football players. Quantitative evidence is part of this story but cannot, in itself, account for the reasons why women play football. Furthermore, an emphasis on this kind of analysis would deny the complexities that the study sought to capture and could be used to construct an uncomplicated picture of the increase in women's access to various aspects of football. In any case, my access to collections of data was usually through indirect means or personal introduction. The representations and perspectives which English society has of women football players, including the views of players and administrators, are not held in centralised archives as such and so the methodology reflects the topic itself.

There is more to women's relationship with football than academics have so far described.[2] What has never been satisfactorily explained elsewhere is a peculiarly English expression of contempt for women who play football. A contemptuous attitude may not only exist in England but it is for another work to describe the precise role of the exportation of the attitude. For this discussion, the perspective has persisted in one form or another for at least a century but has been juxtaposed in the last forty years by an increase in international and domestic interest in women's football. Though the major focus of the argument deals with events from the last forty years, an examination of the recent historical period would be incomplete without considering early development. Britain pioneered the first phase of women's football's during, and shortly after, World War I. The most eminent team, Dick, Kerr Ladies, travelled to Europe, Canada and the United States to play, and audiences of tens of thousands watched women's games. British women's football led the world at this time. The considerable spectator support and media interest from that period is noticeably absent in the present. At home, since the 1960s, large crowds and media interest are not big parts of the women's game but participation rates are considerably higher. At elite level, since the middle of the 1980s, the English national team has gradually become less successful and other countries have progressively overtaken them in international influence.

The axiom that has come to describe women's football generally over the last decade is that it is 'The fastest growing participation sport for women.' Early use of this phrase by the English Women's Football Association (WFA) in the press was instructive (Jardine, 1992). In some senses 1992 marked a watershed; the last of twenty-three years of WFA control before the English Football Association (FA) took control of women's football. The association had been formed on behalf of women and was mainly staffed by volunteers like Flo Bilton, Linda Whitehead and Sue Lopez. But in more significant ways it was a hand-over rather than a take-over. Since its formation in 1969, the association had been led by men who wanted the FA to acknowledge, accept and administer women's football. Sloganeering in the national press was good public relations but the WFA had acted as a pretty leaky umbrella for the sport since 1985. Members were repeatedly asked to leave the 'character assassination of bygone days to the past. Sadly for all of us it lingers on . . . we must start again and implement constructive policies. If we fail our number will decline further' (Stearn, 1987:1).

So the growth in numbers has been neither steady nor unproblematic. For example, the WFA introduced a national league as recently as 1991, the first in the history of English women's football and a crucial step in adopting the structures of the male game. Why and how did women organise play before this time? There seem to be two distinct but interrelated aspects of the idea of a 'fastest growing sport'. The first is that it emphasises consumption: women are *doing* football in increasing numbers we are told. The ways that women own, use and appreciate football are not incorporated into this narrative. The second is that this superficiality tends towards a discussion of an expression of female interest that is recent and has been successfully met.

Women playing football in increasingly large numbers is not a phenomenon specifically of the 1990s. Richard Holt's *Sport and the British* made a point which encapsulated the experience of players consulted for this research and which applied just as much in the 1920s as it did in the 1990s. His central theme is 'The extraordinary degree to which [sport] has been promoted privately . . . People have created their own kinds of pleasure through sport' (Holt, 1989: 346). How do women players view football? Blanket claims for a 'feminine future' and 'women's increased participation' imply that the experience of female players is in some ways similar. Did elite and competitive women and girls view themselves as part of a group of 'women football players' or as individuals?

There remains no single archive for women's football. The WFA minutes and materials were misplaced at the point of take-over or are otherwise unavailable. Records are scattered in various private collections and so it is perhaps unsurprising that some academics suggest that there has been little say about it as a sport, commercial undertaking or as a social activity. Previous accounts of women playing have fallen into two camps. Williams and Woodhouse (1991: 100) and later Holt and Mason (2000: 12) correlate the bureaucratisation of women's football with progress. The second approach has been to focus on the contentious aspects of women's football.[3] There have been a few very useful discussions of body image and sexuality from a European perspective (Fasting *et al.*, 1998) and in the United Kingdom (Caudwell, 1999). But the lack of readily available sources proposes questions beyond these lines of enquiry. For example, why is the number of women who play football important to particular agencies and individuals? There is considerable difficulty in knowing how many female players we are talking about at any one time. What is the relationship between the enthusiasts and the governing body of the day? Why is there no central collection of data?

Administrators, players, coaches and supporters of the women's game have been enormously generous with their time and access to collections of memorabilia during the writing of this book. If identifying these serious amateurs led to many a cross-country paper chase, the warmth of the reception always made the journey worthwhile. Meeting with them as individuals and groups has confirmed my view that the question of a community of women players with traditions and shared memories is an area with considerable scope for further study. The pursuit of physically competitive leisure outdoors by women in football is not just economically and geographically marginal but also culturally stigmatised. If these participants negotiate with the stereotypes in a sport played often in shabby and borrowed conditions, what kinds of pleasure have they created for themselves? It became increasingly possible as I pursued this question to talk about the construction of collective identities but it remains difficult to find examples of the transmission of imagined communities of women players in social and public memory. Some women just play, some also remember those who played in the past. Only a very few commemorate, write about and discuss past and present players.

Documentary evidence I examined in private collections included official reports, minutes of meetings, newspaper and magazine articles and photographs. Personal memorabilia included scrapbooks, programmes, correspondence, medals and other mementoes. The journey into the habitual spaces and places occupied by the women's football community followed leads provided by participant observation, formal and informal interviews and questionnaire responses. Even as a player of some years, I could not have predicted the pattern of these networks at the outset. Nevertheless, they have become one of the most significant aspects of the depiction of a women's football community at home and abroad in this project. The only interviewee who came to see me was a male professional player. My rewards for going to see the players included candid responses and unrehearsed practices that were, by turns, celebratory and stoical. If women players' relationship with their chosen sport was sometimes problematic, they were determinedly optimistic in pursuing solutions. The voices of the participants reflect this mix. Some players suggested the idea of a revival of women's football and others were unaware of the previous popularity of the sport. Either way, because of the general perception of football for females as untraditional, the place of the past in women's actions in the present is a recurring motif. Overall, the contributors highlighted a paradox of women's history: the players of the present era have had, in some crucial respects, to pioneer women's right to participate all over again. Because this has led to different structures of organisation and playing practices from the early popularity of spectator-supported events, the broader analysis will show that the organisation of women's football in England is informed by particular constructions of the social world which maintain the marginality of the sport.

The ambiguous status of women's football was evident in the ban by the English FA from clubs affiliated to the association and Football League grounds from 5 December 1921 to 29 November 1971 (Lopez, 1997: 254; Williamson, 1991: 25). The quasi-legal terminology of a 'ban' reflects a social taboo that is more enduring. Nevertheless, for over a century British women and men have spent many a dull hour on administrative tasks in order to make female football competitions viable. The families of those involved must also necessarily be affected by players' commitment to the game, though participants are more likely to incur costs than financial gain. What makes all this effort worthwhile? The term women's football operates sometimes as a metonym for the belief that female play *is* and *should be* different to male football. This is crucial to the way that women players are treated, but how fundamental is it to their perception of the sport?

Who are the women players? Who are the other stakeholders in this future? Should supporters of women's sport, football particularly, be encouraged by the implied inevitability of Blatter's claim? Some elementary points of reference have been established and the overall tone is one of cautious optimism in the first part of this book dealing with construction and representation of a culture of women's football in Britain. The discussion draws on oral sources to develop a history which includes players' diverse experiences at elite, competitive and recreational level to outline the disputed areas of community and control.

If Part I of the work celebrates an appropriation of football for women's own purpose, Part II is far less encouraging because the attitudes and actions of individual female players and coaches are placed in the broader scope of professionalism in football. The economic, geographical and cultural marginality of women in the world's most popular participant sport means that the recent proliferation of teams has yet to translate into the widespread popularity of spectator-supported female play in England and Europe. Part II places the English model of women's football as a link in an international chain of development in which the United States leads the way in terms of mass participation and elite achievement. In Namibia, in both respects, the sport for women is in its infancy. However, post-colonial sport outreach programmes, such as Voluntary Service Overseas initiatives, have spread at the same time that African women are developing their own formal and informal sporting infrastructures. However, at international level and within nations the ongoing reproduction of the broad division between football for women and men continues. This expression of difference is one of the theoretical issues that questions the idea of football as a globally popular sport for women.

A persistent feature of the scorn shown towards women who play football in Britain is the idea of transgression. Playing a supposedly male game is deemed a masculinising experience and some of our most respected sports writers indulge in this stereotype (Glanville, 1973; Powell, 1996). The following answers to the question 'Do you regard women's football as a separate sport to men's football, as a related sport, or the same sport?' reflect two ways in which women players negotiate a feminine form of football:

> Separate, because not many male teams actually come into contact with the women and don't do anything for the female game.

> I class it as the same game as it has the same rules. I think, though, men's and women's football is played in two different styles.

In most respects English women players are willing to reproduce the structures of male football because the frameworks appear far in advance of the women's game, from mass participation to professionalism. The rise of women's football since the 1960s has undoubtedly been affected by the increasing professionalism of male football during this era. An example of this has been England's recent revision of coaching qualifications, in line with other European countries. To quantify the effect of this change, the research traced women attaining each level of qualification over a four-year period by county of award. The number of qualified women coaches has declined in the late 1990s, in stark contrast to the rise in the number of women players.

In terms of analytical perspective, I wanted to illustrate the premises on which gender division in football is to be predicated. Gender in sport has a growing literature (Hargreaves, 1986, 2000; Messner and Sabo, 1990; Hall, 1996; Griffin, 1998). Gender as the socially constructed aspect of femininity and masculinity is evidently a key factor in an individual's experience of the supposed national game of England from, for example, school-based sporting policy to segregated employment for male players. Other elements are also clearly vital to the consideration of women's experience. Since football in its various forms is so clearly constructed to protect male dominance, the discussion sets out to weigh aspects of what might be called patriarchal behaviour. Though gender and patriarchy are useful frameworks for analysing women's play, the role of social class was more difficult to assess. In the first phase of popularity a defining aspect of women's play was access to relatively well-paid work outside the home and the consequent opportunity to pursue collective leisure. Women's football certainly shared aspects of English working-class leisure generally in that it was born of collective enthusiasm, largely neglected and unregulated by authorities until recently and continues to have a dubious social status. However, the women who play do not, by and large, express a feeling of oppression, compliance or political awareness as a result of their engagement. They express a sense of exhilaration and want to play a game that has the same rules and conditions as the standard form of football.

Women's access to any kind of equality remains hampered by structures that reinforce female football as primarily an amateur and voluntary leisure activity. One conspicuous point is that there are very few senior female executives involved in professional football, but the study of that situation lies beyond the remit of this discussion. Inequities within sport generally and football in particular may be relatively innocuous compared with other economic, social and cultural inequalities that women face, but sport has a particular way of highlighting the sex–gender distinction. In football as a professional sport, an industry, an educational specialism and so forth, women's access to opportunities at the highest level in mainstream bureaucracies is limited. In supposedly meritocratic systems, similarities between the sexes, fundamental individualism and equality of opportunity, the cornerstones of liberal feminism in its simplest form, appear to have a limited relevance. How appropriate is it then to pursue a liberal agenda in developing women's football? The idea of a meritocracy is therefore in need of evaluation. In order to push to more radical conclusions ideas of gender as they are enshrined in football have also been analysed – for example, the pernicious concept of the average man and woman.

Feminist researchers in sport have raised the problem of reflexivity; for example Hall proposes methodological strategies for pursuing research (Hall, 1996) and Griffin discusses the role of the researcher and subject (Griffin, 1998). Both suggest that academics should not withhold information about the research process from those who participate. In this study, memorabilia was particularly valuable when discussing public, familial and private memory as a way of involving the participants in moving from the particular to the general. Photographs, postcards, medals, cups, trophies and clothing became precious links between the past and the present, especially since many of those who played in the 1920s have died. Collection of the items also enabled comparison with the kinds of images, souvenirs and equipment produced in relation to the sport today. The discussion of these items helped to overcome the mistrust of me as an outsider. Being a woman player was enough to allow me access to groups of women players and to establish a warm dialogue but my role as researcher created some suspicion and resistance, especially nearer to the central administration. Such is the hold of the stereotype of transgression that many women players appeared obliged to present a respectable image. The compilation of many voices in women's football, of which mine is one, was crucial to this method.

The lack of schoolgirl football in Britain up to the present day cannot be overstated in preventing the expansion of the sport for the many, from which the few could emerge. Until recently, women regional league players who had not participated in organised football at school outnumbered those who had. This sounds rather bleak but the style of football administration arranged by women until the middle of the 1980s was not very successful both in international and domestic terms. In regional leagues the pragmatic and adult culture of women's football endures. More forceful demands for better playing conditions and more widespread acceptance have yet to be co-ordinated on any great scale. Players have been more concerned with participation than in forming pressure groups. For the researcher this posed a problem because of the dynamic with the participants. If they disavowed a support for feminism generally and specifically for developing a rights approach to (and through) football, how could their contributions be used to do just that? My response is first to form the various opinions into this work to suggest that women have not yet developed a sense of continuity and of history that is consonant with their contribution to the culture of football. Second, the argument outlines the systematic exclusion of women from positions of power within football as an industry and proposes alternative strategies in order to take the debate forwards. As with the memorabilia and information collected during the process of research, reciprocity is intended to reposition individual actions and social structures to suggest that major alterations to the way that we think about gender in football are required.

The stereotype that putting on a football strip indicates that a woman is a tomboy, a lesbian or looking to swap shirts with male onlookers raised particular questions. The interviewees were drawn from women's teams based in one of the national leagues and four of the regional leagues. Some clubs were created to express the sexuality or race of the participant and some reflected student or work identity including school, university, police, army or hospital teams. Jennifer Hargreaves, in her recent study *Heroines of Sport: The Politics of Difference and Identity* used the term 'members of a predominantly lesbian soccer team' (Hargreaves, 2000: 137). Her comments regarding the difficulties of accurately labelling and discussing the sexual identities of project participants struck a chord. The four teams overtly and positively celebrating lesbian identity who agreed to be part of this study suggested it would be a problem to propose that all the players registered for those teams identified themselves as non-heterosexual. As the chapter 'Sporting lesbians' in Hargreaves' book makes clear, gay sport is not a unified phenomenon (2000: 129–74). Nor are individual gay identities fixed and constant, as Jayne Caudwell explores in her work (1999: 393).

Another particular issue was the extent to which race, religion and culture affected participation. The FA has used school-based teams mainly constituted of Asian players for public relations purposes but this is relatively recent and sheds little light on issues of inclusion and exclusion.[4] It was not possible to locate a black or Asian female club, though youth club teams, which reflected the catchment area in which there was a white minority, were willing to participate. Rather than teams formed to express a racial identity, black and Asian players appeared to form significant minorities in teams at elite, representative and competitive levels. It was difficult, otherwise, to be more systematic in ascertaining the racial mix of teams. Playing with and against Muslim women reinforced my view that participation is a series of choices. Women from Muslim and other backgrounds who chose to be modest in their dress were able to maintain a covered head and to wear loose clothing in women-only and mixed situations.

A similar difficulty occurred in identifying and defining disabled players though participant observation enabled me to be aware of those who were partially sighted, had learning difficulties, were hearing impaired, wore prostheses and were subject to a number of temporary conditions from detached retinas to broken backs. In open competition the youngest player was 14 but it is not uncommon for players competing in regional leagues to be in their late thirties or forties: as a long-time player and administrator noted, 'Our back four have a combined age of 128.' The oldest current player who agreed to participate was 52.

The term 'player' therefore refers to a female who is either registered with the FA or signed formally to a team. However, in the case of school-age girls, participation in organised football under tuition, either in curricular or extra-curricular sessions, is included. Useful perspectives to supplement the players' views are drawn from international, national and regional administrators, coaches, medical staff and managers of women's teams. Women officials are not extensively considered. Though they participate on the field of play, the referee is an isolated figure, not playing the game as such. The recent policy in the Women's World Cup to appoint only female officials obviously gave those selected valuable international experiences but it also delineated women's football as a sphere for women. Women supporters to the male game and women who work in the football industry, except in cases where they are also players, coaches, officials or administrators in women's football, fall outside the remit of this book.[5]

The emphasis on organised and affiliated teams is intended to assess the extent to which female players own women's competitive football in Britain. The purely recreational player has also been considered, but less so. For some players at all levels integration with the FA is problematic as it represents an acceptance of the centralised bureaucracy that was historically dismissive of women's football. In some recreational settings there is resistance to the practice of segregating the sexes, including women who play for park teams.[6] The sample in this study included ninety-eight questionnaires and seventy-five interviews.[7] Participant observation became crucial both in testing the accuracy of quantitative surveys and to experience the essentially transitory nature of many games, tournaments and administrative arrangements.[8] As one woman said after a training session in June which involved playing against youngsters in a park, approximately fifteen a side:

> On nights like this it's great. Men couldn't get away with this, playing against kids. It's good training because they are fast, skilful. But with paedophiles and that [*shrugs*] men couldn't . . . and they wouldn't anyway.

The first point of contact for the players in the FA leagues and for those in specialist teams was a questionnaire. Semi-structured interviews lasted for approximately ninety minutes, preferably in the home of the player but on neutral ground if not. The number of clubs from which England players are drawn is so small that specific allusions could jeopardise the confidentiality of the research and so no names have been used. Additional testimonies were gathered from a Canadian female international referee who mainly works in the male game and a recently retired Dutch international player now employed as a national coach.

The question of an international women's football culture is also pertinent.[9] Opportunities to look closely at other experiences were especially useful. Visits to Namibia (1998) and the United States of America (1999 and 2001) enabled me to see how women's football was spoken about, played, marketed and treated by the media in both countries. Three points arise from these comparisons. The first is that in worldwide women's football, England is at best a middling contributor to the current development of the game. The prominence of Scandinavian countries in elite women's play reinforces the point that practices in England lag behind the rest of Europe and much smaller populations have considerably more international success. The second aspect is the widespread policy of football's governing bodies to downplay conflict but to emphasise gender difference. Women's football is hardly a global sport as practices vary a great deal: whereas the Oceania Football Confederation has a woman as General Secretary, in Algeria women have recently contested their first national competition. The third dimension of international women's football culture is the resolute interest and pleasure that women players take in participation.

Women football players have mobilised their claims to sport by forming women-only clubs, but have integrated with bureaucratic organisations. However, whether elite, employed administrators have properly represented the needs of the majority of voluntary participants, without whom women's football would not function in its present form, is debatable. The configuration of patronage and selection by which some women join policy-making elites is obviously in need of explanation. In England, the self-image of those accepted by the authorities has to be subsumed to the public image of the bureaucracy. At international level, in this respect, the case is typical. The section on Namibia examines the role of women's rights advocacy groups in overcoming the processes of historical disadvantage in those countries where women's access to leisure is relatively more problematic. The rare, but considerable, achievement of exceptional women questions the outlook as, in any way, universally female-centred.

The inaugural Confederation of African Nations (CAF) Women's Championship was held in 1999 and marked a moment when all football confederations had sponsored international female competition. The 3rd FIFA World Championship for women, in Los Angeles, 1999, saw the largest live audience for a women-only sporting event with over 90,000 spectators. A professional women's league, Women's United Soccer Association (WUSA), was launched in 2001, owned largely by media companies. However, flourishing interest and encouraging changes hardly constitute women's participation in football as sufficiently commonplace and significant to mark a new dawn. The marginalisation of women at administrative level and lack of widespread support for women players mean that fundamental issues of control are as contentious now as they have ever been. More striking still, women's lack of equality in this area appears to be taken for granted by some women players and by elite administrators. Part I picks up these threads to debate the relationship between changes in quantity and changes in quality in women's football.

In one sense, the story of recent expansion is unthreatening to the football authorities because an increase in the number of players has yet to alter the essentially amateur nature of women's football. The historical summary illustrates that there has been a widespread tendency to devalue the place of women in studies of football, women players in their own game and, by implication, participants in sport. In the midst of this debate, of what should be done on behalf of female players, or by participants or to women's football, comments like the following suggest that this agenda is rather static and in need of revision to examine the values that women players bring to football:

> I came from a little village where my brother had a sports outfitters and at Christmas, they gave me footballs . . . For my tenth birthday he got me a pair of football boots and stood me in a bath of water to make them shrink to fit. I stood for an hour in freezing cold water . . . I was so proud.

Part I

A game for rough girls?[1]

Women's football in Britain

Serious fun

Contemporary perspectives on women's football in Britain

> Our complexions disprove that football is bad for us. Our complexions are our own. We have no need for powder puffs or toilet cream, and we don't keep late hours.[1]

Women's football has been part of the social and cultural history of Britain for over a century. Nevertheless, female players today are most often depicted in the media as unconventional and academics dismiss women's participation in football more broadly before the 1990s as worthy of oversight.[2] When the Sex Discrimination Act of 1975 was drafted to exempt professional football specifically and competitive sport generally from gains in equality by women, then it seems safe to say that women's association with football is about more than sport.

> It seems to me that football is a game that is excepted from this statute. It is a game in which on all the evidence here the average woman is at a disadvantage to the average man because she has not got the stamina or physique to stand up to men in regard to it . . . women have many other qualities superior to those of men, but they have not got the strength or stamina to run, to kick or tackle, and so forth.
>
> (Denning, 1978)

This legislation is now almost thirty years old yet section 44, the clause that limits female access to competitive sport, has endured in its original form in spite of other amendments. Since the purpose of the Act was to address archaic conventions of the roles of men and women, to insist on the preservation of essential gender difference in and through sport is both logically and legally questionable. This is one indication of many that the connection between football and women looks set to remain contentious for the foreseeable future. This contested relationship is the starting point for this work and in particular the body of knowledge implied by 'all the evidence here' in Denning's ruling.

So little work has been covered in the specific subject area that it is difficult to draw upon selected themes from writing about football, about women's experience of team sport particularly or women's sport generally. The most frequently discussed aspect of women's football in England in the 1990s is the growth in the number of participants. For example, Richard Holt and Tony Mason suggest that there is evidence of a recent, rapid expansion to over four thousand women's teams under FA control.

> Women's football . . . grew dramatically in the 1990s. The number of women's teams rose from 500 to 4,500 from 1993 to 2000 and the FA announced plans for a professional women's league along the lines of that in the United States.
>
> (Holt and Mason, 2000: 12)

The figures above refer specifically to England but overestimate the total number of female players in Britain by at least twofold. A decade before, Williams and Woodhouse had also related the rise in participation to patronage from the football authorities, including Premiership and Football League clubs, the Football Trust and the English FA (Williams and Woodhouse, 1991: 100). However, in attempting to find confirmation of a recent, rapid increase a very different view emerged, not least because merely quantifying women's participation does little to reveal the complexity of the players' experiences. Precisely because of the tendency to homogenise women in football it seemed necessary to resist describing players as a set of persons with some common status. The confused but persistent stereotypes that a female football player is likely to be a tomboy, a lesbian or looking to swap shirts with supporters raised particular questions, for example. The contempt shown to English female footballers simultaneously trivialises their sporting accomplishments (as in the pejorative 'play like a girl') and insists on the feminine as the object of masculine desire (women are supposed to play at being a woman, not at football). Out of the discussions with women and girls at all levels about diverse experiences of playing football, it became increasingly evident that an examination of women's participation in an outdoor contact team sport which involves competition, co-operation and skill is long overdue.

The unease between the 'theorists of sport and the ordinary historian' that Richard Holt has described is a tension that I have tried to resolve:

> Sociologists frequently complain that historians lack a conceptual framework for their research, whilst historians tend to feel social theorists require them to compress the diversity of the past into artificially rigid categories and dispense with empirical verification of their theories.
>
> (Holt, 1989: 357)

The challenge was to explore diversity within a structure that enables us to begin to extend our understanding of women's football, and the project consequently began by collecting views of some of the players as this was a fundamental part of my lived experience of the sport. The interpretation of events, people, texts and context which arises out of that starting point may frustrate those who insist on neutrality as equating to objectivity in research but a value-free framework does not exist. Instead the intention has been to capture some detail of players' experiences and to discuss this difference against the backdrop of surrounding factors which bear upon the creation and understanding of those subjectivities. There is an immediacy and a transience that often informs administrators' and players' actions that is crucial to encapsulate as an example of 'history from below'. As an example, two women who regularly coach and play football with men made these comments:

> And sometimes they look at you like, you know, who's she? Then you just have to get your head down and get on with it and after a while they forget and you've got their respect, especially if you pull off skill moves. So you have to have confidence in your ability and play your own game.

> One of them said, 'Are you his secretary?' even though I was in boots and kit and so I thought, 'Right! I'll have you' . . . and I did. I waited until he came to tackle me first time, feinted to the right to go inside and went left and stuck a perfect nutmeg on him. I was laughing so much I couldn't run with the ball . . . [*laughs*] had to pass.

That is, women's football is distinctly un-monumental. Solutions are often designed to work upon the moment and to accomplish something at the time rather than to stand for something in the future. There is, however, much to observe, applaud and commemorate. The player testimonies are like snapshots that are supplemented by textual excerpts and media clippings from which it is possible to compose a collage of English women's football. This piecing together of fragmented sources is both the historical method used to express the diversity of women's football and the conceptual framework, as elements of variety are juxtaposed.

The experience of doing gender in and through football is unavoidable for the male and the female participant, and one reviewer of an early draft of this book offered the perturbed comment, 'There aren't many men mentioned here.' Though not entirely accurate, there was something to this and at several points the evidence suggests that the person who wanted to investigate the place of men in developing women's football would be rewarded with plenty of primary material. Unlike the reviewer, my feeling when reading a book on football is usually, where are all the women? So while clearly this is a gendered topic, men's role is contributory to the focus of this work but not a main theme. Space and ambition preclude including most, let alone all of the women who play football in England and so many men who help them to do so are also left out. The idea of gender division, though, is central because it has shaped ideas of equality of opportunity and, indeed, outcome in football in some peculiar respects. Difference as it is used here is quite distinct and contrary to this meaning, as it incorporates contrasting and overlapping opinions of women's football without this variance necessarily entailing opposition. The strain between the two meanings of difference is significant because at the same time that women express several kinds of freedom when they participate in football, equality is currently contested and unrealisable precisely because there is no consensus about what it means: should the aim be, for example, mixed senior football or separate but equal provision? Should we be developing a professional league for women or allowing elite women to play in the present professional leagues? What kinds of tactics are appropriate in pursuing those objectives? Women interviewees frequently emphasised the similarities between the sexes yet pressed for equal but separate forms of football. This contradiction was intriguing. In trying to examine what was meant, it became clear that participants were not overtly radical in their aspirations for the sport as a whole or in the personal means employed to effect change at club and regional level. Nevertheless, playing football appeared to be more of a lifestyle choice than, say, belonging to a certain gym. For the women who do play, the experience of team sport involving the simultaneous expression of sameness and difference with other players who were usually, but by no means always, also women was sufficiently engaging and celebratory to make it worth taking part. So gender is one of many aspects of players' identity; its fluctuating importance relative to others. To extend the combination of membership and independence that the players talked about, the chapters in Part I provide more detail on how community and memory is constructed and communicated.

The nature of the topic therefore precludes unequivocal conclusions about a radical or liberal feminist perspective in studying women who play football. Some developments appear to support the position that collaboration between women players and established bureaucracies is the way forward. Proponents would point out that women's football under FA control has access to increased resources, more structured playing opportunities and centralised administrative co-ordination. Opponents interpret these benefits as largely cosmetic because they have yet to serve as the basis of more far-reaching alteration to the provision of football for women or to the structures of football itself. As this work makes evident, football authorities have acted as superficially tolerant but tight-fisted patrons of women's football only in the last decade and periods of increased female participation have not led in any direct way to reform of the systems of football itself. So though I subscribe to the view that a radical revision of the place of women, and by extension gender difference, within football is required to bring about fundamental transformation, this will not go far enough for opponents of competitive sport and its values. This line of argument is not pursued here, because most women players who were interviewed in the course of this study did not want to play a different form of football, either as an alternative game or as a critique of the values of sport. Rather, women's right to play the standard form of the game without modification to the size of the field of play, the length of a match, the number of substitutes and so forth remains a moot point. Over and above this, it is not the point of this discussion to outline what a feminist form of football could and should look like but to give a platform to the historical and contemporary aspects of women's participation. This said, the data collected here enable an assessment of the balance of conservatism and progressivism in women's football which could lead to a more widespread discussion of the theoretical repercussions which lead out from the subject.

Part I looks at the historical summary as well as examining two crucial dimensions in more detail to elaborate on the kinds of community and memory in women's football. In order to explore the past, present and potential future of the sport, female players' interpretations are juxtaposed with other diverse texts, from newspaper articles and photographs to personal scrapbooks and match programmes. Widespread support for the idea of a different game for women appears, partly, a function of administrative control by male elites but is also as a means of protecting space for female play. Like the consensus over the growth in numbers of women players, this arrangement appears to suit both the football authorities, because of the dynamic image it presents, and women players as it defends their control over the majority of regionalised activity. This is not compatible with another continuity, which is that the women's game has long called for more financial assistance, media coverage and for female coaches and administrators to be more recognised within the structures of football. One of the broader dilemmas for players and the authorities is about the present and future cultural, economic and social arrangements for women in football in England. In order to summarise why increased participation has yet to translate into more widespread demands for change, some of the popular myths surrounding women's football are deconstructed.

The widely held view is that that there has been a recent, rapid expansion of female interest and play. How many women are we talking about as football players in England at any one time? Even generous FA interpretations suggest that at best there is one female player for every fifty male players:

> There is a total of 2.25 million footballers in England, which includes 750,000 players of school age (say 16 and under) and 41,000 female players. Altogether there are 42,000 football clubs.[3]

The English FA website in 2000 recorded figures of 700 women's and 750 girls' teams. In 2001 it recorded 700 women's and 1,000 girls' teams. This difficulty is also apparent in the context of participation in Britain; for example Sheila Begbie reported the 1991 Scottish women's FA audit as showing 27 affiliated senior teams, 400 member players and 23 qualified coaches. By 1995 this had grown to 194 senior and junior teams, 2,400 players and 184 women coaches (Begbie, 1996: 44–8). In Northern Ireland, the Women's Football Association of Ireland (WFAI) caters for 6,500 registered players, playing in 350 teams and in the Republic of Ireland, the Ladies' Football Association of Ireland (LFAI) has approximately 300 teams. In Wales development has been slower and there are around 150 teams with registered players. The situation is complicated by methods used for calculating clubs, for example the number of girls' teams was immediately doubled by the introduction of small-sided football (in which players under 11 are not permitted to play in teams of more than seven a side) in 1998. To go beyond this emphasis on the number who play, this section develops other narratives about women football players: what are the components of the identity of the players? What do they think they are doing when they play? How do other factors beyond gender diversify women's experience?

In pursuing this line of enquiry, the idea of 'subjectivity' in Passerini's study of memory was particularly valuable. By this she means:

> Both the aspects of spontaneous subjective being . . . contained and represented by attitude, behaviour and language, as well as other forms of awareness . . . such as the sense of identity, consciousness of oneself, and more considered forms of intellectual activity.
>
> (Passerini, 1992: 8)

In attempting to apply this to women's football, both the content and the manner of the players' expressions became valuable. For example, no player identified herself as a feminist or as politically active. However, women contested ideas about physical inferiority, comparative lack of strength and power. In answer to the question 'Do you feel that biological differences affect the way that men and women play football?' the responses included:

> Yes – men are stronger, more physical, faster than women, not just in football but in anything. I think we have a lot of skill and our game is played at a slower pace so it allows you to take time on the ball.
>
> Men have larger muscle fibres to develop which enables them to have more strength.
>
> Biology doesn't affect ability but, obviously, pregnancies are the only difference for a female player.
>
> Men are more physical at the higher levels and more physically agile. Men's football is also a lot faster.

> No – I think because women in other counties train every day and most are becoming semi-pro, we haven't got the capacity to match them physically and fitness-wise.
>
> Definitely not. I think it's absolute rubbish.
>
> I believe women are becoming physically stronger in recent times in comparison to ten years ago.

In this last player's view, a change in women's physical capability enables them to play, rather than a shift in sporting practice or female expectations. There appeared to be a revealing tautology in some comments as players suggested an acceptance of biological determinism expressed through a difference of playing standards which, in turn, supports common-sense ideas of women's physical inferiority. More significantly, the pattern of responses as a whole is indicative of both the production of culture within women's football and the culture of production that is the hallmark of what this project set out to investigate. Each player negotiates and interprets ideas such as strength and physicality and gives them a specific linguistic and conceptual form at any one time. These verbalised definitions may concur, or be at odds with, the physical expression of the same idea when playing football, so are ever-changing and partial. It hardly helps the researcher that the picture is constantly changing but the complexity is itself more representative of what is being depicted than a neatness would allow.

The following chapter debates this relationship between changes in quantity and changes in quality of women's football. In one sense, the story of recent expansion is unthreatening to the football authorities because a change in the number of players has yet to alter the essentially amateur nature of the female game. In addition, the summary illustrates that there has been a widespread tendency to devalue the place of women's football in studies of the sport, women players in their own game and, by implication, participants in sport. The chapter therefore places the views of the players in a broader historical context. Like much of women's history, female football has been poorly documented. There are no yards of statistics to recall great teams, players, events and honours. On the one hand it has passed into football lore that Cissie Charlton (sister of Jackie Milburn and mother of Bobby and Jack) coached her young sons in the back yard.[4] On the other, some commentators are so offended by the idea of women playing football that they talk of it as a modern-day equivalent of a dog on hind legs.[5] In lacking both a sense of history and a link between local and national memory, the failure of women's football may be less to do with inferior play than an inability to grasp the popular imagination. This, in turn, affects the social memory of women's football. Consequently, the mediation of culture by interviewees is treated as very much of a period in the sport's development.

The most difficult nut to crack was to assess the extent to which women are agents in the rise of women's football beyond the organisation of their own club. A further but related matter is whether participation was primarily social, competitive or otherwise motivated. The value of these individual and collective memories to women players and administrators raised questions about a sense of a common past, present or future. For the foreseeable future, the female body as 'other' in football will remain. What is the relationship of the individual woman to the 'football family' (to women footballers, women athletes, to male players, a particular team)? One player summed up the gap between the public image and her own experience as follows:

> The image of women's football on TV is that most women in football are gay, which is untrue, and that we are in it to escape our families, which is also untrue.

There has yet to be a fulsome account of how this popular view developed. Not only have the systematic attempts to prevent women from playing received scant treatment, the women who have played and the forms that participation have taken are long overdue for discussion.

1 A brief history of women's football in England

Women's football has had an unstable and uncertain existence. This instability intersects with a broader historical continuity. Whether or not it has been the working man's religion or linked to proletarian community life, it has clearly mattered to many people that football, whatever the code, should be synonymous with masculinity. This myth has been perpetuated in terms of club ownership, playing and coaching personnel, and in ancillary industries like the sporting press. The development of this 'tradition' has tended to be seen as self-evident and unproblematic. In discussing women's involvement in association football as players the first intention in this brief historical account is to show what was happening at the time. The second is to provide an introduction to the influence of these events on contemporary forms and issues in Part I and the book as a whole.

Although football authorities began to intervene in women's associations from the late 1960s, the practices upon which this built can be traced back throughout the twentieth century. The Football Association and Football League have been characterised as a family and a semi-democratic commercial collective (Tomlinson, 1991: 35; Goldberg and Wagg, 1991: 242). The administrative structure, rules, regulations and policy imperatives, however, reflected quite particular social and cultural values in the late nineteenth century. Metaphors of inclusivity and representativeness are therefore misleading. Anxiety, lack of interest and, at times, incomprehension over where to place female players are much more in evidence in molding the present administrative niche out of which women's football has yet to break. It is within the context of systematic exclusion that the football industry began to deal with women more directly during the 1990s. Until this point, it seemed that the football authorities had neither the inclination nor the infrastructure to oversee women's play. There have been benefits for female football in that there has been an independent tradition of women's play, led by managers and administrators with knowledge, skill and commitment. One of the most significant disadvantages is that teams, regional leagues and central administrations have been, and can still be, cut back, closed down or restructured quite quickly. Another separate but related issue which football as a sport and industry has also found uncomfortable is how to represent women players and in turn, how this representation will reflect on football itself. Both the organisation and the depiction of women's football in the present is more influenced by the past than has so far been acknowledged.

Since sport is typically defined as an institutionalised, highly structured, rule-bound physical contest, essentially a creation of the nineteenth century, women's first participation in football is difficult to pinpoint. In nineteenth century upper-class Japan women played a courtly form and Native American women played folk football, but the British examples are the most significant in the tradition of women's football as sport. In the final decades women were agitating for improved economic, social and political conditions in an era of popular entertainment and there were many new 'healthful' forms of recreation covered in the pages of the *Athletic News*, from boat polo for ladies to a feminised form of football on roller-skates. Inverness, Scotland appears to have hosted the first recorded women's football match in 1888. This can be interpreted as distinct from folk football, like the late eighteenth century women's games, or mixed holiday activities such as those that took place on Shrove Tuesday in Atherstone, though it did pit the married against the single women. The two teams had colours, fixed goals, a fairly stable and even number of members and the game had a limited time span. The first match within Scottish Football Association (SFA) guidelines was held at Shawfields Ground, Glasgow in 1892 (M. McCuaig, SFA Museum, telephone interview). An association for women was founded in 1894 and a tradition began of attempting to link football with ladylike behaviour that persists today. Nettie Honeyball, the Secretary of the British Ladies, organised the English North versus South game at Crouch End, London in 1895. It was followed by games in the Midlands, the North and in Scotland; the most significant of which was the Newcastle fixture with a crowd approaching 8,000. Lady Florence Dixie, the President of the British Ladies' Football Club, youngest daughter of the Marquess of Queensbury and a keen advocate of women's rights, sponsored the tour with the declared aim:

> I am in hopes that the British Ladies' Football Club will be able to furnish teams to travel about the country, and endeavor to popularize the sport by playing some matches in different localities.
>
> (Sheila Begbie, SFA Director of Women's and Girls' Football, private correspondence 2001)

Dixie's touring team played games at Cappielow (Greenock Morton FC), Love Street (St Mirren FC) and Reaburn Place in Edinburgh, amongst others.[1] Though the trip attracted great publicity from the press, the coverage was not confined to the sporting contest. One way that women's football acquired a dubious status for the bourgeois girl was a link with the 'Rights question'. Though there had been some change in public opinion about the place of games for girls in public schools, women who participated in individual and group sports were likely to have their motivation discussed and criticised. Whether early women players were politically motivated, fashion conscious, or tentative enthusiasts, the authorities viewed their involvement as a nuisance. Resentment had become sufficiently widespread by 1902 in England for the FA to issue a ruling preventing male clubs from playing against 'lady teams'.

Gender division was an issue from the outset and extended beyond the nomenclature of 'Ladies' teams' to the physical appearance of the participants. The relatively large crowds would have seen a spectacle reflecting ambivalence over how to dress women football players. Photographs of the time suggest that dress codes were open to interpretation. If rational dress allowed for some freedom of movement, it can hardly have been conducive to strenuous or pleasurable play to wear

> Red blouses with white yolks, and full black knickerbockers fastened below the knee, black stockings, red berretta caps, brown leather boots and leg-pads . . . white gloves and . . . a short skirt above the knickerbockers.
>
> (*Manchester Guardian*, 1895)

Playing football in a skirt or baggy breeches would as much disadvantage the working-class girl who wanted a kick about in the street as the young ladies of Roedean. Female sports enthusiasts could wield a hockey stick or cricket bat with relative freedom but would have had greater difficulty in receiving a ball to feet while wearing a dress. The 1890s cycling craze had spread the popularity of bifocated garments for women as both highly fashionable and risqué. If sport was the enemy of femininity, then the symbolic significance of playing in uniforms which risked compromising women and girls' status as ladies could only make football challenging to public reaction.

Work, rather than leisure, revived the acceptance of trousers as practical in some circumstances when women moved into new occupations in World War I. The increase in the number of women's football games was partially assisted by a change in women's costume as more teams of munitionettes opted for shorts, long socks and a jersey. The notoriety of wearing trousers meant that not all women's teams were prepared to make this transition. Into the 1920s, some women played in skirts and stockings, under-skirts, blouses and sweaters with the only concession to a football uniform being shin-pads and boots. Unlike European players, British women covered their heads in mob caps, tam-o'-shanters or woollen hats until the mid-1920s. Beyond that, other aspects of the physical appearance of the players gives a particular identity to the individual in stylistically diverse ways that would, in itself, reward future study. There were differences within teams as well as between clubs as individuals negotiated ideas of feminine modesty.

Dress has continued to affect the image of football for women in contrast to sports where shorts began to replace skirts for female players only more recently. With the exception of covered heads and lighter footwear the uniform for women has changed very little, though it has been subject to changes in fashion which have influenced male and female participants, such as tight shirts and brief shorts in the 1970s. Football is also fairly unusual in that most women today play in the same kit as male players, albeit some in junior sizes. The beauty of the football strip for participants is that it accommodates most body shapes and can be adapted to suit personal taste and belief. In an era where female athletes are not necessarily made famous by their sporting prowess, and those who are routinely display their physique as an aspect of self-promotion, the lack of differentiation between the male and female player's uniform is now unfashionable. In the charge towards commercially backed legitimacy, and specifically the vogue for revealing female sports costumes, the functional aspect of the uniform, however successful in enabling a wide range of women to play, could be threatened. So the issue of dress reflects a series of decisions about how individuals participate in addition to highlighting broader cultural practices that connect with women's involvement as a group.

Girls' football in schools at the end of the nineteenth century was much less in evidence than adult women's play and this has yet to change (small-sided football and duplication of player registration aside). One consequence is that the female uniform was not feminised or infantilised like some games' clothing. Another effect was to prevent the transition to football as popular sport for school-age females. James Walvin has assessed the influence of public and state schools at the point of the creation of the FA and during the codification of laws in the 1860s as the pre-eminent force in modern as opposed to folk football:

> Time and time again this public school hegemony determined the course of football in these early days . . . Indeed the new emphasis upon football in state schools by the turn of the century was perhaps the most important factor in guaranteeing the future of football as a mass game and was undoubtedly a determining factor in making football the national game.
>
> (Walvin, 1994: 44)

The lack of organised school-based play for girls has undoubtedly been a major factor in encouraging women *not* to play football for over a century. A more systematic inclusion of football in the female physical education curriculum is a very late development beset by disagreement regarding the relative role of individual teachers, educational institutions, the Football Association, the English Schools Football Association and local authority sports development officers.

This said, girls of all classes have played football in school since the 1890s.[2] Gatekeepers of feminine respectability including Miss Lawrence of

Roedean, Jane Dove at Wycombe, Emily Davies at Girton, Dorothea Beale at The Ladies College, Cheltenham and Frances Buss at North London Collegiate thought football too rough for girls. Nevertheless there were teams formed by the pupils at Brighton High School and Nottingham High School in 1894 and 1895 (Sondheimer and Bodington, 1972: 35). Like hockey and cricket, football was perceived by some woman educators as leading to possible injury and the medical theories of the day, as Fletcher points out, held that bruises, especially to the chest, could become cancerous.[3] Middle-class girls may have had some access to games in school, but for working-class girls and boys space was probably a constraining factor, as was poverty and ill health. Typically, an early working-class girls' team, based at a Reading school where the boys' team won the English Schools FA Cup of 1905–06, was mentioned almost as an afterthought in a contemporary newspaper article.[4] We know little about whether girls played football in single-sex groupings or with boys at this time. We know even less about street football involving females. What remains clear is that schools, colleges and universities have been far less important to women's football culture in Britain than regional adult female competition. A player who had been a child in the late 1920s confirmed the school as the first institutional barrier preventing female play:

> There were separate playgrounds for boys and girls. Football wasn't allowed in the girls' playground but they didn't seem to play the games that I was used to.

The semantics of separation have been as enduring as ideas of physical difference. At its foundation in 1904 the English Schools Football Association (ESFA) had as its primary objective 'The mental, moral and physical development and improvement of schoolboys through the medium of Association Football' (Alatt, 1988: 2). For seventy years the organisation was untroubled by any sense of omission before a misunderstanding about the wording of the 1975 Sex Discrimination Act led administrators to consult legal experts about whether mixed football was required by law. The mystification about where to place girls was evident in the protracted negotiations to include females after 1975. It took until 1991 to change the constitution to include schoolgirls so that the ESFA could potentially administer all school-age football. Initially, lawyers with experience of the law of trust and charities advised the association:

> You have a discretion . . . you are not compelled to allow girls to play in mixed competitive teams . . . though you are entitled to do so . . . We therefore do not consider that the association is in a position to vary its Rules to permit schoolgirls playing football under the aegis of the association or in mixed teams.
>
> (Goodger and Auden, 1988)

The wording of the Charities Act meant that including females, whatever the intention, would contravene the original articles of the association.

The process of changing the constitution raises two main points. The first is that the ESFA, like other football authorities, did not gradually become more enlightened.[5] In this case, one individual was adamant about the need to include girls in the work of the association. The General Secretary, C.S. Allatt, first sent around a *Curriculum Time Questionnaire* mentioning females and mixed football to schools in September 1986. His motives were, it appears, partly to ascertain how much female football was played, partly to clarify the situation regarding sex discrimination and, additionally, a response to more frequent requests by girls to take part in football (Allatt, 1988: 2–3). Allatt then sent out a further *Girls' Football Questionnaire* in 1988 and successfully revised the articles of the ESFA three years later. Though expansion is hinted at in the legal advice, the ESFA certainly had a more progressive approach than the FA who merely continued to uphold section 37 of the Rules of the Football Association banning mixed football.

The second point raised by changing the ESFA constitution is that this led in an indirect and belated way to the modification, ten years later, of FA Rule 37 to allow mixed football among children under 12 years of age. As schools have joint facilities, they were perceived to be the major site of development for single and mixed football in the late 1990s. However, the number of teams competing in the ESFA National Girls' Competition (with transport and accommodation fully paid for by the association) has more than doubled from 318 in 1995 to a still modest 835 in 2000. So this potential is as yet underdeveloped, for reasons including the local management of schools and the sale of pitches, resource pressure on curriculum physical education, extra-curricular activities and the resistance of some teachers, students and parents to football for girls.[6]

The two players speaking in the following excerpts attended school forty years apart (the first in the 1950s, the second the early 1990s). Their experiences show how persistent the antipathy to girl's football has been:

> Well, they wouldn't let us play football at school; it wasn't ladylike. But now and again we would play in the schoolyard . . . 'Cause we had separate schoolyards, you know? Lads were in one schoolyard on one side of school. It was a mixed school but playgrounds were on separate sides, so I'd be playing 'The Big Ship Sails through the Alley Alley O' and all that stuff. So, yeah, I didn't play – we didn't really bother in the school. Perhaps we might have had a kick about now and again, but it wasn't sort of encouraged. We had to do drill and deportment; you know, 'Backs straight girls! Brush your knees together as you walk'.

Q Did you like hockey and netball?
A I just didn't like those games. I'd rather be kicking, rather than . . . you know, it felt strange handling a ball?
Q School was probably the first time that you can remember being discouraged from playing football?
A I wouldn't say we were discouraged but we weren't encouraged. It just wasn't on the agenda so you just accepted that, because that's how it was.

If there is little evidence that schools inspired girls to play football throughout the century, there is much to support the view that playing football was an activity initiated by women. The expansion of women's football organised by workers after 1914, sometimes on the initiative of female welfare supervisors in various industries, was more pronounced in Britain than anywhere else. Teams included Aberdeen, Belfast, Cardiff, Edinburgh, Glasgow, Llanely, Newport, Renfrew, Rutherglen and Swansea, in addition to English munitions sides like Bennets of London and Dick, Kerrs' Ladies of Lancashire.[7]

In the absence of personal patronage and sponsorship, which doesn't appear to have continued after Florence Dixie's involvement, football for women was promoted in small collectives based around work or leisure interests that became competitive networks. The early split between administrators, entrepreneurs, managers and players, evident in the formation of the Football Association and Football League, did not take place in women's football in the same manner. Nettie Honeyball was typical of the pre-war player in that she was an enthusiast who took on the role of secretary in order to organise games and is, in that sense, more like the contemporary participant than the munitionettes. The lack of female administrators and managers appears partially due to the nature of women's work and leisure. Working women were unlikely to move into bureaucratic roles as separate from, or an extension to, their playing career because time was at a premium and they had to support themselves and, in some cases, home-based dependants. It is one thing to take part in healthy recreation as an individual and another to facilitate the play of groups of women at the expense of other obligations. For example, Joan Whalley played for Dick, Kerr Ladies for almost twenty years. Her scrapbook indicates she played an average of forty-two matches a year in addition to working full time. Many of the matches involved overnight stays and social duties. Football endured when the nature of work changed, for example Joan and the formidable striker Lily Parr were among eight Dick, Kerr's players who retrained as nurses at Whittingham Hospital in order to continue supporting themselves during the inter-war years. Some remained there the rest of their working lives, though some took up alternative careers again after World War II, Joan, for instance, as a bus conductor.

In the period of the rise of work-based clubs the secretary/manager was not usually a player and it was comparatively rare for Atalanta, from Huddersfield, to be run entirely by and for women. However, though more sharply differentiated in roles than at times immediately before 1914 or after 1960, the secretary/manager such as Alfred Frankland of Dick, Kerr Ladies (later Preston) usually dealt with a counterpart to arrange fixtures, in addition to training the team, organising transport, publicising fixtures, scouting for new talent and dealing with cash. Photographs often show a female chaperone or physiotherapist who accompanied players to matches and so it would be good to know more about the interaction between the supervisory roles and the relative balances of power. It does indicate that, as representatives of the firm or club, women's play was under constant scrutiny in order to enforce respectability.

Though munitions football was the most visible dimension to the women's game around this time it was not the only aspect of female competition. Other industries that employed large numbers of women, for example retail, light engineering and food manufacturing, also played a part. The secretaries and teachers of Atalanta indicate that female football players were not necessarily industrial workers. Nor were they solely based in the North. Ley's Ladies of Nottingham, begun as a munitions team, continued to play for approximately six years from 1916 to 1922 (after World War II the factory produced lawnmowers and a team was revived in the 1960s). Up to five Lyon's Ladies café teams around London played at any one time in the early 1920s. Plymouth Ladies, was a local representative team and renowned for a serious approach to competition. Club members trained in all weather on the seafront and games drew large crowds, for instance against a Bath XI there were 12,000 spectators in 1921.

What continues to challenge researchers is, why football? In attempting to answer this Melling suggests a mixture of ad hoc and formalised activity that was cheap, flexible and able to cater for different groups. That is, it was one of many collective and social activities women took part in during and immediately after World War I (Melling, 1999: 10). This is more convincing than the FA factsheet *Women's Football History* which describes women's football before the 1960s as a wartime exception: 'During the First World War, women's role in society began to alter. Women's football teams began to spring up, using the games to raise money for charity' (Football Association, 1998g: 1). 'Spring up' suggests an uncoordinated activity. In support of this version of events, Lopez explains women's interest during World War I as follows:

> Grace Sibbert worked at the Dick, Kerr factory while her husband was fighting in France. She organised the first proper match . . . For no fee, on Christmas Day 1917, in front of a crowd of 10,000 they raised in excess of £600 for wounded soldiers at the Moor Park military hospital.
>
> (Lopez, 1997: 3)

The sums of money raised equate to millions of pounds today but it was not just charities that benefited. The Football League had continued with fixtures during the war in the face of much press criticism. Tolerating games played by women for charity was one means by which the members of the Association and League could reclaim some credibility through the appearance of patriotism. With the war three years past, an alternative strategy was required.

The official memory of women's football was set by the 1921 English FA declaration that the game was 'unsuitable' for women and its ban on them playing on the pitches of FA and League affiliates. The ruling was not a dramatic about-face by the FA, which had debated the financial repercussions of continuing with women's matches for almost a year. Two months before the decision, the FA had given host clubs authority to take over the gate receipts from women's games. So the decision appears to be about the League and Association's continued attempts to recoup and defend a masculine image for football. It was impossible to stop women playing per se but those who did participate were simultaneously seen to behave in an inappropriate manner, in places where they ought not to be. The ban spread across Britain quickly. One Scottish newspaper, for example, reported the decision with unreserved approval:

> The action of the Football Association in passing a resolution considering the game unsuitable for females, would appear to have a good deal of support. Even among women generally, the playing of football by the sex is far from being popular . . . A proposal to form a football club for the women of the staff of Messrs Selfridges went before the Athletic Committee, but was rejected due to lack of support . . . In America girls are not allowed to play unless they have been medically tested and the gymnastic instructor is always a qualified medical man. The trouble is that the type of woman who wants to play football here won't be medically examined.
>
> ('The Football Playing Women', 1921)

The decision has had a profound effect on women's football culture in England and still shapes the sport in material respects today. One consequence is that there are no fixed or discrete local or national sites to place the memory of women's football.[8]

The often referred to peak of 55,000 spectators at Goodison Park on Boxing Day 1921 aside, there has been a lack of information about the contribution of those agencies who continued to assist women's play in histories of football. In addition, the perception of women's football as a wartime enthusiasm fails to deal with two vital questions: why would the governing body want to impose a ban and why did they maintain this policy for half a century? The relationship between the League and the Association and their relative rights to control the game are facets of the answer to both. In his study of the relationship between the two administrations, Matthew Taylor describes the mutual dependence and antipathy of the mainly northern-based League (Proud Preston) and the southern-based Association (Taylor, 1997: 56). As Taylor points out, the relationship between the League and Association was characterised by negotiation as issues arose rather than entrenched positions (Taylor, 1997: 97–8). Therefore the ban on women players was partly a response to the way that football as display was developing during World War I. As a parallel form of entertainment with male professionalism, women's football had established itself as a female sporting spectacle, watched by a mainly male audience whose entrance fee was donated to charity. The expanding network of the women's game in England had led, not to a shabby amateurism, but adept entrepreneurial organisation in terms of raising large sums of money as the result of consistently attracting large crowds. Banning women as a group could be interpreted as a rather clumsy attempt on behalf of the Association and League to reinforce the masculine image of football. With the return of men from the front line, following on from the uproar during the war, the administrations could not afford to alienate their prime supporters; the large crowds at the 1923 FA Cup Final suggest this was a crudely effective strategy, though some of those supporters would have been female. It also suggests why the policy was pursued until another point of crisis in the English professional game.

Women's football has never recovered its early popularity in terms of status or support. Having established itself as a show, frequent and regular access to grounds with the capacity to hold large crowds was vital in order to cultivate a substantial live audience. Moreover, the idea of improper behaviour is still pertinent to the reputation of women's football today. More players participate in less spectacular surroundings, but women's football remains a minority activity by comparison with men's football and female leisure activities generally.[9] Nevertheless, the reasons for the general effectiveness of the ban cannot be explained by sport alone. The relative change of the status of working women and in welfare policies during the 1920s was also a contributory factor. During the immediate post-war period, women who worked in munitions and on the land were especially affected by recession (Braybon and Summerfield, 1987). The defeat of the General Strike in 1926 further worsened working conditions for women and the 1931 election saw trade unionists predominate in the Parliamentary Labour Party; at least half from the Miner's Federation (Hinton, 1983: 14). The dominance of the miners and other trade unions and the lack of political leverage of those occupations dominated by women, such as nursing, retrenched the position of women as leisure consumers outside the home.[10] As a non-school sport requiring teams of eleven to be transported to places where pitches were available, football was perhaps not best placed to continue its popularity with women at this time.

Also in terms of the wider context, immediately after 1921 came the reprise of a debate in the *Lancet* and in educational circles over the effects of athletics and sport on women. Dr Arabella Kenealy's *Feminism and Sex Extinction* of 1920 outlined the sterilising influences of competitive games, at the same time as the National Birth Rate Commission expressed concern over the fall in the rate of childbirth. The Board of Education's Chief Medical Officer endorsed physical education for girls and called for more of it at the same time as other contributors to the *Lancet* suggested that women's health had been permanently damaged by athletics. In summing up the episode Fletcher suggests:

> The 'Sexless gymnast' reached the national press, a focus of complex anxieties about the appropriate role of women, and potentially as damaging to the movement for women's physical education as the Victorian 'overstrain' argument had been to their academic training.
>
> (Fletcher, 1984: 76)

The arguments show that the FA was not isolated in its view that strenuous sport was inappropriate for women, it was a theme in the general and specialist press. However, even if the board members were genuinely of the conviction that football was harmful, as Dave Russell suggests, it was a convenient excuse (Russell, 1997: 97). The possible misuse of charity money by managers, for example, was also given as a reason to ban women as a group rather than expel the individuals responsible. Football as authentically male, in particular the unfeminine effects of energetic exercise, continue to influence the public. Unfortunately, the cajoling and persuasive tone of the commentary in this 1950s programme, here presented as a form of educational plea, has a contemporary relevance:

> Should ladies play football? Can they play the game? These and other questions are often asked. Today you have the opportunity to judge for yourself. Many people go to ladies' football matches out of curiosity, but we feel sure that before half time you will admit that the girls play the type of football that entertains the public; the attacking game with the ball on the ground. The girls play for the love of the game. To them football is a serious matter. They play with a full-size ball on the regulation size field for the full 90 minutes. So please give them every encouragement and in return they will give you a good afternoon's sport.
>
> (*Corinthian versus Lancashire Ladies Programme*, 1951)

If there were 150 women's clubs playing football by 1921 would the formation of an association have overcome the worse effects of FA prohibition?[11] A second association for women's football, the English Ladies FA, *was* formed but only twenty-five clubs met in Bradford in 1921.

Though Williamson has the numbers at the second meeting at sixty clubs he also suggests that the decision to prevent any club affiliated to the association from playing against non-affiliated teams was crucial in its demise in 1922 (Williamson, 1991: 82). The ruling meant that teams could not advertise for opponents in the local press and the number of potential opponents would have been severely limited. Without wealthy or middle-class patrons and with the majority of players coming from working-class or representative teams, women participants perhaps had little time to give to an association or money to fund expensive tours. Tournament-style fixtures and series of matches continued without a formal association after 1922 but also without restrictive policies.[12] Player testimonies suggest that there was considerable strategic planning involved in the co-ordination of matches. Indeed the forms of competition and the kinds of communities created in women's football are treated in their own right in the next chapter, but there are some comments that are worth making at this point.

The withdrawal of FA support did not, in effect, end women's football. It rather misses the mark to suggest that 'The charitable causes and the social context of wartime Britain upon which the female game was built, and which remained its raison d'être, were by 1921 beginning to fade from the collective memory' (Williams and Woodhouse, 1991: 92). Otherwise repeated reinforcement of the ban, such as Williams and Woodhouse refer to in the case of the Essex FA, would hardly have been necessary (ibid.: 94). From 1921 to the end of the ban in 1972, players and managers of women's teams were creative in their use of space to play. Public areas were frequently used and many matches were played on local recreation grounds. A Weymouth side played against Preston at Portland Borstal in front of a crowd of 500, followed by refreshments at the British Legion Hall. This use of private and public space reflects the dubious status of the game; it is unlikely that the players would otherwise have visited a young offenders' centre, but, presumably, at least some of the supporters attended of their own free will. In the years 1946–8 Dick, Kerr Ladies played on recreation grounds and parks including Longford Park, Chatham and Gillingham, Erias Park in Colwyn Bay, Souacre Fold in Stalybridge, Lockyer Avenue Playing Fields, Giant Axe Field and Longfield Park. In addition, matches were held at Co-op sports grounds, Clitheroe FC, Burnley Police sports ground, Fulwood Barracks, Walmer Bridge Council school ground, Bamber Bridge Training College sports ground and an ICI sports ground.

Competition was stylistically diverse and quite a contrast from the stable, bounded development of male football through hierarchies and leagues. The organisation of the matches shows the quite explicit appropriation of existing aspects of the game, such as spectator-supported events, and their reconstitution as a form of entertainment with a female focus. Fixture secretaries presented women's football as an altruistic, harmless activity to cultivate these audiences. The Hulton Getty Picture Collection has photographs of a Marks and Spencers' team leading out to play against Invictas in 1933 and soldiers coaching women players in 1939. However, during World War II, because of rationing and travel difficulties, Dick, Kerr's manager Alfred Frankland refused to play the team, even for fund-raising events, because he felt it inappropriate. Most players were also involved in war work and had little time for leisure. World War II was consequently less of a turning point for women's football than World War I had been, though women players remained popular with the public. In three years, in the late 1940s, in addition to the weekly fixtures already listed, Joan Whalley played in three international tournaments, and attended over twenty civic receptions and a memorial service.

Ali Melling has suggested that the 1950s and 1960s was a turning point in the rise of gay women taking part in football.

> After the release of the Kinsey Report in the 1950s the situation was complicated by a growth of public awareness regarding homosexuality. Women were sometimes jeered at during matches, with the result that many women players became victims of homophobia from both inside and outside the game. From the 1960s onwards, gay women have indeed become increasingly involved in women's football. A number of writers have argued that lesbians are attracted to football because the characteristics required to play are contrary to the dominant ideal of femininity. Whatever the motivation, it has not been uncommon for confrontations to arise between the heterosexual majority and the gay minority.
>
> (Melling, 2002: 328)

The first part of the statement appears to support the findings of this research in that both when playing and in association with football, women and girls are still likely to receive homophobic comments. However, the final three sentences would be pretty hard to substantiate and appear to border on an acceptance of football's masculine qualities. In contrast, evidence from privately held material suggests that besides the single tournament, the pattern of works and representative teams playing regular fixtures persisted throughout the decades. In the 1950s Corinthians, Fodens (based at a hauliers in Sandbach) and Bolton toured extensively and the Dick, Kerr works team became a representative Preston team. Scottish team nomenclature of the 1960s was more creative than most and many of these sides played against English teams. The names combined representative and works titles, including the Cambuslang Hooverettes, Johnstone Red Rockets, Johnnie Walker and Fife Dynamites, Holyrood Bumbees, Tayside Toppers, Aberdeen Prima Donnas and the Glasgow Gay Eleven (based at the Gay's biscuit factory). In England Fodens reached dominance in 1971 and played against new teams like Warminster and Southampton (originally the Cunard shipping company team). At non-elite level, the Raleigh bicycle factory in Nottingham played in the East Midlands League from 1972 to 1988. The full account of the inter-war or post-war development of women's football in English society remains to be written and lies beyond what is attempted here but there remains a considerable body of work to be done on placing women's teams. The arrangement of matches, at once a self-conscious activity, a form of leisure and a social practice throws quite a different light on the idea of creating women's football teams in response to a transitory and ad hoc situation requiring an amusing fund-raising gimmick.

During the 1960s the status of football altered immeasurably following the removal of the maximum wage in 1961, and the abolition of the 'retain and transfer' system in 1963. Against this background of emerging professionalism, participation football for women grew, crowds dwindled and the sport became less about spectacle and more about taking part. Some attribute England's World Cup victory to be the major agent of change. How important was 1966 to women's football?

> The England victory in the 1966 World Cup proved to be the catalyst for a dramatic renaissance in the women's game and this time the upsurge of interest would be sustained. For a group of women football players in Southampton, it was to be the beginning of a long and successful career.
>
> (Lopez, 1997: 31)

However, the independently held material suggests that there was no pivotal change in female attitudes and a more gradual transition. Manchester Corinthians were formed in 1949 and disbanded in the early 1970s. Fodens had begun playing around 1955. Stewarton Thistle first played in 1961. The last game of a depleted Preston came in 1965 before they folded due to a lack of players. EMGALS began in early 1967. The Doncaster Belles began to play in 1969 after selling Golden Goals tickets at Doncaster Rovers because the job gave them free entry to watch the club they had supported all their lives. Knowing that they could not join a men's team, the women clubbed together and initially played at five and six a side until sufficient numbers joined to form a full team. So 1966 was not as significant as it has been held to be, not least because football for women became popular at around this time in other countries.

Another feature of women's football that had evolved over time became a set pattern in the 1960s as men became the elite administrative influence but women dealt with organising play on a daily basis. The list includes the manager/coach Alfred Frankland, Harry Batt, the unofficial England team manager in the late 1960s and early 1970s, the so-called Father of English women's football Arthur Hobbs, who was founder of the Deal Tournament and WFA pioneer, to the present FA. This ascendancy has been both direct and less obvious. Women have led teams and leagues and for this reason can be seen as the owners of female football to the extent that competition does not depend on central administration, but they have relied on male leadership in major bureaucratic posts. One example of how this has shaped the sport is the case of Pat Dunn as, briefly, Chair of the WFA between the November meeting in 1969 to convene a women's association and the first assembly in June the following year. The qualified referee had contested FA rules regarding women officiating at affiliated matches and they let it be known that she was considered to be a liability. Her reluctant resignation was followed by the appointment of a male chair, Pat Gwynne. Infighting in sporting and voluntary associations is not unique to women's football but it does point to a weak role in decision-making. It also seems astonishing that those in women's football have been careful to accommodate the reactionary element of the FA since integration, and would rather exclude individuals who have fought for women to have a place in football than address the issue of embargo.

This is more significant when considering the lost opportunities for women's football because of administrators' modest hopes for the future of the sport. Hughie Green was perhaps as unlikely a champion for women's football as it is possible to imagine but an 'Opportunity Knocks' contestant in 1967 challenged him to see Scots women players in action and he took her at her word. The Butlins Games, as they came to be known, had £300 prize money, attracted crowds of 5,000 and were supported by the *Daily Mirror* in England and the *Daily Record* in Scotland. There was one predictably salacious tabloid photograph of Joan Tench supposedly taking leave of her shorts as she jumped to head a ball but Green was not apparently promoting a powder-puff image for the sport:

> These women are terrific. We've had some tremendous games since it all started. If they don't want the kind of publicity and the big attendances and great games we've been giving all over the country I couldn't care less. Our girls have played hard; they deserve all the encouragement we can give them.
>
> (*c*. June 1969, Margaret Rae Collection, SFA Museum)

The critics to whom he was responding were WFA members, particularly Arthur Hobbs, who did not approve of the matches at all and discussed banning affiliated teams who participated. Hobbs obviously felt his own Deal Tournament to be more respectable than one fronted by a showman, however affable and enthusiastic: 'Our aim is to get women's football recognised by the English and Scottish football associations. People used to laugh at women's football. We want it to be recognised as a serious skilled part of a great game' (*c*. September 1970, Margaret Rae Collection, SFA museum). Again due to infighting, the WFA also squandered an opportunity to televise a Women's World Cup based in England and backed by Moore, Hurst, Peters and Ramsey, sponsored to the tune of £150,000 in 1972. Though not a professional league, the tournament, which Hobbs tentatively supported and Pat Gwynne opposed, would certainly have presented women's elite play as entertainment to potentially millions of viewers with the backing of national football heroes six years after England's World Cup victory. The WFA committee had initially accepted the idea before a dubious procedure cast a revote against the proposal (Lopez, 1997: 62).

Rather than leading progress, directives from the Union of European Football Associations (UEFA) regarding the co-ordination of women's competition in the 1970s were strongly resisted by associations in the United Kingdom. In contrast, the WFA programme for the 1971 Mitre Challenge Trophy shows how widespread women's interest in football was; teams included Stewarton and Thistle (Scotland), EMGALS (Leicester), Wanderers (Nuneaton), Kays Ladies (Worcester), Amersham Angels and White Ribbon (London), Thanet United (Kent) and Southampton. An unofficial World Cup in Mexico in 1971, where beach volleyball could have learned a lesson or two about presenting women players in revealing pink sports uniforms to television audiences, in particular led to some concern about the place of the feminine in football. Change, though, has been painfully slow, for example the FAI in Ireland formally adopted the LFAI into its structure in 1991, the English FA and the Football Association of Wales (FAW) took control of women's football in 1993 and the Irish Football Association agreed a partnership with the WFAI in 1995. The Scottish FA took over women's football in 1998. The tentative phrasing of the agreements reflects a conspicuous lack of enthusiasm which means that, after integration, home country women's teams have increasingly struggled in international competition. In contrast, women were welcomed rather more warmly into administrative organisations in Germany and Sweden in 1970, Denmark 1972 and Norway 1978, and all are in the top-flight.

Professionalism was also a mixed blessing in the 1970s when British women players like Sue Lopez, Edna Nellis and Rose Reilly had to choose between travelling to pursue a career in football and representing their nation. Rose Reilly and Edna Nellis both had professional experience in France and Italy which led them to suggest that the Women's Scottish FA choice of manager in 1975, a poorly-qualified amateur male, was not the ideal solution. In return both received a lifetime ban which they feared would end their professional careers. Fortunately this was not the case; Rose captained the Italian team after being given citizenship and continued to live in Italy for some years. Sue Lopez returned to England and gave up a professional career to pursue an international one. The issue of female professionalism has only recently resurfaced in England with the breakaway launch of SASI (Seven-a-side Soccer International) and the FA's own league both competing for ITV funding. The situation is complicated by resentment from Nationwide League clubs in financial difficulty after the collapse of the ITV Digital £180m deal early in 2002. At the current time, like in the 1970s, travel is the only option for the fully professional player. Though Fulham and Arsenal run semi-professional teams, the United States Collegiate system is still the best showcase for young British women players who hope to make a career out of playing, coaching and related activities. In spite of having world-class players, British women's sections within associations continue to be prone to internal sparring, particularly about how to make female football acceptable to obstinate and fusty bureaucracies.

In spite of the increased regulation since the 1960s it has been difficult to conduct a systematic study of the numbers to arrive at a judgement of exactly how many players and how many clubs operated in women's football at any one time. In order to test the hypothesis of a steady rise in playing numbers that has accelerated since FA control in the 1990s Table 1.1 attempts to summarise current knowledge from 1969 to the present. The 1969 figure of forty-four clubs came from two WFA administrators who suggested that the number of clubs should have been forty-nine but five clubs did not join for various reasons. At this time competitive leagues began to replace the calendar of tournament style or annual fixtures. Though they were regionally based, the formation of the leagues was subject to change. For example, the participation by Chiltern Valley in the second unofficial Women's World Cup in Mexico in 1971 led to the expulsion of the whole East Midlands Ladies Alliance (of which Chiltern Valley were the champions). Therefore the figures may underestimate the established but unaffiliated clubs around. In 1977 the *WFA News* gave the number of clubs as 257 with over 100 youth teams. Bale appears to support this approximate number with 260 in 1978. Lopez gives a figure of 300 clubs with 6,000 players in 1979. Dorothy Miller has the 1987 figure as 187 clubs, a figure she obtained from WFA Secretary Linda Whitehead. The Football Association has the 1989 figures as 263 clubs with 7,000 players. In 1991 and 1992, Lopez has 334 and 380 clubs respectively. The 1991–2 *WFA News* development report says 'Such is the growing interest in women's soccer that by the end of this next season we could be looking at a total of 500 affiliated clubs' (Women's Football Association *c.* 1992: 33). Table 1.1 summarises the sources referred to here and the uneven growth year on year.

The most significant pattern from this data is that in one decade, between 1969 and 1979, the number of clubs affiliated to the WFA increased sixfold. Compared with the FA figures in 2000 of 35,000 females in 1,500 clubs, it has taken twenty years for women's football to grow a further six times. The attempt to chart the growth in numbers year by year has been possible to a limited extent. By compiling lists of clubs affiliated to the WFA in the years 1980 to 1990, including those mentioned in minutes, league fixtures, cup matches and feature articles, it was possible to arrive at figures which reflected perhaps the minimum number of clubs. The names of clubs were checked against previous years, in order to examine continuity but it was not possible to track the withdrawal of teams.

The figures compiled from this source, shown in Table 1.1 as asterisked numbers to the right of the second column, when compared with the other sources detailed in the previous paragraph, have two uses. One is to show

Table 1.1 Number of women's football clubs 1969–96

Year	*Number of clubs*	*Number of registered female players*
1969	44[1]	
1971	100[2]	
1972	182[3]	
1977	257[4]	
1978	260[5]	
1979	300[6]	6,000
1980	250*	
1982	267*	
1984	260*	
1985	263*	
1987	187[7]	
1988	166*	
1989	263[8]	7,000
1990	251*	
1991	334[9]	9,000
1992	380[10]	
1996	600 women's, 750 girls' teams[11]	14,000 and 7,500 respectively
2000	700 women's, 750 girls' teams[12]	35,000

Sources: (1) Football Association, 1998f: 1; (2) Lopez, 1979: 60; (3) Williams and Woodhouse, 1991: 96; (4) Lopez, 1997: 62; (5) Bale, 1982: 26; (6) Lopez, 1979: 40; (7) Miller, 1987: 5; (8) Football Association, 1998f: 1; (9) Lopez, 1997: 86; (10) Women's Football Association 1992: 4; (11) Football Association 1998f: 1; (12) Football Association 2000b

Note: *Figures derived from clubs affiliated to WFA in these years.

a similar pattern of growth until 1985, which roughly corresponds with Miller's figure of 187 in 1987. The plateau of numbers and the subsequent drop reveal irregular development in that the 300 clubs in 1979 appears to be a high point, not exceeded for over a decade. Whether this reflects a dip in actual participation or inaccurate procedures for recording the number of teams, or both, remains to be established. What is clear is that at a time when television was becoming interested in the sport and when England's success on an international stage was recognised in the press, the numbers challenge interpretation.

The asterisked figures also suggested a further complication, in that, though the number of clubs in 1989 is fewer, the number of players is greater. This is even more exaggerated in the 1991 figure, with an increase of 3,000 registered players, though only thirty-four more clubs. The combination of increased administrative competence, more clubs with reserve and junior teams, the expansion of girls' school-age football and an established structure of regional leagues which facilitated growth in the early 1990s after the apparent decline in the mid-1980s could account for this.

The number of clubs was particularly difficult to ascertain between 1979 and 1989. As this was the decade of increased popularity in the media and success in international competition, the notable lack of documentation reinforced an impression that increased participation was not matched by, let alone created by, increased bureaucratisation.

The mid-1980s was a turning point for the organisation of women's football in England though there was very little direct or immediate impact on the majority of players. In response to increasing pressure from FIFA and funding bodies, such as the Football Trust and the Sports Council, the WFA affiliated to the FA in 1984 and appointed Tim Stearn as Chair. The installation of experienced and FA sanctioned personnel with little understanding of the women's football community produced mixed benefits so that by 1985 the association had seriously under-forecast its bid for the Sports Council Grant Aid support. Participation consequently grew at a time when the management committee misunderstood the scale and scope of interest. In domestic football 1985 was also a turning point for the establishment of Football in the Community in League clubs and so, as women's football began to undergo a period of financial difficulty, the attitude of the football establishment began to change towards females as potential customers. The community officer's role was to co-ordinate commercial, voluntary, and public activities and as an easily identifiable 'minority' women, but more importantly girls, became included as part of the football family. They were categorised in a way that distinguished them from male professional football but which enabled them to consume that product. Almost twenty years later, many women's teams who ostensibly hold the name of a League club can expect to play their games on practice pitches and to be self-funding to the extent of raising sponsorship. The WFA Chair in 1988 was Richard Faulkener, the first deputy chair of the Football Trust, and the involvement of other agencies in women's football was cemented in 1991 when the Sports Council insisted on a closer relationship between the FA and WFA as a prerequisite for future grant aid. Whether the Sports Council intended to be free of the financial cost of grant aid to the WFA, or was alarmed by the financial difficulties after 1985 remains unclear. What is evident is that equality of opportunity was taken to mean integration with the existing structures of football.

In summarising the legacy of the WFA, it has to be said that though conservative and prone to infighting, the organisers as a whole were progressive in other respects, such as providing varied competitive opportunities for women players and being mindful of the broader international perspective. The association also sponsored two women for a full A Licence coaching award and developed junior representative sides.[13] As a focal point for regional league and elite representative success, the WFA was successful in its achievements; as a unifying authority and as an engine of good public relations for women's football it was ultimately a failure. Some, but by no means all, within the women's game remain optimistic about the access to expertise that alliance with the FA offers.[14] The pragmatic arrangement of where, how and when girls and women participate in football suggest that a voluntary network continues to arrange most female play.

The reactionary sporting world clearly needs to include some women as members in order to be culturally legitimate in the 1990s in ways that apparently were not necessary in the 1920s, and in exploring some aspects of this, it seems that this historical overview has raised more questions than it has answered. Consequently, claims for a recent rise of female interest retain the idea of natural gender difference and at the same time reposition women as consumers of many aspects of the sport, of which playing is just one. This is clearly at odds with the privately held material and this theme of women as the co-producers of their own experience of playing football is developed in the next chapter. One of the wider issues from this disparity is the need for a critique of the process whereby a sport is equated with masculinity as feminism gains footholds in popular culture, as it did in the early part of this century and in the second wave in the 1960s, and Part II begins to extend the analysis. Evidently women football players and administrators acting on their behalf did not meekly accept the FA ban that prevented women from playing on Association or League pitches after the collapse of the English Ladies' Football Association. However, crucially, resistance has not taken the form of sustained or collective action except for women continuing to play. Therefore tradition is fragmented but traceable and many of the gaps will be filled by those who wish to discuss aspects of dress, social background, team formation and maintenance, travel and so forth. Meanwhile, the idea of a prohibition remains but applies to mixed rather than female football.[15] In spite of the early and widespread popularity of the British touring teams, English football has hardly been at the vanguard of the change and football for women under the control of both the WFA and the FA is symptomatic of the wider conservatism of officialdom. The formal parameters at national and international level that have been applied to women playing competitive football, from 'banning' women to presupposing their physical inferiority in the laws of the game, are by no means rational or inevitable.[16] In addition, since the 1960s women's attempts to enter football have corresponded with a new and emergent professionalism in the sport. The use of associations for various specialisms particularly and the process of patronage generally have served to include a few exceptional individuals at the expense of a critical mass of women.

Unlike this top-down view of female participation, using privately held material has made it possible to characterise some processes of the construction and maintenance of community in women's football. The collections reveal a co-operative of contacts with clubs at once local in identity and widespread in rivalry, with several teams claiming themselves 'the best' or 'foremost' exponents of the women's game in Britain until, in the 1990s, the women's game mirrors the structures of the men's in the accumulation of double or treble honours.[17]

2 Competition and community in English women's football

The previous chapter gave a brief overview of the history of women's football and discussed a number of popular narratives about players. This chapter focuses on the period of transition as the spectator-supported forms of women's football as entertainment gradually gave way to a more prevalent participatory culture. The kinds of competitive arrangements reflected specific senses of community better understood in terms of a long tradition. Continuities are evident, however the meanings attached to these activities would have also changed over time. During the period when sport generally became more commercialised, women's football became less popular with audiences. Women players who were fêted as local dignitaries from 1895 onwards may have found it interesting and enjoyable to tour the country in order to play in front of large crowds but they would not have thought of this as a viable alternative to full-time paid work. Yet the practice of 'finding' jobs for very good players that would enable them to play frequently without being too tired was commonplace until the 1960s. Thereafter, women's football as spectacle progressively became less familiar and the idea of it as primarily a leisure activity took hold. This is not to say that the motivation of the players was any different and for this reason the production of community through competition and vice versa are the most enduring aspects of women's football culture in England.

This issue has been treated as a chapter in itself because it is one of the most disputed aspects of the subject and has affected the sense of tradition and memory in women's football. The scarce athletic opposition and sense of affinity appear to be a point of widespread academic consensus, for example Fishwick concludes that in the period 1910–50, 'Women almost never played organized football'(Fishwick, 1989: 17). Also writing in 1989, Richard Holt said of women and clubs more generally, 'This sociability has been largely male. Female participation in sport has been negligible until recently. Men have kept women out of sport except as helpers . . . Female *social* participation may have been more widespread than has been realized' (Holt, 1989: 348).

As is evident from the interviews, sporting sociability, playing because it is fun, is the most frequent response of players surveyed for this study.

So though Holt is right in suggesting that women's football was and is a minority activity, female participation has been both more common with players and more popular with the public than 'negligible' implies. However, the prevailing view is extended by the supposition that if the teams are largely unknown to us, they will have been isolated in competitive terms and without a sense of community:

> Estimates suggested that towards the end of 1921 there were around 150 women's clubs in England . . . Many of these clubs probably knew little of each other's existence because of the localized nature of charity competition . . . The fate of football for women in Britain over the following forty years or more remains, as far as we can tell, almost wholly unresearched.
>
> (Williams and Woodhouse, 1991: 93–5)

Derek Birley's account of British sport shrugs off the popularity of the munitionettes and post-war games as a fad. 'The fervour was not sustained, partly because wartime mores did not last, and partly because the FA, with troubles enough from male professionalism . . . felt [women's football] had little to do with soccer proper' (Birley, 1995: 204). Dave Russell resisted this idea and, though brief, the argument places the development of the sport for women as 'One of the most striking aspects of the inter-war and the immediate post-war game' (Russell, 1997: 95). As one of a number of topics covered under the chapter 'Football, Economy and Society 1919–1939', the argument sets women's football as related to wider patterns of social change. The discussion of regional and occupational unemployment against an overall improvement in material conditions is useful for the analysis of the community of women players and how this compares with competitive structures today.

One component that endures, but which academics have overlooked, has been a large number of tournaments, both preceding and then supplementing regional or national leagues. In the 1920s the circulation of players around the country forged an embryonic national community, with some international ties. It was not a system that appears, at first glance, suited to those with families or to working women. Nevertheless the arrangement of fixtures in blocks allowed for social and competitive activities which players fitted in with these responsibilities. In contrast to the idea of charitable fund-raising being the main point of these fixtures, women's challenge contests were rarely arranged for purely economic reasons. For example, twenty-six teams competed in the English Ladies' Challenge Cup of 1922 and it was specifically designed to foster local pride based on the pre-eminence of Stoke, the home side. It was a tournament invented and administered by ex-Sunderland player Arthur Bridgett and his brother Len. England international Arthur Bridgett had a reputation as a gentlemanly player who refused to play on Sunday. Len was a local employer, had been a Director of Stoke City FC (at the time of their re-election to the Second Division of the Football League in 1915) and a local council member for twenty-two years. Bridgett's United, later known as Stoke Ladies, overcame Newcastle, Manchester and Grimsby sides to reach the June final at Port Vale's Cobridge stadium, beating Bentley's of Doncaster 3-1 to win.

Arthur coached the Stoke players, and the team appears to have been formed originally because Len had seven daughters, several of whom worked in the family business. With Len's money, and Arthur's know-how, the Stoke team was well placed to ignore the FA ban from 1921–3. As Arthur's son tells it:

> So Len put the money up and it was his team – Bridgett's Eleven Ladies. He had five daughters playing in the team and then they had the coal merchant's daughter who was a good strong girl 'cause she could carry bags of coal, so it made sense that she would be a good strong girl to play football: they were like pit ponies really. Then they had the Captain of the Titanic's niece – Smith. Lily was the oldest, and after a few years she moved with another brother to Liverpool, where the fish was. She went up to look after [the shop]. She was like the secretary for Len and she wasn't married. I think most of Len's daughters were involved in the fish business. I can remember the lot of them working down the Stoke fish market. Apart from that, the girls that were in the team were outsiders; the coalman's daughter, the milkman's daughter . . . Oh yeah, I found that I did, these strapping girls of yesteryear. That was Dolly Cooper, she was Captain of the ladies' team. You've got [a newspaper article] there on Daisy Bates haven't you? [*pointing*] Daisy continued her association with football [*laughs*]. She married Bob Dixon, Stoke's first team goalkeeper.[1]

The various groups that helped women's matches to take place seem to have been carefully casual in their approach. Len sponsored the women's team to travel to Spain in 1923 to play against a French team and the organisation involved must have been considerable. However, when fish became more readily available from Grimsby, several of Len's daughters moved there to develop the business and Arthur was offered a contract back in professional football, so the team folded. Stoke's last game was played against Dick, Kerr Ladies, billed as 'Winners of Seven Silver Cups and Two sets of Gold Medals' on 22 September 1923 at the Horsfield Ground, Colne. The club doesn't appear to have been created for any resistant, oppositional or counter-cultural expression by the brothers or the players. There was a little rational recreation associated with these games and much to do with enjoyment and entertainment.

The Stoke team were not unique: before there was a league structure, regional or otherwise, women's teams played frequently against one another for the accumulation of honours. It is only in the last thirty years that administrators have chosen to imitate the amateur or professional structures of male football. The continuity of tournament-style fixtures and cup events across the country and across decades is sufficient to suggest systematic organisation. For example, Bolton were formed in 1938 and Manchester Corinthians in 1949, with a second team, Dynamo Ladies, created in 1950. There is evidence from souvenir programmes of repeated competitions, year on year, between these teams.

A 1951 programme has the Corinthian Ladies (acclaimed as Britain's Premier Ladies' Team) against Lancashire for the Furness Trophy at Craven Park and reports that twenty-six teams were participating in the tournament. Whilst it wasn't possible to confirm that these were the same twenty-six teams operating in 1922, and it would seem unlikely, we know that some women's clubs endured for decades. It also suggests some strength in depth in the level of competition. The Corinthians, 'modelled on the famous Corinthian style of old', were listed as having won the Southern Cup, Manchester Area Cup, Sports Magazine Cup, Roses Trophy, Midland Trophy, Cresswell Trophy, Odeon Championship Trophy, Belle Vue Trophy and the Festival of Britain Ladies' Championship Trophy. A 1952 programme for Bolton versus the Corinthians at Manchester Athletic Club, Fallowfield for the Rogers Trophy claims the home team were undefeated from 1938 to 1948 and winners of the Estra Henry Trophy in 1946, 1947 and 1948. The Bolton manager declares himself as 'Ever ready to put the Team on for any Charity' in England, Scotland and Wales, and the Corinthian team as having 'travelled over 9,000 miles and raised over £8,000 for Charity' (*Corninthians versus Bolton Programme*, 1952). Though we know something about the form and style of tournament play, research has still to ascertain further details about the patrons of the various competitions, like Estra Henry. There is also a lot more to know about individual teams like the Edinburgh Dynamos of the 1950s and early 1960s, who played in the trophy final on three occasions and played in England against Bolton and Manchester.[2]

Though games were often played for charity, the range of organisations for which fund-raising took place indicates that this was rarely the sole reason for competition. Part of the legitimacy of women's games played on professional grounds was based on support for the working or the fighting man. In the 1930s and 1940s players were sometimes overwhelmed by support. So many supporters slapped Joan Whalley on the back in congratulation after she scored a hat-trick in 1949 that her skin was seriously bruised. In the same year the Dick, Kerr's team were invited as guests of honour to Freckleton to lay a wreath of red roses in memory of thirty-eight children killed by an American Liberator which had crashed on their school in August 1944. So the public recognition of players extended beyond games to include a degree of civic respect. However, the target audience varied depending on the circumstances of the time. For instance two matches, in 1951 and 1952, raised funds for the Printers' Pension Corporation Fund.

Printing as a highly unionised, male-dominated occupation is a distinctive example. Put another way, working men had the necessary expendable income to pay the 3d cost of a programme to facilitate female play on large, sometimes League, grounds.

In this respect, women's football successfully cultivated an element of working-class support until the late 1960s. Many of the matches took place in a ceremonial atmosphere, with welcome parties comprising local dignitaries. Teams were often accompanied out onto the pitch by brass bands who provided half-time entertainment, it was a convention to have a celebrity 'kick off' and the games were followed by civic receptions. As examples of public recognition of female competition and sustained spectator support of women's football, this arrangement demonstrates the pitfalls of projecting ideas taken from the male structures of football onto female play. The meanings given to the activities of women players in these circumstances were quite different to the lack of respect they receive today, though the sporting press may well have been less than constructive. The instrumentality of those who hosted women's teams and the free choice of supporters in opting to attend games over another leisure activity were part of the construction of a reciprocal relationship which linked players with the wider community.

Alethea Melling, in her work on the French and English teams, supports the point that international competition has long been a part of women's football (Melling, 1999: 42). Teams representing the home countries played one another and Dick, Kerr's travelled to Canada and the United States in 1922. The Stoke tour to Spain in 1923 also suggests autonomy and self-sufficiency. In short, there was no need to go to Spain to play, but there was sufficient awareness of women's football as developing a European dimension that English teams wanted to extend the range of competitors that they played against. The setting of the Spanish game is likely to have been the FC Barcelona ground between 1909 and 1922, Carrer Industria. Known locally as L'Escopidora, 'the spittoon', because of its small pitch, the ground was considered the best of its time in Catalonia and the first to have artificial lighting. The possible capacity and the crowd reported in the local newspaper at the time was 6,000 spectators. The Stoke Ladies played the French Femina side, over two fixtures. Why they should play in Barcelona remains unclear beyond the fact that the French side toured extensively in search of opposition. The event was significant in terms of the construction of a memory of women's football, because it is one of the first in which a woman player is captured in photographs while playing football. The fixture echoes the British form of wide-ranging competition but also contrasts with the number of home-countries teams against which British clubs could compete during this phase of popularity.

Sports tourism in women's football involved travel, friendship and competition. For some women it involved more. Alice Mills Lambert left England for the United States after the 1922 Dick, Kerr's tour, where she had purportedly tried to 'jump ship'. On a return visit to Preston Guild in 1952 photographs show a 48-year-old Alice, then mother of six, shaking hands and reminiscing with Alfred Frankland (the manager), aged 70. After her death, Bill Parillo, writing for the *Providence Journal* prior to the Women's World Cup 1999, wrote:

> If Mia and her friends want to call themselves pioneers they have every right. However, if you're looking for the real pioneers . . . included in that group was a feisty 4 foot-11 young woman named Alice Mills, who spent the greater part of her life living in Pawtucket raising a family of six daughters . . . Alice Mills' soccer career ended when she returned to America, got a job and began sending for her relatives – her mother, brother and sisters.
>
> (Parillo, 1999: 2)

Other women travelled because of developments more obliquely related to football. Nancy 'canonball' Thomson initially played for Edinburgh City Girls in the 1930s before moving to England to play for Dick, Kerr's in 1939 where she took a job out of necessity.

> Wherever we went we had the best treatment . . . all this was going to my head, I sent a letter to my married sister saying, 'Please send my things down, I'm not coming back'. I didn't learn immediately how distressed they were. Then came the problem, I had to work . . . I didn't fill a form in, I didn't have an interview and I suddenly realised it was a mental hospital . . . in no time at all I became interested . . . I was 41 when I finished playing football in 1957 and moved to Gibraltar to improve mental health care. It was a very exciting time . . . All this started through football don't forget.
>
> (Thomson, 2000)

In the private collections of these players there is development of a consciousness of a community of players that goes beyond club or region. Players' access to transport and the ability to compete were directly linked because of the geographical spread of teams. Players travelled by public or hired transport and sometimes took days to reach a destination in order to play football. Character notes about the participants in programmes give some idea of the various social backgrounds of visiting players. For example a French team was described in a Preston versus France programme from a match held on 23 June 1949 as:

Cecile Sorel (Captain) Fearless tackler and makes a splendid captain.
Aline Dingee A very fine college girl, plays many games and likes soccer best of all.
V. Nelanney Teacher of Physical culture in several Public Schools in France.

Anne Boutin Excellent swimmer and runner, a Milliner by trade and wears her own hats.
Paulette Le Blond Secretary to one of the largest Motor Firms in France, a fine all round sporting girl. Winner of several skiing Championships.
Ranle Cadi By profession a photographer. Her speciality is Spanish Dances of which she is a teacher.
Jeanette Graindar Recently won a French National Championship which included all Sports. She is Secretary to a well-known Congressman.
Yvonne Renald Basketball International. She is a Clerk in the French Post Office.
Arlette Reni A Masseuse specialising in sports massage. Represented France at Basketball.

The French tours were usually annual events and, though less frequent than tournament-style fixtures amongst British teams, sufficiently significant to suggest that competition was not just local or dependent on other fund-raising or leisure activities. This said, it is more difficult to find out about the social background of English players than touring participants from programmes and this may in part be due to an assumed knowledge on the behalf of the sporting public. For example, these 'pen pictures' of players taken from a 1923 programme, Stoke versus Dick, Kerr Ladies, 22 September:

Miss Alice Kell (Dick, Kerr's Captain and Goalkeeper) Modest and unassuming off the field, cool and capable on it. Kicks with beautiful accuracy and judgement. Strangers who meet her express surprise that she is a footballer. They little know that the quiet, charming girl to whom they are speaking is captain of the most famous girls' team in the world and that she only occupies that position by virtue of her consistent and excellent play.
Miss Dolly Cooper (Stoke's Captain and Centre-Half) Young, tall and robust. One of the best centre-half backs playing. Kicks powerfully, can trap the ball like a man, and feeds the forwards judicially. Is largely responsible for the success of the Stoke Ladies.
Miss Lily Parr (Dick, Kerr's Outside-Left) A phenomenal player, and quite young. Big, fast and powerful, is tricky and can take corner kicks better than most men and scores many goals from extraordinary angles with a left foot cross drive, which nearly breaks the net. Is the tom-boy of the team, who always says exactly what she thinks about everybody and everything – often to the amusement and embarrassment of the other members of the side.

We feel we know something of the players' personalities but little about their personal and social background. Nevertheless, football-related travel is an example of how sport brought the participants into contact with a wide range of people in a variety of social situations. The players were, by turns, local dignitaries, the object of spectator support, co-competitors, local representatives, friends, co-workers, rivals and so forth. Then, as now, sports tourism and hospitality formed an integral part of the engagement of participants.

The example of Homestead Ladies, from North Hykeham, Lincolnshire, shows continuities with the way that new clubs became established and closed again: an ongoing situation in women's football, as with other locally based and volunteer-supported sports. The club is also a typical challenge for the researcher as it was formed for a relatively short time. The team originated at the local garage where several women worked as administrators in early 1960. They played on Sundays on Home Ground Memorial Pitch and trained under floodlights nearby. The largest crowd of supporters, 3,500, was recorded at a match against the Boston Bombshells at the Mayflower Sports Ground in 1961 but Homestead also played against teams including Gainsborough Worthies, Oldham Ladies, Corinthians and Ripley. They lost the use of the Memorial Ground site in 1964 and ceased to play soon after. The team's performance was the subject of a local history piece, still to be published. Excerpts include Linda Dring knocking herself out on her own goalpost; a collision involving Hykeham's Shirley Reid in which a visiting centre forward's arm was broken; a 7-1 defeat at Ripley played in teeming rain and ankle-deep mud; the feats of leading goal-scorer, Audrey Mole, and the leadership of Captain Barbara Duncombe (M. Hird, local historian, personal communication 1997). By cross-checking with Gainsborough or Ripley team members, for instance, a more comprehensive picture could be compiled about why the team did not obtain an alternative home ground or whether players went on to play for other teams.

The competitive network of women's football is a distinctive and characteristic aspect of involvement that regional leagues formalised to an extent after 1969. Some teams have been one-off collections of women playing for various reasons, as Homestead's ninety-one goals in their first eighteen matches suggest. Others, like Corinthians and Ripley, remain formed for several years. This may appear somewhat fluid compared with county-based and regionalised leagues with rules for promotion, relegation and so on. But this loose alliance of interest provided enough of a foundation for women's participation to grow without central regulation or a great deal of officialdom in the 1960s. A lot more work remains to be done on the continuity of clubs, and the involvement of administrators and managers. By extension, the movement of players between clubs and the playing careers of individuals are also areas that have yet to be given a more sophisticated treatment.

Unlike the period up until 1921, there is no way at the present time that women's football could challenge men's football as a professional elite sport in England or Europe. In contrast, the Women's USA (WUSA), the professional league in the United States, has the potential to at least equal the popularity of Major League Soccer (MLS) but as a non-indigenous, often ethnically focused sport, this is not comparing like for like. Attempts by global and national associations to control women's access to the game now, might indicate a relative weakness in their status at a time of rapid change in employment law and financial interest from outside sport. The financial support and patronage of the FA and FIFA who, in turn, enjoy an enhanced public image because of their apparently progressive attitude forms the basis for the mutual support of the development of a feminine-appropriate sub-brand. In England a split system has developed as a consequence, whereby the majority of participation is still organised through the regional leagues run by and for women, but the elite representative squads are increasingly under the control of the FA. This is beginning to shape aspects of ownership and the distribution of power within the women's football community in line with this split.

Sheila Rollinson's playing and administrative career is a useful example because like most women players in the 1960s, 1970s and 1980s she began playing in organised competition when she started work. At 17, Sheila was a founder member of a club which is also, in some senses, representative of how the pattern of the split between elite and regional teams became established from the 1980s onwards. Rollinson and a work colleague formed Burton Wanderers in 1978 and became Beacon Wanderers in 1985 (sponsored by Beacon Hotel). The club was then adopted as Derby County Women's Club in 1992. In the early, three division Midlands Women's League, Burton were mid-table of Division Three as at December 1978. By 1980 Doncaster Belles had joined the League and were mid-table of Division One. At the end of that year Doncaster won the league and continued to dominate the headlines for successive years. With respect to Wanderers, they had some success and were promoted but were less successful than the Belles, perhaps reflecting a more participatory rather than a competitive ethos. Sheila continues to play for Derby County, and she has coached, administered and supported women's football in the intervening decades. After initially being closely involved with both international tours with the representative squad and regional administration, the creation of succesive layers of bureaucracy has placed specialists like Sheila at the edge of decision-making structures. Increasingly, the job of the regional leagues is to deliver FA policies rather than to inform or create them. In this sense her career in women's football is representative too of the shift from formulation to implementation of centrally devised strategies. However, this devolved model continues to provide significant leeway for administrators to employ time-served and hard-won discretion in developing the sport to the advantage of regionally based players.

Private collections of memorabilia and WFA newsletters, such as those held by Sheila, dispute the view that 'By the 1980s . . . the women's game in England had enjoyed little success in its attempts to establish a strong countrywide base for the sport' (Williams and Woodhouse, 1991: 99). For example in the 1980 season, in addition to the regular matches of the

Midlands Women's League (three divisions, twenty-three teams), Burton Wanderers also participated in the WFA Cup, the Midland Region Cup, the Majestic Cup, the Lloyds Cup, the Geoff Gibbs Trophy, friendly matches and tournaments. A 1982 edition of *WFA News* characteristically reports on games against Japan and Norway. In a single edition advertisements appear for competitions in West Germany, Denmark, Norway, Holland, France and Scotland, in addition to UK tournaments for international teams and tours by foreign teams who were searching for English opposition. Widespread local and national co-operative competition remains a key feature to this day, with teams regularly travelling for two hours for a Sunday game and the more occasional international tour. However, there are signs of change from 2000 onwards: the FA Women's Football Committee intends to ally women's football more closely with the structures of men's football and introduce county-based leagues in order to reduce the amount of travel. This is logical if one does not accept the existence of a women's football culture in its own right and is perhaps more motivated by a move towards developing youth football rather than adult competition.

Another way that funding has been directed towards infantilising elite play is that Centres of Excellence, with fifteen girls in each squad, are central to the FA's plan. Is this likely to benefit the overall standard of women's football or is it a means of diverting money to already wealthy league clubs where the centres are located? Whatever the intention, women's clubs based outside Football League and Premiership grounds do not receive equivalent subsidy to those that integrate. FA administrators see independent women's clubs as an extremely low priority. For example, Doncaster Belles' plans to build a stadium are therefore vital, as without it, the club will not be granted a licence to host a Centre of Excellence. If this situation develops further the representation of independent women's clubs at elite level is likely to be reduced. The Belles' players are keenly aware of this and they describe their situation as follows:

> In my first year at the Club we did the treble – FA Cup, League Cup and the League. Before that we won lots of things including the League many times. We are not associated with a men's side – so I think we lose out. Belles were in the North Notts league, then we went to the Premier league. We fund ourselves – we're not affiliated to a men's club which makes it harder for us. ZARA sponsor our kit and tracksuits, T-shirts, shorts . . . they send everything free. Belles have won the cup and league many time, the last being the 1994 double season . . . we haven't won anything since then.

> Club founded for women 1969 . . . Our first sponsor was NPS Healthcare and Forester Health. Our major sponsor for 1998/99 season, Optima International, provided a training ground and other numerous facilities . . . it was a major financial input.

> The Doncaster Belles were founded in 1969 on the Doncaster Rovers terraces by a group of women who sold the 'Golden Goal' tickets for Doncaster Rovers' promotion. For the Doncaster Belles to maintain their high profile on and off the pitch we need to be financially secure. This security can only be sustained by sponsorship.

To withhold support for independent women's clubs without a certain standard of facility, when these clubs have achieved success despite not having these resources is, to say the least, arrogant. In future plans to develop women's football there is little recognition of tradition that these independent teams represent. There is also a feeling among some women players that county-based leagues will actually reduce the level of competition that regional leagues have fostered, because of the emphasis on local opposition. Currently the county leagues are more useful for youth and reserve teams who have travel concerns or just want to play an occasional game; the vast majority of women's teams have chosen to remain in regional leagues because of the quality and frequency of competition.

The points made so far about the absence of women's football in our urban and rural landscape look set to continue. Loughborough teams are a useful example of both the pressure on pitches and the uncertain nature of the integration with men's clubs. The rules of the Football Association state that 'No Club, Player or Official, Referee or Linesman shall be compelled to participate in Football on Sunday'. In practice, lack of pitches means that playing on Sunday is the only viable option for the majority of League and Cup matches. Games usually take place on Sunday afternoon, generally on pitches already used that day, and the day before, by senior or junior male teams. In the case of Loughborough United the women's afternoon fixtures take place at home on alternate weeks, with a junior male team playing on the remaining afternoons. Another junior male team uses the pitch on Sunday mornings and the senior male team has sole use of the pitch on Saturdays. It is not unusual for facilities and clubhouses not to have been cleaned after the men have used them, or for match officials to cry off after refereeing in the morning, or for the playing surface to be extremely cut up.

The integration of women's teams with men's clubs has been, at best, partially successful. Loughborough Dynamo Women were funded for three years from 1999–2001 by the male team who shared the same name, who in turn received lottery funding as a result of having a female team affiliated. In 2001 the women moved to Loughborough United due to their dissatisfaction at having over half their fixtures cancelled the previous season by Dynamo club officials concerned about the 'state of the pitch'. As a result, United will be able to apply for lottery funding for an additional three years. Another local women's team moved to Loughborough Dynamo in 2001 to become Dynamo Women. This is just one of the ways that players' experiences are grounded in small collectives, even if the image of women's football is marketed by bureaucracies. So although the Lincoln team discussed earlier were based in rural surroundings thirty years ago and the Loughborough team play in a small market town with a significant student representation, the continuity over place and time is that of the priority given to female play as a whole. The struggle over access to pitches and clubhouses also affects the social memory of women's football, as the next chapter discusses. For many male clubs, the fact of having women affiliates in order to be seen to observe equality of opportunity is more significant than who they are or how the sport is developed.

In elite terms, Table 2.1, listing winners of the WFA Cup, later renamed the FA Women's Cup, presents a picture of teams affiliated to Football League clubs, particularly based in London, beginning to dominate competition in England over a thirty-year period. However, throughout the history of the cup there are examples of independent teams reaching the finals, particularly the encouraging endurance of Doncaster Belles.

One of the questions raised by this shift to the dominance of London clubs is the relative role of the FA in administering funding, especially for independent clubs to bid in their own right. Following Southampton's dominance in the 1970s, Doncaster Belles were *the* team of the 1980s and early 1990s within English women's football. However, the prominence given to London-based clubs in promotional material is clear in this commentary on the FA Women's Premier League (FAWPL) and Women's FA Cup.

> In 1995 and 1996 the winners (Arsenal and Croydon respectively) have completed a double by also taking the FAWPL title . . . All teams in the 3 divisions enter the FAWPL Cup. Arsenal have been the most successful participants . . . Southampton has been the most successful side in the FA Cup competition, appearing in 11 finals and winning eight of them. They hold the record winning score in a final (8–2) and are the only side to win the Cup three years in a row (in 1971, '72 & '73). The Doncaster Belles have competed in the final a record 11 times [*sic*], winning six, but Arsenal have the most successful recent record, winning three of the last five finals.
>
> (Football Association 2000b)

In this excerpt the kudos associated with established men's teams is borrowed to add some glamour to the women's game as a whole. The subtext appears to be that if Arsenal and Croydon are taking women's football seriously then other League and Premiership clubs can and should too. In point of fact, Belles' five wins and two second places in fourteen finals gives a different kind of 'recent' perspective, with Arsenal having a total of four wins in these years. Beyond this, Doncaster's importance in the women's game is such that United States and Australian internationals apply for trials; during one of my visits, the daughter of a US Air Force

Table 2.1 WFA Cup winners 1971–2000

	WFA Cup winners	*Finalists*
1971	Southampton	Stewarton and Thistle
1972	Southampton	Lee's Ladies
1973	Southampton	Westhorn United
1974	Fodens	Southampton
1975	Southampton	Warminster
1976	Southampton	QPR
1977	QPR	Southampton
1978	Southampton	QPR
1979	Southampton	Lowestoft
1980	St Helens	Preston North End
1981	Southampton	St Helens
1982	Lowestoft	Cleveland Spartans
1983	Doncaster Belles	St Helens
1984	Howbury Grange	Doncaster Belles
1985	Friends of Fulham	Doncaster Belles
1986	Norwich	Doncaster Belles
1987	Doncaster Belles	St Helens
1988	Doncaster Belles	Leasowe Pacific
1989	Leasowe Pacific	Friends of Fulham
1990	Doncaster Belles	Friends of Fulham
1991	Millwall Lionesses	Doncaster Belles
1992	Doncaster Belles	Red Star Southampton
1993	Arsenal	Doncaster Belles
1994	Doncaster Belles	Knowsley United
1995	Arsenal	Liverpool
1996	Croydon	Liverpool
1997	Millwall Lionesses	Wembley
1998	Arsenal	Croydon
1999	Arsenal	Southampton Saints
2000	Croydon	Doncaster Belles

Sources: WFA Cup Final programmes 1971–1992 and FA Women's Challenge Cup Final programmes 1993–2000

worker had flown in from Germany for possible selection. The Belles have adapted well to new FA structures and the reserve team is continually at the top of the lately formed Reserve League. Though there is evidently a successful club structure to develop younger players, the financial benefits given to Croydon, Arsenal and so forth are not otherwise available to Belles or other independent women's clubs. This makes recruitment and retention consequently more difficult, with players leaving Belles in order to access coaching and sponsorship; some transferring to Arsenal! The structural inequalities make this issue more than a case of independent clubs as the ugly ducklings to the swans of the League and Premiership-based women's teams. Though it appears an increasingly southern-based sport at elite level, the official view overstates the importance of London clubs particularly and the role of the south generally in the women's football community. Whether the methodology for funding women's teams will change the constituents of that community in the future to become a self-fulfilling prophecy remains to be seen.

One area of steady growth, for instance, that could lead to a degree of semi-professional preparation has been female university football in England. Tables 2.2 and 2.3 show an overall increase in the number of teams from which it is reasonable to conclude an increase in the number of young women participants. However, university football is not anything like as important to football for women (or men) in this country as it is in the United States. For example, eleven-a-side competition was not formalised until 1988. Table 2.2 illustrates how the uniform rise in the number of eleven-a-side teams from 1988 to 1992 is followed by a dramatic increase, due to the merger of the University Athletic Union (UAU), the British University Sports Federation and Brit. Colleges (made up of the British Colleges Sports Association and the British Polytechnic Sports Association). Though the number of teams involved in the competition since that date has continued to increase, participation has remained at a plateau for the last three years. Likewise Table 2.3 shows a steady increase in five-a-side football until the year of amalgamation, followed by a considerable increase. The apparent dip in numbers is due to the regionalisation of competition in a preliminary round and the figure in the table is the number of teams at the Finals tournament.

In both tables Loughborough dominates, with Crewe and Alsager, Birmingham, Manchester and Reading also prominent. However university football for women is an addition to the regionalised club competition rather than fostering talent in its own right, as College football in the United States does. Because the Sunday Leagues operate at different times than the traditional Wednesday afternoon and Saturday morning slots for university sport, a team like Loughborough can enter the East Midlands Women's League by arranging fixtures from mid October onwards *and* play in university competition (see Tables 2.2 and 2.3 beginning on page 60).

The contribution of higher education to the production of elite representative women's football players is poised to shift, perhaps rather belatedly, in response to the success of teams which have extended periods of training together as tournament preparation, like China, the United States and Norway. There is also something of a skills/brain drain that the English FA has to seal or risk losing players; for example, three of the current England senior squad are based in colleges in the United States.[3] However, directing elite women players to the United States to develop their playing career is in part due to financial pragmatism, in so far as it places the economic burden on the American education system. However pragmatic the intention, change is coming gradually. In September 2001 nineteen players joined the newly created National Player Development Centre at Loughborough from across the country and will continue playing for club sides on Sundays in addition to training at the centre during the week. The plan is to coach this squad of players to win the Women's World Cup in 2007. Accordingly, all the players are under 21 years of age. Julie Spearink, for instance, has reversed the journey across the Atlantic. The 16-year-old goalkeeper was born and bred in California, but English parentage qualifies her place. Attracting bright, exceptional female players to this kind of initiative involves persuading them that the course would benefit them beyond sport. As yet in England, viable careers in football for women are scarce. Over and above this, English female players will continue to go to the United States for some time because of the relative professionalism of the collegiate model, the less acknowledged role of university teams, plus the stipulation that those at the National Development Centre have to have played representative football. From the role of football in education the discussion moves to the ways in which education has also had a key role in the increased rationalisation and consequent increased specialisation of football. However it is not just the identity of the women's football co-operative that is open to amendment, as women's services football indicates.

The place of women's football in the army is a good case of the use of the sport to enhance the public image of certain organisations and also makes a point about wider shifts in culture. From WAAF Sergeant Wilkinson who played for Preston in the 1940s, to the captain of the newly formed Combined Services team, women working in the military who wished to play football have had to play for civilian teams until the 1990s. Given the nature of postings and the kind of work involved, this has made a consistent involvement difficult. As two interviewees put it:

> The typical Army attitude affected my playing career for the best years I had; you know, between 18 and 28 when you're at your best. We could have a kick about with the blokes but those of us that wanted to play competitively had to join civilian teams and that made training difficult . . . you couldn't always make a game on Sunday.

> Yes – there was also that thing about women football players being lesbians and 'course you couldn't even have a hint of that on your record so [*laughs*] I grew my hair long. So did some of the others and I can't believe it now . . . as if there are no long-haired lesbians! But that's what you were up against until the Army wanted to promote a more inclusive image and it was a godsend to them when Alex [Cotier] joined.

The key game in the broader acceptance of women's football was the British Army on the Rhine (now British Army in Germany) against the Army UK side in February 1995 at Aldershot. This was the first eleven-a-side match, which had been preceded by a number of six-a-side tournaments, notably at Bassingbourne. Though there were no organised women's teams at regimental level, the six-a-side tournaments demonstrated a clear interest among women, as the interviewees suggest. This led to the formation of an

Table 2.2 BUSA Women's eleven-a-side association football competition 1988–2000

Year and final venue	*No. of teams taking part*	*Quarter-finalists*	*Semi-finalists*	*Winners*
1989 Cardiff	16	Birmingham Sussex Swansea Southampton	Exeter* Bradford Lancaster	Loughborough
1990 Bath	19	Sussex East Anglia Birmingham Lancaster	Exeter* Swansea Sheffield	Loughborough
1991 Bath	25	Lancaster Leicester Imperial College, London University College of North Wales, Bangor	Loughborough* Warwick Sheffield	Exeter
1992 Bath	27	Leicester Lancaster Birmingham Warwick	Exeter* Reading Manchester	Loughborough
1993 Warwick	40	University College of North Wales, Bangor Hull Loughborough West London Institute of Higher Education	Manchester* Liverpool Bedford	Birmingham
1994 Stafford	78**	Aberdeen Royal Holloway/North Bedford College, London Sheffield Birmingham	Crewe & Alsager* Cambridge Brighton	Loughborough

1995 Loughborough	 88	Aberdeen South Bank Greenwich Birmingham	Crewe & Alsager* Marjon Brighton	Bedford
1996 Warwick	 87	Trinity and All Saints, University of Leeds Loughborough Marjon Brighton	Birmingham* Cambridge Liverpool Institute of Higher Education	Crewe & Alsager
1997 UCL	 88	Heriot-Watt, Edinburgh Birmingham Brunel University College University of Wales, Cardiff	Brighton* St Marys Liverpool John Moores University	Crewe & Alsager
1998 Birmingham	 99	St Marys Cheltenham & Gloucester Heriot-Watt, Edinburgh Birmingham	Leeds Metropolitan University* Liverpool Hope Chichester	Loughborough
1999 Ilkeston	 98	Birmingham Liverpool Hope Brighton Royal Holloway College, University of London	Marjon* Oxford Loughborough	Edinburgh
2000 Stevenage	 99	Liverpool Hope Brighton University of Wales, Cardiff Wolverhampton	Loughborough* Manchester Crewe & Alsager	Brunel UC

Notes: * Runner up. ** The number of teams increased due to the merger of UAU/BUSF/Brit. Colleges.

Table 2.3 UAU (1980–9) and BUSA (1990–2000) women's five-a-side association football competition

Year and final venue	*No. of teams taking part*	*Quarter-finalists*	*Semi-finalists*	*Winners*
1980 Nottingham	14	Loughborough (II) Nottingham Nottingham (II) Reading	Bath* Essex Swansea	Loughborough
1981 Keele	10	Keele (II) Loughborough (II) Nottingham Nottingham (II)	Keele* Bath Swansea	Loughborough
1982 Bradford	12	Bath Keele Manchester Keele (II)	Swansea* Birmingham Sheffield	Loughborough
1983 Sussex	13	Aston Hull Keele Loughborough (II)	Sheffield* Sheffield (II) Southampton	Loughborough
1984 Keele	13	Sheffield Southampton Surrey University College London	Salford* Keele Loughborough	Lancaster
1985 Birmingham	15	Lancaster Manchester Sheffield Surrey	Salford* University of East Anglia Keele	Loughborough
1986 Durham	15	Aston Birmingham Leeds Manchester	Loughborough (II)* University of East Anglia Surrey	Salford

1987 Essex	21	Bradford Bangor Manchester Sheffield (I)	Loughborough (I)* Warwick Birmingham	East Anglia
1988 Bangor	21	Loughborough (II) Exeter Manchester (I) Birmingham (I)	Bradford (I)* Loughborough (I) Keele (I)	Bangor (I)
1989 Keele	23	Lancaster Loughborough (I) Sheffield (I) Warwick (I)	Bangor (I)* University of East Anglia Keele (I)	Exeter
1990		University College of North Wales, Bangor	Keele*	Loughborough (I)
Keele	22	Exeter (I) Lancaster (II) Warwick (I)	Leicester Sheffield	
1991 Southampton	22	Brunel (I) Exeter (I) Sheffield (I) Southampton (I)	Lancaster (I)* Exeter (II) Loughborough (I)	Leicester (I)
1992 Aston	23	Lancaster (I) Leicester (I) Liverpool (I) Sheffield (I)	Manchester (I)* Bangor (I) Exeter (I)	Loughborough (I)
1993 Hull	26	Exeter (I) Marjon Sheffield (I) Sunderland (I)	Loughborough* Bedford Manchester	Leeds (I)
1994 Cheltenham	32	Brighton Birmingham Exeter	Marjon* De Montfort (Leicester)	Manchester

Table 2.3 (continued)

Year and final venue	*No. of teams taking part*	*Quarter-finalists*	*Semi-finalists*	*Winners*
		Kent	Loughborough	
1995 Cheltenham	42	Cheltenham & Gloucester Sunderland Glasgow Reading	Bedford* Northumbria Crewe & Alsager	Marjon
1996 Keele	14**	Loughborough East Anglia Lancaster Leeds Metropolitan University	Crewe & Alsager* Cheltenham & Gloucester Birmingham	Reading
1997 Keele	13**	Exeter Marjon Sunderland ***	Liverpool* Lancaster Leeds Metropolitan University	Reading
1998 Keele	12**	Marjon Newcastle Queen Margaret University of East Anglia	Leeds Metropolitan University* Loughborough Manchester	Keele
1999 Keele	20	Coventry Loughborough Keele Liverpool	Marjon* Crewe & Alsager Staffordshire (Stoke)	Manchester
2000 Keele	15	Portsmouth Wolverhampton Liverpool Cheltenham & Gloucester	Manchester* Reading Exeter	Crewe & Alsager

Notes: * Runner up. ** Number in finals tournament. Regional groups not tabulated. *** Three groups only. Source: Dr Colin Aldis, British University Sports Association files army representative side with an executive committee to oversee women's football and Joe Roach acting as Director of coaching on completing his commission. Acceptance of women's football by the Army FA and the armed services more widely led to the inclusion of match reports and articles in *Soldier* magazine, which has an international circulation, and in the more local corps magazines. In turn, the services appeared to be more progressive and the decision of Alex Cotier, with six England caps, to enlist was something of a public relations coup.

Representative football has developed the profile of the sport in flourishing periods of interest followed by some decline. Regimental squads play tournaments, which also act as selection events for divisional teams from which the Army representative side is formed, for instance. However, as with civilian football associations, the enthusiasm of key individuals has varied considerably across divisions. From February 1995 to 1997, under the administrative lead of Kevin Reardon and the management of Joe Roach, women's football in the Army became perhaps the most established of all the services. In the pre-season tour of Cyprus in 1997 the representative side played against other Army, RAF and civilian teams which ended in victory for the former in each case. The same year, the Inter Corps Challenge Cup was contested at eleven-a-side rather than the small-sided form and demonstrated an increasing number of women prepared to participate in Services football. Matches have also been organised with other services including the Civil Service, the Prison Service and civilian teams such as Julie Hemsley's Brighton and Hove Albion.

When it assumed control of the government in 1997 the Labour Government pledged to reconsider the ban on gay and lesbian service in the British Armed Forces within the next five years. In 1998 it was reported that senior officers in the British Armed Forces were drawing up rules to integrate gay men and women into the Army. A European court ruling in September 1999 added weight to the case and in January 2000 the British Defence Secretary, Geoff Hoon, announced that the ban on gay service in the UK armed forces was abolished. The rise of women's service football has coincided with these events and it is difficult to assess whether the stereotypes have been weakened or reinforced by the type of recognition shown to women players in the forces. Endorsing women's football as part of an active, collaborative ethos in the military has been the combined result of personal influence by individuals, recruitment markets which include women as the role of peacekeeping increases in importance, and promotion of the forces as a career and healthy lifestyle. In the years since the Aldershot match the informal processes of women's play have been replaced by more systematic organisation which appears to benefit both the participants and the sponsor. Nevertheless, women's football has not been co-opted in the high-profile way that, for example, athletics has and in that sense it remains more firmly rooted in civilian life.

The lack of women players in decision-making roles at the top level in their own sport has influenced not only the community of women's football, but also the construction of memory. The head of women's football in the RAF and chief administrator of the Combined Services Squad for 2001–03 made this point during our interview. The first woman to attend the football committee meeting at RAF Uxbridge (where the Chair marked the novelty of the occasion by referring to 'lady and gentlemen'), she inherited the administrative position from a male colleague rather than being appointed. Though eminently qualified in terms of football expertise (as an ex-Fodens player, and part of the team that won the Mitre Cup of 1974) her assignment to this post was incidental to her other duties. Like volunteers in the regional leagues, she had been so busy organising play that little time had been given to compiling records:

> Your letter prompted me at our committee meeting last Tuesday to raise the point that we should be keeping records and when the RAF take over the Chair of the Combined Services team for its two year stint in August, we intend to begin to do that.

In moving from a chapter which concerns itself with the competitive and social traditions within women's football to one that discusses several kinds of memory, there is a rather obvious point to make that the invention of custom has been central to the popularity of men's football. This has accelerated since the formation of the Premiership so that teams and individual performers can now accrue a large part, in some cases the majority, of their revenue from endorsing products and creating their own lines. There is also the rise of the 'anorak' fan, sometimes a celebrity, who glories in the detail of what can hardly be described as general knowedge. The business of football can embrace all manner of consumer products where tradition and memory are given visible and audible from, from retro shirts to the playing of the Post Horn Gallop when Leicester City run out of the tunnel to name but two. My point in pursuing this is not to indicate the gulf between the two: it is that this situation is symptomatic of broader social relations and beliefs about what women's relationship to football has been, is and should be. It is a pretty uncomfortable experience to sit with my nieces in crowds of twenty-plus thousand at Premiership games and watch cheer-leaders (a recent experiment in the tradition of football as entertainment) of roughly their age dance around in revealing costumes. In one sense we are willing female consumers of the spectacle since we've paid for our tickets and we're sitting on seats which supposedly represent a move towards a more civilised era of support. Nevertheless, the presumed feminisation of football after Hillsborough requires much more theoretical and empirical work because the young women who display sanctioned but newly fashionable spectacle in tangent to the match demonstrate one way in which the masculinist tradition is also being recycled in new forms. Would Major League Soccer-style double headers (occasional events in which women's teams play their games before the male match) broaden the scope of support and media attention for women's football? Those few double-headers that have taken place suggest that it could be a successful strategy but only if they were constructed to demonstrate the wider backing of the club, FA and surrounding bureaucracies in a more sustained effort.

The lack of recognition given to female performers is not merely a response to 'the world out there'. As the examples of historical and contemporary sponsors used in this chapter indicate, the construction of group identity by women players has been neither at the mercy of corporate production nor as necessarily outside of, and 'other' to these influences. In addition to focusing on the structures and organisational constraints shaping memory, the following chapter discusses activities that are devalued when women's involvement is reduced to a question of novelty or number. Indeed the emphasis on these two points is a way of deflecting attention from the more fundamental issues of women's involvement. The next chapter develops the critique of these dual narratives by showing how women players and their supporters have expressed recognition, fellowship, respect, sameness and difference through football. If socialising and travelling to meet the opposition is an upside of participation, dealing with anxious individuals and bureaucracies uncertain of the effect of female involvement on the image of the sport as a whole is a downside. The belief that women's play *is* and *should be* different retains currency, so the next chapter deals with contradictory perceptions of the women's football community. Though there is not a widespread public awareness of women playing football for over a century this does not mean that there is nothing memorable about women's relationship to football, as the first two chapters of Part I have made evident. However, even today, the forms of commemoration owe much to informal customs of remembrance. It is to the more readily apparent media representation of women players that the next chapter turns before looking at the less obvious oral history.

3 Memory and English women's football

Collections of the lived culture of a sport memorialise certain dates, places and people, and academics interested in football, for example Redhead (1997), Allison (1998), Tomlinson (1999) and Hill (2002), have explored the link between sporting leisure and popular culture. This reflects a welcome move toward inter-disciplinary and multi-disciplinary research. However, though the history and sociology of women's sport have been progressively developed as subjects in their own right, little analysis of the culture of women's sport has been undertaken.[1] Specifically, there is a pressing need to collect and analyse artefacts associated with women's football if we are to establish and commmunicate a sense of the autonomous tradition which the previous two chapters have outlined.

The early high points of women's participation (folk football in Caledonia; British ladies' football club matches; the 1915–21 games) are important in themselves but also because they contextualise contemporary women's football culture. Therefore Holt and Mason's distinction between social history and sociology has been questioned in this study:

> A key difference between a sociology of contemporary British sport and a social history is that history takes an interest in the past in its own right rather than using it as a source to explain the present . . . we have tried to piece together what mattered *then* rather than what matters now.
>
> (Holt and Mason, 2000: ix)

The public, local and private sources examined here are representative of the view of women's football at any given time *and* as part of a longer tradition, which has had considerable impact on the current state of the female game. The pre-1960s material shows that the female player passed into popular culture in ways that are now largely hidden from public view. The place of these items in local and private memory then is one issue. Present-day players' attitudes towards these items of memorabilia is another. Do newspapers and photographs suggest a gulf between the pre-1960s players and contemporary participants or do they lend to an understanding of previous aspects of the sport?

In English cities and villages, a variety of paraphernalia establishes and confirms the public memory of male football, from road signs to club houses to goalposts on school playing fields. We can take a stadium tour to visit the site of the game even when there is no action, or entertain corporate clients in the restaurant of Premiership and Football League grounds. Fans can, and do, become aficionados of the facilities of each and every Football League ground in the country. In contrast, there are, as yet, no memorials or separate grounds for women players until Doncaster Belles' stadium is built. With the possible exception of the Belles' national reputation there is little evidence of women's football in, say, signage, widely known club names or the landscape. During World War I and up to 1921, women's teams could fill League grounds past capacity, but from that time to the present the public have generally known little about the form and style of women's football. In conversation, people frequently ask if women play for ninety minutes, on full-size pitches and so forth. The common-sense idea that women can't play is evident in these, mostly innocent, enquiries. The assumption that the sport must be very different from the men's game is also a factor. This sense of the unusual is reinforced by the human geography of Britain: male participation in football is so ubiquitous that we know about it and will probably have seen at least part of a game even if we don't want to. To appreciate when, where and how women play, we have to take the time to find out.

The tone of material which sets the official memory of women's football is decidedly forward-looking and self-serving in its praise of recent initiatives. In attempting to control the public face of the women's game, the Football Association in England and FIFA globally must have a perceived 'client' cohort which may or may not reflect those who play. In order to explore contemporary women players' view of their actions, valuable sources lay in private compilations, which typically included newspaper reports of matches, programmes and images, usually from postcards or photographs. Tracking down these materials enabled an examination of the components which contribute to the public and private memory of female participants.

A defining feature of women's football is that it continues to be characterised by a struggle for space in the broadest sense. The gradual pace of assimilation and partial accommodation of women players into men's clubs can be reflected in aesthetic forms, as well as in sporting terms. For instance, in the 1980s Highfield Rangers in Leicester supported a netball team before a women's football team was created in 1991 by attracting players formerly with Leicester Ladies FC (Highfield Rangers, 1993: 113). Rangers have no images of the netball team and two photographs of the women's football team in the clubhouse out of approximately twenty items of memorabilia. In both *Highfield Rangers: An Oral History* and the clubhouse itself, women are memorialised in a tenth of the available space even though there have been females affiliates for half of Highfield's history. This local example is indicative of a more widespread lack of representation of the female player in all kinds of media. Another significant aspect of the depiction of the 'woman footballer' is a difficulty in describing female participation.

The dilemma of how to talk and write about female players has continued from the earliest days of women's participation to the present. These 'pen pictures' of players taken from a Festival of Britain programme characterise this dilemma as the exclamations manage to be both highly specific and yet vague:

Muriel Jones R.H.B. School Teacher. Coaches the boys. Always Reliable and Steady.
Flo Cloake Age 17. (Withington). A Rock of Gibraltar. Natural left-footer and splendid header of a ball.
Alma Nixon Age 19. (Manchester). Steady type of player. Very hard to pass, and a great student of the game. Likes to referee.
Doris Ashley Age 27. 'Skipper' is captain and schemer in chief. Always seems to be where the ball is. Odeon Lady footballer of 1950 gold medal award. Played for England and France.
Irene Hebron Age 18. 'Legs' is an ardent Denis Compton and Arsenal fan. A fine exponent of the sliding tackle.

(Corinthians versus Lancashire *Ladies Programme*, 1951)

The approving terms 'always', 'splendid', 'great' and 'fine' are rather abstract ways of describing female play and the closest references to athleticism are the rather immobile 'Rock of Gibraltar' and 'steady'. This diplomatic praise is a response to, but is also informed by, a more pervasive public awareness of anecdotes and clichés about the suitability of football for women and men.

Myths which prescribe football as a masculine preserve are an enduring part of English culture. For example, whether male or female, we learn at a very early age that to perform football 'like a girl' is something to be avoided: it is better not to play at all. Invariably parents, teachers and coaches insist on protecting masculinity even when appearing to defend female play.[2] For instance, it remains quite common to hear that 12-year-old girls, who might be bigger and better players than their male counterparts, have been withdrawn from a mixed side 'for their own protection' or 'because it's an unfair advantage' because boys are too chivalrous to tackle a female or 'because she might feel like the odd one out'. The idea that football is an unsuitable game for ladies has been given a contemporary form as girls who play are called 'tomboys' and women who play risk being objectified as 'lesbians'. The 'dykes' tag combines homosexual inference (because players change in the same room in order to play a sport involving contact) with, besides, a reference to the common-sense idea that lady-like women don't like football and prefer shopping.[3] Otherwise sophisticated females have, in this social fiction, an innate inability to understand the offside rule which no amount of patient explanation can tutor. Thankfully, tired old remarks about women players sharing a post-match bath have faded due to health and safety regulations but the equally boring speculation about changing shirts has not quite died yet. Male or female players who clash are said to be 'drawing handbags at forty paces' to indicate the lack of authenticity compared with fights which take place off the pitch without rules and a referee. If particularly innocuous, the diminutive equivalent of 'girlfight' is emphasised and players draw their 'purses'. When what looks like a particularly promising shot is sliced high and wide the crowd will wolf-whistle to indicate a feminised approval, as sarcastic disapproval of a male player's efforts. The unspoken insult 'Good shot . . . for a girl!' takes us back to a logic where good female players are 'butch' and poor players of either sex are 'girly'.

The insults are often light-hearted and accompanied by a wry smile because they are a kind of shorthand of insider knowledge. However, seen from another perspective, idiomatic fabrications are one means of insisting on essential gender difference in, and through, football which are also recycled geographically, commemoratively and linguistically. Meanwhile, the recent focus on racism and attempts to 'kick it out' of football have led to some re-evaluation of how language, representation and common practices have led to a degree of institutionalised intolerance which the sport is trying to address. Racist conventions, especially those relating to black players, could not now be repeated with a knowing smirk and be rewarded with general approval, though much more remains to be done. Nevertheless, there is something more than playing a particular sport happening when worn gender distinctions, rather than being forgotten or seen as uncomfortable aspects of the past, are instead cherished as part of the fabric of custom.

The first part of this chapter looks at the depiction of women players in the media as, to a large extent, informed by the problem of representation. In moving from conventions which constitute playing football as expressive of gender, the aim in the second half of the chapter is to present female players' comments in order to question the idea of 'woman', 'girl' and, worse, 'lady' as universal categories. The multiplicity of, and discontinuity in the responses indicate that players are performing and negotiating shifting identities, of which gender is itself a plastic element. In this I am mindful that some feminists would argue that, strictly speaking, women cannot be said to exist and categorising gender enables oppression to be structured along dual lines (Kristeva, 1980: 56). However, so far, the experiences of women players have not been discussed nearly enough and the view that is articulated is of my experience of talking to some contributors to that diverse community. So the oral testimonies are not an attempt to redescribe football from the point of view of women, because there is not a singular normative vision of a shared cultural reality that is 'women's football'. Acknowledging the theoretical insufficiency of categorisation is one point of the position that is defended throughout this work and this critique is, I believe, furthered by collecting the views of women players together. However, the excerpts are no more than a starting point in a longer process of releasing the stabilised and polarised fabrication of gender difference both in football and beyond it.

The idioms discussed above reflect values that form the basis of the organisation of male and female participation and so are not just a question of semantics. This is exemplified in the convention of 'football' and 'women's football' and in the Laws of the Game by notions of 'gentlemanly' conduct. In the last decade particularly, the reactionary sporting world has become aware of the need to be seen to facilitate female play for its cultural legitimacy. Football as a business and industry is traditionalist but ambitious and keen to enter new markets (Tomlinson and Sugden, 1994). Consequently, natural difference, as expressed through play, has led to the development of discrete provision which serves a policy of gender regulation and control. This, of course, is not unique to association football: in *The Stronger Women Get, The More Men Love Football* (1996) Mariah Burton Nelson critiques the process whereby a sport is equated with masculinity as feminism gains footholds in popular culture in her study of the code of American football. In England, football authorities have become more public relations oriented, if not less cautious, as they market their sport to women in a feminine-appropriate form, or risk losing an important segment of the leisure and entertainment audience. So the apparently positive slogans of fast growth and the future are projections rather than firm commitments to fundamental change in the here and now. Implicitly, the memory of women's football is affected because the really historic events appear to be very recent, such as the crowd of 96,000 at the 1999 Los Angeles Women's World Cup Final, or have yet to materialise, like the first English women's professional league.

In exploring what some contemporary women construct the meaning of their play to be, this chapter discusses the oral history of the 'ordinary' participant to show that private and local forms can, and should now, begin to affect this public memory. A mother of five, life-long player and local administrator described her experience of football as follows:

A It's a problem if you've got short hair and you are skinny, like me, because sometimes blokes, and women, call you a lesbian. But if you've got long hair and boobs they think you can't play and make out you are running around for attention . . . like, you'll hear them whistle and give dirty laughs when some players run. You can't win. If you go in for tackles you're a she-bloke and if you stand off you're a sissy.

Q Why do you play then?

A [*Surprised*] Well, because I love it. You've seen me play. Anybody who has seen me play knows . . . and I'm not going to let some idiots

> stop me [from playing football] by calling me names. I'm better than that. But it upsets my kids if they come to watch and someone in the crowd is giving the players a hard time. [*Shrugs*] They want to go and shout back but I tell them, 'We're better than that'.

Other players also appeared to draw reassurance from, and yet feel stigmatised by, their participation in the game. Responses to the question, 'Is there a time you stopped playing football?' reflect this paradox.

> Never stopped because I love playing. Some people sometimes take the mickey out of me but I'm not bothered.

> People still view football as a man's game and this won't change overnight. I believe that in order to encourage new girls into the teams we need to show them that girls who play football are still feminine. This could be done by using the media to focus on professional teams and focus on two main things: (a) the game, (b) the girls.

So what motivated women players to continue? Most valued 'fun' as the primary reason for participating. Football is a team sport, requiring levels of particular skills. Players who choose to wear a uniform with several others and take their exercise collectively, outside, in a contact sport that is also an invasion game, place themselves in a public arena. This contrasts with individual sports and other forms of exercise popularly undertaken by women (for example, swimming, tennis, and aerobics) and with school-based team sports (like field hockey and netball) which are usually played at private clubs or on school grounds. As Richard Holt has written in connection with a shift to sport participation in Victorian culture, 'The gratuitous expenditure of energy in organized groups according to carefully drafted laws is a very special way of having fun' (Holt, 1989: 87). Before moving on to unpick the complexity of enjoyment, the discussion turns beyond sport to look at the mediation of women's football and, in particular, the creation of an undignified reputation that leaves players open to insult. Like other cultural forms that require great financial resources for their production, distribution, consumption and reception, the media has been relatively closed to women. As Victoria Bennett has written in her thesis on women sports journalists, by the time of the modern era, media industry structures were in place which made sports writing, as well as the business of spectator-supported events, a male preserve (Bennett, 2002: 27). The construction of a public memory of women's football has been adversley affected by this because of both general omission and the rare, and rarely impartial, coverage of the game.

There have been some isolated incidents of national pride in English women football players. For example, following the victory of England's women in 1985 and again in 1988 in Italy in the unofficial World Cup, the 'Mundialito', was subsequently recognised by *The Times* newspaper who awarded them 'female team of the year'. Media acknowledgement of international success undoubtedly raised awareness about domestic women players in the 1980s, but this has not been sustained or systematised. Sports reportage is conventionally trivial, sensational and highly opinionated and women's football has been depicted as endlessly novel, as shown by the laboured puns 'Women to boot!', 'Agony for the goal-den girls', 'Women get a kick out of soccer!' and 'England aim to dominate Europe by fairer means than foul'.[4] Articles on women's football predominantly support Bennett's conclusion that women's magazines and newspaper supplements provide much of the coverage of female sport generally, rather than newspaper sports pages. Since the 1960s, therefore, women's football has been discussed as an aspect of lifestyle rather than as an entertainment spectacle. A common-sense view would tell us that women's football is infrequently represented in the media. However, the trends in the reportage of women and football tell us rather more about the basis of these shared understandings.

Fishwick has suggested that the press and public opinion of female football spectators in the 1930s, 1940s and 1950s was highly critical (Fishwick, 1989: 58). However, material in the private collections of players reflected a range of texts in which the responses ranged from unreserved admiration through reticent approval to contempt. Some contemporary articles may span two or even incorporate all three views. Jimmy Hill, writing in the *News of the World*, for example, urged, 'Take a tip Revie . . . it's time to follow the girls!' (1974). This is a typical case of using women's football to criticise the knowledge or ability of a professional male player or coach, in this case the then-England manager, by characterising women's football as unsophisticated and therefore closer to an amateur, purist style. At a time when coaching in England was mistrusted, Revie's attempts to experiment with formation and tactics were seen to be needlessly complicated. Hill protests rather too much in applauding the shorter passing game of the women, the use of left-footed players in left-sided positions and solid defensive play.

Praising women players for their lack of refinement is also a backhanded compliment in this *Daily Express* article:

> I went with all the usual male prejudices about soccer being 'unfeminine'; that the girls would break down and cry if someone kicked them or if the referee was a bit nasty and did not allow a goal. I saw instead the best game of football I have seen since those famous Wolves managed by Stan Cullis terrorised Europe in the 1950s . . . no 'aggro' . . . no 'acting' or cheating . . . and soccer of a standard . . . [I] remember watching as [a] schoolkid.
>
> (Morgan, 1977)

The article is superficially about women playing football but the barely disguised subtext is a nostalgic examination of the author's masculinity. He demonstrates specialist knowledge by referring to Wolves in the 1950s; displays patriotism by the choice of 'terrorised' to describe England's supremacy; reinforces ideas about girly behaviour and in particular the sporting rather than skilful reference to school-age football before concluding with a reference to his own youthful idealism. Both Hill and Morgan use women's football in order to critique what is wrong with the male professional game and Sepp Blatter continued this theme in a *FIFA News* press release prior to the 1999 Women's World Cup entitled 'Women Don't Cheat', in an essentialism combining moral virtue with femininity.

Another style of article, not necessarily only in the tabloids, is one which focuses on the sexuality of the players. This can take the form of football as a masculinising influence as in Peter Batt's 'Dates have the order of the boot' piece,

> Ask them to pose for glamour pictures . . . and you are odds on to wind up with a punch up the throat. The dedication to the sport is nothing short of fanatical. Only one of the team is married, the rest quite simply haven't got time for it . . .
>
> (Batt, 1973)

Though apparently positive, the following article from the *Guardian* uses descriptive devices for Algerian girls which also emphasise confrontation and gender difference almost twenty years on.

> Coach Mohamed Dubabas makes his girls bend forward with arms spread-eagled. This coach is held in great esteem (the Kouba coach, Mohammed Chalal, confesses to being envious of him). His players listen intently, but remain on the wild side when they implement his orders. One player breaks her hand, howls, and is then back on the field. Dubabas says that there is no difference in terms of strategy between men and women. But 'the girls play a purer football. I cannot push them physically as much as the men, but they are technically better players'.
>
> (Jones, 1999)

In both of the above extracts stereotypes about sport as an expression of female disorder bordering on coarseness are rehearsed. In contrast, some journalists suggest that women should play more 'like girls' and revert to an equally cliché-ridden style where titillation is the undertone, for example in this *Guardian* article which ran under the headline 'Bridge of thighs'.

> What they need to do now is to redefine [football] in feminine terms, not ape the men so much . . . especially those gum chewing players, holding their groins in the defensive wall for instance, and appealing for every throw in as a matter of course.
>
> (Keating, 1977)

Much more rare is reportage like that of Chris Lightbown in the *Sunday Times*, where the only reference to a player's body is a genderless remark,

> Spacey, who had tremendous control for a tall player, weaved the ball past three, sometimes four, Doncaster players . . . Spacey's turns, dummies, changes of pace and sheer instant control helped to make the game into a spectacle . . .
>
> (Lightbown, 1990)

Kate Battersby in the *Daily Telegraph* and Jean Simpson in the *Daily Express* have attempted to cover women's football in the form of a more regular, detailed review of the sporting action. However, more articles appear like the following:

> Eleanor Friel was kicked out of a taxi and left on the streets – because the driver found out she was a referee. 'He said women should not be watching football at all, they should be at home doing the cleaning and washing,' Friel says. 'And he was being serious!' She was left with a mile-long walk home; the union that represents Leeds taxi drivers says the cabbie could lose his licence if he is identified. Friel, meanwhile, has just started refereeing Leeds Sunday League matches.
>
> (Viner, 1997)

The association in the national press of women's football stories with crises in male football on the one hand and with incidents where women challenge ideas of feminine-appropriate behaviour on the other contributes to the myth of impropriety that continues to surround the sport. Many studies of sports history use the national and local press as substantive sources; however, relatively little of the information for this study came directly from newspapers and given the examples above it is easy to see why. There is more evidence of a cross-over from reportage to autobiography, as in *Astroturf Blonde (It's a Man's Game – Sometimes)* (Rudd, 1998) and the paperback edition of the same work, *Astroturf Blonde: Up Front and Onside in a Man's Game* (Rudd, 1999) which give the author's experience as a player. Rudd's criticism and rejection of women's football in favour of being the only female player in a parks team ignores issues around mixed sport more generally. In order to pursue a career as a sports journalist Rudd had to move into related areas first and build up a profile of sports writing, often by less than obvious means. Bennett has pointed out that this need for a persistent and indirect approach is typical of the experience of women who wish to establish themselves as sports writers (Bennett, 2002). The example also makes a point that some women journalists will distance themselves from women's sport and maintain an individualistic approach to work and play.

In spite of the relatively small percentage of national and regional press cuttings dedicated to women's football, the latter can be used to trace the expression of local memory and much more work remains to be done on this. The *Stoke Evening Sentinel* is worth particular mention as, after subsequently contacting the family mentioned in the articles, it became possible to contrast the use of the newspaper article as a source of local pride, borne of nostalgia, and the photographs held in a private collection as part of the remembrance of loved ones. The press clippings follow the same line in retrospective articles which appear every few years.[5]

> It took Stoke City 99 years to bring a national soccer trophy to the Potteries, but these footballing females of the 1920s covered themselves in glory and won the English Ladies' FA Cup without too much trouble.
>
> (*Stoke Evening Sentinel*, 1976)

The excerpt portrays the past as a way of framing the present. It is therefore possible to be proud of the women of the past without the obligation to support individual women players, teams or the sport as a whole in the present. Other local newspaper reports include captioned photographs, individual descriptions, statistical histories of teams and reports of honours won:

> A crowd much larger than the organisers had hoped for turned up at the Walker-Lane ground, and at the start of the game there were large crowds behind both goals and on the natural grandstand provided by the hill at the side of the pitch. The spectators were lined six and seven deep round the touchline. The Mayoress of Hyde was cheered when she kicked off for the match with a well directed punt down the field. The play was followed with terrific interest by the spectators. There were many professional touches which were eagerly recognised . . . within five minutes, Joan Whalley, easily the finest player on the field, equalised with a shot from 20 yards.
>
> (Joan Whalley's scrapbook, Hyde 1947)

Just as the treatment of Dick, Kerr in the press is perhaps the most well-developed example of a women's team being actively supported by the local media before the 1960s, Southampton in the 1970s and Doncaster Belles in the 1980s and 1990s would also provide significant examples for researchers of this topic. The cuttings in the centrally held Belles' club file, for example, include reports from Scandinavian tours, local and national newspapers and magazines, international programmes and so forth. As the most directly and indirectly mediatised women's team, the variety of attitudes conveyed in these pieces is in itself deserving of a study; for some writers Doncaster Belles are supremely skilful athletes, for others they are working-class women who exhibit feisty characteristics through playing football.

> Kaz and Gill, they've been halfway round the world, and what would they have been without football? Gill Coulthard, she was a rogue, she'd probably be in trouble . . . she'd be going nowhere, anyway. Like too many women in pit villages, three or four kids, grossly overweight, down club every weekend, nothing in her life. Or what would Kaz have done? Go round Goldthorpe and Barnsley getting drunk on a weekend – and that's the summit of your life as a young woman?
> (Davies, 1996: Foreword)

There is a significant history of women writing about women's experience of sport, as the excellent anthology *Crossing Boundaries* demonstrates (Bandy and Darden, 1999). However, women's football has a small but growing literature. Early fictional accounts of women playing football were written by men and were especially popular in the decade between 1915 and 1925, including 'Ray of the Rovers', 'Bess of Blacktown' and 'Nell O' Newcastle'.[6] As the working-class, and hence resourceful, heroines, Ray, Bess and Nell are not only eye-catching because of their football skills. The formula ensures that the unwelcome attention of an unscrupulous, and therefore unsuitable, suitor requires the inventive heroine to engineer her way out of a difficult situation, often aided by an obviously appropriate partner. After the troublesome episode is resolved and marriage accomplished, the footballing heroine is not necessarily required to give up the sport that is the hallmark of her dashing character. In comparison, recent fiction writers can be seen to recycle the essentially masculine nature of the sport. For example, Richard Allen's *Skinhead Girls* (1972) related playing and supporting football with attempts by young women to enter and imitate male sub-cultures. *Gregory's Girl* (*c.* 1983), originally a drama piece (often adapted for school productions) then a film, and more recent children's books such as *Joanna's Goal* by Michael Hardcastle (1990) and *Dulcie Dando* by Sue Stops (1992) see the female player as an exceptional individual. This image has been transferred to advertising campaigns to market a range of products from soap powder to orange juice drinks, as if the lone girl player somehow captures the Zeitgeist. In the sense that football is being used to sell all kinds of products it does capture what is currently happening. Over and above this, the symbolic use of the single girl player places the sport as so very fashionable that young women would want to participate and so is also referring back to the novelty of female participation. In another example, when a women's team was implied by a television commercial, the 'players' were in post-match showers eating chocolates. *Hem and Football* (Bhattacharya, 1992) is another text which pursues the same theme in that it attempts to use football as a symbol of resistance to the traditional role of women in Indian society. Hem is a truculent character, the playing scenes are brief and the overall style rather hackneyed. Football is evidently not the avenue for self-discovery or self-fulfilment that it is meant to represent in the character's life. Her immaturity is indulged through football and, though she is unlike the stereotype of the submissive Hindu girl, she is also unlike the other players who are prepared to be disciplined in their attitude to the game and work as a team. Hem's wilfulness eventually costs her a place on the squad and her independence but there is little to feel sympathetic about. In summary, the exceptional girl footballer is more in evidence in fiction and non-fiction cross-overs than the women's teams and this aspect of social memory has yet to change.

The essentially masculine nature of sport has been satirised by Simon Cheetham in *Gladys Protheroe . . . Football Genius!* (Cheetham, 1994). Not only does the diminutive Gladys earn sixty-five 'bonnets' for national women's appearances, she plays professionally for Watford, becomes England manager, manager of Real Madrid and helps England to win the World Cup. The excesses of the style can be seen from this excerpt which teases the reader with bogus facts and analysis: Cheetham would be pleased, and no doubt bemused, that I was originally introduced to the book by a colleague who recommended it as source for my research.

> It was the beginning of an era when women played a part in English men's football . . . Gladys actually went on to appear 28 times for Watford . . . Nancy Dixon played at right back for Fulham in the 1947/48 season, and Emily Cuthbert made one appearance for Aston Villa.
> (Cheetham, 1994: 16)

This text is also noteworthy because it makes links between other cultural forms and football, for example popular music. Much of the humour derives from in-jokes which require the reader to know the significance of the Bernabau, the bracelet scandal in Mexico in 1970 and the patronage of football by stars such as Elton John. This again reinforces the idea of anomaly in the playing, administrative and coaching sense as Gladys is exceptional in many senses. This has passed into the media more broadly as something of a cliché. If you want to speak to a woman managing director, for example, there's Karren O'Brady, if a celebrity director then it has to be Delia Smith, and so forth. The repeated use of those individuals as rare, often singular, examples of women involved in football does little to steer us toward the real issues. Though their achievements are nontheless outstanding the informal and formal structures which maintain their status as a minority are a focus in Part II of this work.

The consolidation of playing grounds for male clubs during the course of the century has been mirrored by the condensation of power in the print and media industries, and the disparity, if anything, continues to grow. The amount of printed and electronic material on male football has become so overwhelming that sub-genres continue to flourish. For instance, the football comic, from the original *Roy of the Rovers* strip to the non-fiction magazines *Goal*, *Shoot!* and *Match*, was a genre distinctly aimed at boys, but it also provides useful images of women's football from the 1960s onwards. The industry as a whole may have contributed to the expression in popular culture of the idea that girls don't like football by providing them with their own publications like *Twinkle*, *Jackie* and *Just 17*. But though fantasy, romance, fashion and pop music may have been what little girls were meant to be concerned with, the consumers of the weekly editions were likely to be boys and girls, men and women. The WFA certainly knew this when advertising for players in *Goal* in the early days, and the coverage of the first Women's FA Cup Final in 1971 included some excellent photographs.

However, these magazines also affected the perception of the sport for women in ways that were perhaps not intended. For example, a 1973 *Goal* article, 'Men only?', is very positive about women's participation but, as the title suggests, the tone is one of justifying women's right to participation rather than taking this as a given. Pieces are often based on continued attempts to either confirm or confute the stereotype of the woman player. WFA use of boys' magazines such as *Shoot* and *Goal* to advertise for players and the occasional reference in these magazines to women and girls playing did little to change the gendered nature of such publications, whomever their eventual reading audience might be. A good example of this is *Football Today*, which regularly ran either a single- or double-page article on women's football in the mid-1980s but again reflects a confusion in how best to present the players.[7]

As the sports pages in the national press have increased in number, women's sport generally and women's football particularly have been given scant coverage, especially in sporting rather than personality terms. Many of those women reporters and commentators who are now to the fore in professional sports media as presenters and writers followed the route of journalist to sports journalist, or had a famous male relative in sport. Few past or current women football players have access to a media profile except for via discrete events such as the Women's World Cup or the Women's FA Cup. Nor, as yet, do women's matches appear regularly on television. This reflects the wider state of affairs of the marginalisation of women's events and amateur sport in broadcasting, but it does contrast sharply with events in the recent past when television had a demonstrable role in increasing interest in the community of women football players in the 1980s.

Television is a primary tool of individuals, disciplines and codes attempting to establish themselves with wider audiences and can make heroes and heroines overnight, regardless of sporting specialism. The 1991 Broadcasting Act ended the restriction on competitive bidding and major events are now sold to paying audiences. By the end of 1998 the Olympic Games and Wimbledon Finals are the only two 'A-List' sports where women compete that are guaranteed to be shown live on terrestrial television. The World Cup, European Championship and FA Cup are three of the eight other 'A-List' sports events, indicating the primary importance of football in televised sport. The repeated theme of women's sections of football associations internationally is that more media attention and higher levels of sponsorship would help to develop the game (FIFA, 1997b). This appears to be borne out by the case of Channel 4 in the 1980s, whose coverage included a series of one-hour programmes on women's football which consistently sustained a very respectable number of viewers. It is also strongly indicated by the role of television companies in owning Women's USA, the professional league in the United States. The English FA wants to mirror this to use television to create a women's professional league by 2003. The paradox at the heart of this plan is that a media form that has studiously ignored women's football, with the exception of Channel 4 in the 1980s, is supposed to foster a new era of professionalism in a very competitive market. The relationship between women's football and television remains undetermined, more so in the case of digital TV, but is likely to be crucial in the future of the sport.

The launch of Channel 4 in 1982 with a remit of covering minority interests in sporting terms led to the inclusion of popular items on Italian League football, the Tour de France and American football. In addition, Australian Rules football, Sumo wrestling and women's football were part of this format but now appear less regularly. The Sunday afternoon scheduling of WFA matches and England internationals provided continuity of coverage and games were watched by up to 3 million viewers. It looked as though women's football would support itself as media spectacle on the combination of a round-up of the week's highlights and more in-depth coverage of a particular fixture. However, Sky took up where Channel 4 left off but initially showed the games on UK Living, leading to a million viewers for Cup Finals but excluding highlights of the later rounds as Channel 4 had done. Both used men and women presenters. The crucial difference was that UK Living was a female lifestyle format and so women's football became compartmentalised as an interest story, rather than appealing to sports fans.

Women's football has yet to re-establish itself as a sport on television. Even when, for example, in 1998, Sky was persuaded to cover the England versus Germany World Cup qualifier at Milwall, the consequences are debatable. Naively, the organisers stationed cameras on the same side of the ground as the 5,000 supporters, leaving the TV audience with the spectacle of empty stands. Yet viewing figures were very good, drawing higher figures than WWF wrestling, golf and some male soccer programmes. In a week in which the sixth round of the FA Cup and a five-day test between England and the West Indies were also contested, the programme came seventeenth overall (X25 Partnership Report, 1998: 2).

This has affected the depiction of the sport because television drama based on women's relationship to football is at least as evident as sports coverage of matches. In terms of the process of TV dramatisation over the period, the 1970s and early 1980s saw *Gregory's Girl*, *Those Glory, Glory Days* and *The Manageress*. These three examples dealt humorously with women's involvement in football within traditions of heterosexual narrative, for example the domestic conflict a woman manager experienced as a result of her power over an all-male workforce. The most recent serial, *Playing the Field*, uses women's football as a metaphor for northern working-class female grit, heavily influenced by Pete Davies' book, *I Lost My Heart to the Belles* (1996) and the production values of the documentary *The Belles*, which depicted the players as uncouth ladettes. The drama shows little football and lots of socialising. The reception of both programmes in women's football was mixed. For some players, including a few Belles, it upheld stereotypes of mannish women players consuming lager as enthusiastically as playing football. For others it was more positive:

> *The Belles* programme was good, but didn't really do women's football any favours with some of the ways the players were seen and it seemed to be cut to bring out one side, like it was always muddy and there was a lot of swearing and then the play fights and so on. Some of the players' families were upset by that because these are respectable women and they were just letting off some steam in an atmosphere where we all trust one another.

> The programmes were OK, but not true to life in some bits and we felt a bit tricked by that, some of us . . . I mean in *The Belles* they made you look a certain way by cutting it so that it isn't you you're looking at but more like a character in a soap.

> They are both very good, I was in both of them [*The Belles* and *Playing the Field*]. The filming was good fun. The actresses enjoyed it and we are still in touch.

In *Playing the Field* attempted suicide, family secrets, affairs between team members and their spouses, fraud and violence are interspersed with scenes of singing, dancing and heavy drinking. One character has affairs but wishes she hadn't; another pretends she is the sister, not the mother, of her child; a third bullies her husband in fits of rage, a fourth is gullible, and so forth. In this programme football is the source of tensions but also womanly togetherness to overcome problems that are, in essence, created by the flaws of the characters themselves. The formula has proven to be so popular that it has moved to a prime time slot. Again this provoked mixed reactions amongst players.

> *Playing the Field* I felt was very good as a drama series. Some of it summed women's football up, some of it was nothing like what goes on, but it was good to watch – I enjoyed it.

> *Playing the Field* showed women's football in a true sense.

> Although I enjoyed seeing a programme on women's footballers (and the fact that it was based on us, and some of us starred in the football action shots) the programme gave the image that female footballers are alcoholic lesbians who sleep around and has done no good for the sport.
>
> It's too soapy and dramatised. Women playing football isn't the main issue on the programme – it's just a novelty topic dramatised into a TV programme.

The most recent feature film, *Bend it like Beckham!* produced by Deepak Nayar and directed by Gurinder Chander, has the fictional Hounslow Harriers getting to the Women's FA Cup Final against the odds, in a style recognisable from Chander's earlier work, *Bhaji on the Beach*, as a 'chick flick'. This formula has been applied to women's football rather than reflecting the subculture itself, though Shaznay Lewis (the ex-singer/song-writer of the group All Saints) who has a cameo, was at the Arsenal academy. *Playing the Field* and *Bend it like Beckham!* tap into the novelty of women's football and the idea of bending the rules rather than breaking stereotypes does little to take forward the image of the female player or the game as a whole.

This led me to ask would women's football have to change to become television-friendly entertainment or would the attitude of television producers and audiences have to change to accommodate female players? There is a great deal to be concerned about if the unofficial Mexico World Cup proved to be such a great success with TV audiences partly because players wore revealing pink uniforms. The next section elaborates on the issues implicit in a change of women's football to suit a television audience. A fundamental change in media attitude would have to take place were television to popularise women's football in England. The Women's USA League in the United States had the success of Atlanta 1996 and Women's World Cup 1999 on which to build. Even with the considerable backing of AOL, Time Warner and Comcast, television audiences of 5 million and average gates of 8,000 in the first year indicate some way to go before the league is established. With the disappointing live attendance at the 1995 World Cup in Sweden and the strength of men's football in Europe, the omens for television-supported professional league in England are not good. In summary, mediation has brought some awareness of, and recognition to, women's football but a more uncommon view of the portrayal of players and the ways that participation has been articulated in popular culture have been collected largely in private.

The postcard on the cover of this book, *A Fine All-Round Player*, indicates that women's football in the early part of this century was sufficiently established to pass into popular culture and Fred Spurgin cards are now collectable. The eroticised player, the large crowd and awe of the male players tells us that the public view of women's football at that time was not wholly disapproving. The familial propriety of the Chapman postcard (see Plate 2) provides a very different image of women players. The admired individual Spurgin player is given curves which belong to an era before the flappers made a 'skinny' bodyshape fashionable but she is also of that moment as her hair is bobbed. The mobcaps, tunics and full-sleeved shirts of the Chapman card mark the players as belonging to the workplace and their shapes are hidden by such rational wear. The setting of this picture suggests restraint and order, including the central placement of male trainers and a female chaperone at the back of the group. Given the likely ages of the players, some of whom do not appear to be adolescents, this perhaps suggests the protection of female modesty. There are many more postcards of this kind from which a visual history could be compiled, from Plymouth training on the beach in the early decades of this century to Dick, Kerr's taking part in inter-war holiday parades.

The depictions in the images intended for public distribution compare with those for private consumption, for example personal photographs. In Joan Whalley's scrapbook and the collections of Peter Bridgett and Nancy Thompson these snaps include sporting and social events, tour and travel shots plus portraits of individuals with whom friendships clearly became established. For instance, Joan annotated each photo, 'Having tea with the mayor at Stalybridge', 'On the Pleasure Beach at Blackpool with the French team' or just 'Kitty' or 'Madelene'. It would be rewarding to compile and juxtapose these images and artefacts of remembrance in a collection which could also include the moving image and sound (though I have been unable to track down much in the way of radio coverage of women's football to date).

Archived collections which present women's football in contrasting contexts add something to our knowledge of how players were portrayed but there are an unknown number of home movies and videotapes which capture women's games which could supplement this understanding. For example, the North West Film Archive Collection, based at Manchester Metropolitan University, holds films from the period 1945–80, most of which show five-a-side games in pageant settings; respectively at Haslingden Carnival 1950, a Garden Party and Pensioners' Picnic 1960 and at Salford Festival 1980 (which marked the 750 anniversary of the Salford Royal Charter and over 250 cultural, sporting and educational events took place between 23 August and 6 September).[8] Since Manchester Corinthians, several of whom came from Salford, had for many years vied with Preston (previously Dick, Kerr's) for the claim to be England's premier team, local memory and pride appear to be less present than participation in holiday celebrations.[9] In contrast, Ronald Frankland, son of Alfred, produced a more competitive film of Dick, Kerr Ladies playing eleven-a-side matches and visiting the Territorial Army Barracks at Cross Lane, Salford which is also in this collection.[10]

This is another area where development has been neither progressive nor steady. On the whole, though, while there have been repeated attempts in a variety of formats to collect and transmit a sense of tradition in women's football, there has never been a sufficiently systematised or sustained means of creating a sense of community. The match programmes indicate that an entrepreneurial spirit was part of women's football before the 1970s. The games were sponsored, and match progammes included affectionate, if patronising, nicknames and pen pictures of individual players as part of the entertainment. Beyond the immediate event, writing about women's football is an example of how the relationship between sport and supporter has been less than successfully cultivated. The reasons may in part lie with the attitude of the WFA and the FA regarding the women's game as amateur, reflected in the format of the publications developed at this time. In 1969 the WFA's ambition to create respectable domestic and international competition led them to use the technology of the photocopier and line drawings of a woman player on the cover of their programmes. The authorities misunderstood the relationship between the print media and television as mutually reinforcing channels for public relations.

The publications of the WFA are revealing in this context. After the paper-based amatueristic publications, a more business-like *Official Magazine of the Women's Football Association* ran from 1978–81. The international focus and action photography combined with a glossy cover and several pages of in-depth coverage of league games and internationals, only to be replaced in February 1982 with *WFA News: The Official Newsletter of the Women's Football Association*, with broadly similar content condensed onto four photocopied sides. The financial difficulties of the Association in November 1985 led to a typewritten, rather than typeset, newsletter without photographs but with the same mix of national and international results. However, the editorial for several editions appealed for unity on behalf of the Association. The headlines ran, 'Financial state of the association', 'Are we doing enough?', 'A new era is about to start' and 'Report on the future development of the WFA and the new regional set up'.[11] As the administration sought to deal with internal disagreement, it is easy to see why the dissemination of a community of women footballers through magazines, newsletters and fanzines should have been so problematic at the time:

> It is my fervent wish that one day I will go to a WFA Council meeting and report, that at long last we are striving and progressing together to achieve our goal of increasing participation . . . I have been your Chairman for two and a half years and have seen the membership decline, something the working party on women's football predicted eighteen months ago . . . The Future Rests With You. [*sic*]
>
> (Stearn, 1987: 1)

This is hardly light reading for players or for the non-playing public and the rather headmasterly tone suggests the aim was to speak to those within women's football, rather than to greet newcomers. By July 1990 the *WFA News* was re-launched in typeset form, this time as *The Voice of Women's Football* and reverting to the mix of photographs, national and international news and newspaper clippings. The changes reflect not only the confusion of the association and the direction it should take but also re-packaging of women's football, which continues today. Other magazines demonstrate both an awareness of the gap in the market on behalf of players and the same problems of distribution that official titles experienced. Independent titles, such as *Spot Kick* ('England's hippest new women's football magazine') launched by Vic Atkins with the support of Coventry City Council, and *Action Replay* ('The women's soccer magazine') launched in 1992 by Havant Ladies FC, also failed to gain currency with a wide enough audience to support subsequent editions. Like other women's sport, women football enthusiasts complain today about a lack of media interest without having access to the mechanisms or a coherent message about women's football as sporting spectacle.

Perhaps the most successful publication, *Sunday Kicks*, began in April 1995. As with other fanzines and magazines, circulation to, and consumption by, a fractured audience affected its longevity though it did run for at least fifteen editions.[12] *Sunday Kicks* expressly attempted to educate readers about women's football, and to give local contacts, but it also included topical and humorous articles. Using Sports Pages bookshops in Manchester and London, Sport in Print in Nottingham and the Independent Bookshop in Sheffield, it tapped into the conventional non-game outlets for fanzines. The action photograph on the cover of the magazine was followed by an editorial on, for example, changes to the rules for women such as the notorious basketball-style 'time out', and criticism of the England regime and of clubs unwilling to take promotion opportunities. In-depth player and team analysis, international news, regional League results and news items were standard.

In contrast, *On the Ball* was initially an independent magazine with glossy production values, which was taken over in 1999 by the FA as the official magazine for women's football. In 2001 it was renamed *She Kicks*. In comparison with *Sunday Kicks*, *She Kicks* has production values more consistent with a teen magazine. There are profiles of players, equipment promotions and briefer articles mainly concerned with future projects. For example the Diary coverage of March and April's fixtures in *Sunday Kicks* listed weekly results and a commentary of the effects of these on team position in May 1995 in a three-page article of densely written text. The April 1999 edition of *On the Ball*, however, asked a 12-year-old player her nickname, likes and dislikes and plans for the future. The format of *She Kicks* suggests that the intention has been to ally playing football with non-sport teen activities. The writers of *Sunday Kicks* were enthusiasts and had the support of many players and administrators. This kind of publication was of most benefit to the people who played and were already in the community. As a small-scale enterprise it also had the objective of improving communication, knowledge and commentary but is clearly for the declared fan. Given the difficulties of *Women's Soccer World* in the US, an independent magazine with world circulation but again with production difficulties that have limited circulation after the Women's World Cup Final in Los Angeles in 1999, *She Kicks* magazine will at least ensure a means of publicising recent developments. With the appointment in 2001 of a public relations executive for women's football, the considerable resources of the FA could now begin to make up some ground in the print and broadcast media. As with the difficulties of language shown in this section, the women of the United States team are, for example, sometimes infantilised to link with their audience in titles like *The Girls of Summer*, *All American Girls*, *Go for the Goal*, *The Game and the Glory*.[13] The image-makers are also astute in using teen-based marketing to describe players, as one title declares, *Mia Hamm Rocks!* (Weber, 1999). So it would seem that this use of a youthful, fashionable image for women's football looks set to continue.

Nevertheless, as one 21-year-old elite player put it in interview:

> Q You speak to a lot of girls over here and they don't know who Mia Hamm is or who the current England players are?
>
> A That's because they just play for fun, they don't read about football or watch it.
>
> Q Do you get *Women's Soccer World* or *On the Ball* or any other magazines?
>
> A I get *On the Ball*, or *She Kicks* as they're calling it now. I just get it for support really. It's getting better. I prefer magazines which focus on football, you know? Ones that talk about the tactics and aspects of the game to improve my understanding of, you know four, four, two versus three, five, two. Because although I'm a winger my manager sometimes tries to play a wing-back system and it's an aspect of my game I'm working on . . . to be able to adjust to tactical changes.

The question of how much the publication speaks to the players remains but in a differentiated market *She Kicks* is aimed at young competitive female players, *Team Talk* is aimed at non-league male football and *Kick it Out* at those interested in addressing racism in amateur and professional football. So the administrative policy of integrating women players is not replicated, by and large, in football-related media. Nor is this the only area where women are virtually invisible as players and it is to this oral history that the chapter now turns.

Jennifer Hargreaves, in her latest work, uses the term heroine to describe traditionally marginalised groups of women and used ethnographic methods to show that, 'Identity embodies sameness *and* difference' (Hargreaves, 2000: 2). This resembled the pattern emerging from interviews with women football players. It would be difficult to conduct research of this kind without feeling considerable admiration for women players who are also often coaches, lead junior teams, raise funds, and so forth. How do those women who do become players, get involved in football? Each player, in response to the question 'What are your earliest memories of playing football?', had a vivid recollection and retold this with confidence.

> I played with my father when I was about 8. He used to take me to a local football field and taught me different tricks and skills. I liked it when he could see I'd got a move down because there were four of us [children] and it was his and my time together.

> In the school playing ground, kicking tennis balls around at break times with my best friend Jackie Dingley and so I was Bobby and she was Jack. [The player's first name is Roberta]

> I was about 5 [years old] in infant school – with lads at break times . . . Wearing a shirt too big for me, scoring a goal and my team mobbing me.

Older siblings and relatives were often both the opponent and coach, and interviewees were customarily amused by their early recollections. At a very young age most players began to 'kick a ball about' with male relatives and only gradually learned that it was not suitable for older girls and women to play. In response to the question, 'What's you earliest memory of playing football?' the responses from elite and non-elite players were similar.

> Kicking a ball about with my brother and dad in the garden aged 4.

> Seven or 8 with the lads at primary school, but my dad informed [*sic*] me, he taught me to kick a ball when I was a toddler and I played a lot with my elder brother.

> Playing in the streets at home with my dad and next door neighbour – Louise – probably age 8 upwards.

> Kicking the ball about with my dad and brothers.

> With my dad and family when growing up in Scotland.

> In the back garden with my dad and sisters.

A father or older brother was most frequently cited as the person responsible for influencing girls to play the sport. In the case of only children, playing began frequently as an exceptional girl in a small gang of boys. It was seen to be one of many games and not perceived as more important than others. One player spoke about the mystique of the Dick, Kerr tradition in Preston as a primary factor in encouraging her to play in the 1960s:

> So many people lived in such a small area . . . we used to play on concrete and chuck yourself just in the street or a place where there's a bit of grass . . . [*pause*]. We played centring or heading, bringing in stuff like that and I always played out me tree [*sic*]. I had always heard people talk about the Dick, Kerr team. About this mysterious women's football team. I never saw them but heard there was this legend in Preston and I remember playing on the park and people saying, 'You know, you've got more ideas than all these lads' so I thought I'd look for them.

Sometimes male cousins, neighbourhood playmates or friends' fathers were also influential figures.

> I first remember playing with my brother and his friends when he was about 8 and I'd be just over 6.

> I had two male cousins and we would play football whenever I visited them. The first time I remember is when I was about 10 years old.

> When I was about 4 years old, I used to play in the street with all the boys until mum would shout me in for tea.

> At 13, I started to play with my younger brother to keep him amused and it just carried on from there.

> I first used to play football with boys from our street in 1989 but you had to take part in all the games. British Bulldog was the worst. Someone always went home with a bloody shirt.

> I used to play with my cousins at weekends on a caravan site when I was about 7 years old.

When the move was made from prepubescent, usually mixed, recreational football to structured school or junior leagues the accounts diverged depending upon whether local female teams had been established. The role of sport in family life in general elicited differing responses with some very active parents and some less so. In answer to the question, 'Does any one come along to support you at games?' responses included:

> Yes, my father attends every training session, my mother attends occasionally, but both of them attend every match I play.

> My father and mother never miss a match, plus my grandma and sister come along when we're at home. Lots of my friends come frequently.

> My parents come along and watch all the time. My brother and his friends are there sometimes. My friends will be there if it's not raining.

There appeared to be similar patterns in generations of players and the questionnaires and interviews yielded views that were broadly in agreement. In interviews, however, for those with less supportive parents, mobility and access to transport was a major issue, to the extent that an unemployed England player was collected and returned home by her coach when she could not afford her own transport. Approximately two-thirds of the non-elite players regularly took lifts from other players. This raises the point that access to transport may be as important a factor in continuing to play as other commitments.

Testimonies of family members gave a perspective on how the family see themselves in relation to the player's sporting career. For example, an elite player's mother felt that her daughter was right to choose football only after she had been picked for international duty. Mother and daughter negotiated the initial resistance and then support of the family during the interview.

> Me and my brother would kick about in the back garden for a laugh and mum would try to get me to go to dancing classes and girl's things like that . . . but he was into running more than football and I only ever wanted to play football. So I got better than him.

A player with dual nationality cited her family's disapproval of her choice of sport and part-time career as a reason for moving away.

> Yes, my family thought it wasn't normal . . . even after breaking into the National and Olympic side. Frustrated – burnt out. [For] one and a half years . . . when I first came back to England I didn't speak to them.

The point about family attitudes is substantive since male relatives often initiate girls' interest in the sport as play. A dual process then seems to take over where on the one hand, girls are socialised as they mature to see themselves as different than boys, and on the other, as children grow older, footall comes to be about competition rather than play. This therefore influences gender segregation as a means of ensuring a protected arena for boys *and* girls.

Some women emphasised social reasons for playing but rarely at the expense of the sporting contest. In sporting terms whether the players feel that winning is the important element or whether participation is about self-expression, for all but a tiny minority the activity remains a decidedly amateur affair. This led to questions about how players perceive their team and their personal contribution to it. The answers to the question, 'How would you describe your team?' combine competition and collaboration:

> A great mix of over-30s and under-18s. Experience counts. We battle together, never give up.
>
> High spirited, determined, fun loving, fair, following the motto: all for one and one for all!
>
> A friendly team, with a good atmosphere and we have the greatest parents to support us.
>
> Excellent. We get along well, we can play good football and we all have fun.
>
> Fun, friendly and always willing to try, we are all friends and everyone helps each other.
>
> A hard-working and young team, with fun and friendship along the way.
>
> I see my team as friendly, fun to play with and there are some very talented players playing around me.

Women players are also clearly drawn to the more rigorous elements of football, including an important measure of physical and intellectual skill. Part of the attraction is that football combines physical skill with judgement and elements of chance. Strategy and risk are mentioned repeatedly. Physical participation is fun but it is also an education, as is indicated by these non-elite responses to the question 'In your own words describe how you see your team':

> Improving with every game. We are all very committed to the club and our football.
>
> A young team, who are eager to learn and still committed in the 90th minute whatever [the] result.
>
> As a young side which is learning and progressing all the time.

> We have good potential if we can keep going as a club and keep playing as a team.

> In most teams I have played the women were serious and committed about their football but this team takes that to a new level.

> A team which plays good football, will not lower themselves to the 'hit and run' tactics of other teams. Friends.

The intellectual challenge is part of the fun. Conceptual engagement with the tactics and technical aspects of the sport are another dimension of women's involvement, like time spent thinking about and talking about football, that make the concept of participant more complex. If the cerebral and emotional elements of partaking in the sport at regular competitive level are taken into account, the players' connection is, at times, intense.

However, in some responses the internalisation of patronage in the sport more generally and the split between player and coach is more evident. As a student of the game, the subservient position of the players is a means of obtaining licence to play. In connection with the idea of fun, education and play the terms used by non-elite players conveyed eagerness in response to the same question:

> Young, committed, inexperienced and enthusiastic.

> A group of girls who love football, who want to show anyone willing to watch that women can play football.

> A bunch of enthusiastic girls out to play a good game.

> Not that serious, or too bothered about whether they win or lose, but there is quite a good team spirit – particularly off the pitch.

In part this emphasis on willingness conveys the seriousness with which the players approach their activities but it also appears to be defensive of women's right to play, as skill is hardly mentioned. Beyond these relatively few responses, there was a connected pleasure in play; examples from elite and non-elite players demonstrate that, for some, the enjoyment is of a more serious kind:

> We are all very close, and you would not see this in any other club. You've got to be something special. Players have come and gone after a season, whereas some will come and stay forever and they'll not go and play for anyone else. It's more than a camaraderie, you feel like you belong to something, it's not just a football team.

> Like a family – we all stick together. If someone is having a bad game then we all try to lift that person. You can talk to any of your mates with anything and the atmosphere is first class. All the squads mix. It's not them here and them over there. We are all as one and I don't think you'll see that at any other club in the country.

> The Doncaster Belles are a team who it has always been my destiny to play for. I never thought I'd get the chance, and now that I do I intend to stay with this Club until I am at an age where I can no longer play. But even then I will still take women's football further, by either going into physio[therapy] or management.

The expression of closeness and similarity in clubs formed primarily to play a sport is remarkable. Though several players also participated in individual sports they expanded upon the importance of teamwork in interview. That the club becomes something larger than the sporting endeavour is on the one hand significant and on the other perhaps less surprising if one considers that in order to play football the participants must spend hours together.

How do players make time to play? This emerged as a clear difference between elite and non-elite players as expressive of their playing identity. At the point of change from recreational to elite performer a conscious dedication to the pursuit of athletic excellence has to be made. The degree to which players specialised was a correlation of this dedication to one sport. For example, in the non-elite questionnaires the response to the question 'What other sports do you play?' included a significantly wider range of activities than for elite players, though team sports such as hockey, netball and basketball feature strongly across both groups, as do activities with a tradition of female participation such as swimming. Several international and elite players suggested that participation in other sport is usually to assist with fitness, agility or rehabiliatation for football and, in turn, this posed the question whether other sports could be considered alternatives to football or as part of a sporty lifestyle. However, though it was difficult to ascertain the extent to which football attracted women players who may not participate in other sports, one interview with an elite player struck me as particularly expressive in describing time related to football activities:

> Friday night I go out and have a drink with my mates and we're talking about the match on Sunday . . . who it will be [against] . . . what we'll do . . . having a laugh. Saturday I'm thinking about it and it's great because it's the weekend but I want the time to go quick [*sic*] so it's Sunday. I'll get my stuff ready and I won't go out . . . I'll eat pasta and go to bed early but I don't sleep easily because I can see myself playing and hopefully scoring [*laughs*].

The interview carries on in this way with the player describing how her experience of each day of the week relates to the Sunday game. For example, Monday involves a dissection of the previous day's action and physical recovery; Tuesday is a club training night involving nutritional preparation and organisation of time and travel; Wednesday is for personal training; Thursday is a club training night and Friday involves some personal training followed by socialising. In addition to the time spent in physical preparation, the interviewee spent a considerable amount of time talking and thinking about football. For some women in terms of commitment, time and focus of effort, football is central to their leisure and influences other recreation. To develop this line of research further, analyses of players' use of time at different levels of the sport could be developed.

Respondents also described their identity in the team as being formed by nicknames, their particular quality as a player and the role they contributed in terms of group cohesion. The majority of nicknames do not support the adoption of stereotypically male traits as characteristics of women's football culture. The names included contractions (Harj for Harjit, Staff for Stafford, Tommy for Tomlinson), features of play (Skip for a forward, Hedge for a sweeper) or a physical feature (Red, Smurf). Such names should be understood in relation to the game as rules prevent players from shouting 'My ball' but a one or two syllable title is a necessity for speed and accuracy in fending off a tackle, calling for a pass or claiming possession. Notably not one of the players claimed to be excellent by their own judgement; self-praise was often prefaced by comments such as 'X often says I've got excellent balance', X frequently denoting the coach, or 'The team always relies on my sliding tackles'. Performance was very rarely described in absolute terms. The process of assimilation of younger players by older players into the club hierarchy is also noteworthy. It was not unusual to find a mother and daughter or siblings playing for the same club and there was one exceptional team in which three sets of mothers and daughters played.

At elite level, several respondents explored the theme that competitive team sport is a preparation for life. Most differentiated between club experience and international selection. Club experience was emphasised as being less a competitive relationship with team-mates than a co-operative and parallel relationship characterised by promotive interdependence. In part, this would seem to be supported by the responses of recreational players, several of whom listed a captain or older player as their main influence. In contrast, at international level the mutual benefit of the collective involves competition for places so the separate accomplishments of individuals are paramount. Players are proud to play for England but playing representative football rests on individual accomplishment and outperforming others for selection. Both male and female coaches at this level reported a need to speak differently to women – 'Women are like sponges. They're great to coach . . . they've got no egos to massage like blokes.'

Specifically, coaches reported the need to motivate by encouragement rather than criticism ('women take things personally') and to comment specifically on the performance of skill rather than on attitude or approach. The most feared form of verbal abuse was laughter and several senior coaches discussed the difficulty of getting players to express themselves sufficiently so that they might try manoeuvres which required mental and physical courage like overhead kicks or diving headers. Even obviously skilled players felt at risk of being laughed at if the move failed:

> Well, even though you're all 'girls together' sort of thing, at England the pressure's on . . . so it's alright to say, express yourself, enjoy yourself and those other clichés they trot out but if you go for a big one and fail, you look a right plonker. Keep it simple . . . do the simple things well.

For those who have had a break from the sport at any level, accident and injury are relatively high on the list of reasons. Schedule constraints and transportation were other key factors. Over half answered the question 'Was there a time you stopped playing?' by saying there had been no interruption to their playing career. The following replies explained temporary disruptions.

> Yes. School would no longer allow competitive play between girls and boys. (I did, however, continue to play outside school.)

> Yes – when I was about 11 as I could not play for my school team or boys' teams and there was not too many girls' clubs around.

> Yes. I stopped playing seven years ago for one year as I made a trip from Australia and lived in England for twelve months. As we didn't have a car, I was unable to get to/from training and games so I stopped playing while I lived in England.

> Yes, I had a year out due to working and also for a break. I had played every Sunday for eleven years.

> I came back from London where I had played for Arsenal Ladies. I also worked at Arsenal FC for two years so when I came home I took a year out – basically to get settled with other things like work.

> Yes. I stopped playing seven years ago for one year as I made a trip to hospital with a broken leg.

Even the very young girls aged 8 and 9 were aware that football was not something that adult women did conventionally. In answer to the question,

'Were you ever stopped from playing while at school?' the following young respondents were surprised by the interruption to their playing career.

> Yes, for six months because I went to a new school and girls there didn't play football. It was an all-girls' school, I was only there for six months.

> Yes. Having played in the team at primary school I was stopped from playing at comprehensive school – they said it wasn't 'appropriate'!

Football was rarely a casual exercise option; on the other hand school-based opportunities in some cases facilitated participation, as one 15-year-old player replied, 'I first played football when I was 11 at school'. However, amongst those who had given up the sport it was rare to hear that another sport or recreation had replaced football; usually the decision to give up was explained as a change in priorities.

In terms of dealing with the stereotypes around women's football, a range of strategies were employed by individuals. For example, an England regular denied that there were any homosexual players in the sport, 'I have never seen any lesbian behaviour and I don't know any lesbian players. I think that's a stereotype.' The topic was also frequently and obliquely raised by young interviewees, often quite early on in the process. For example, a repeated comment was that the combination of training and school left little time for boyfriends.

> Well, you know, some boys don't understand that you have to train twice a week and I want to do well at school so I work most nights on homework. Mum says it's their loss! But then they say things at school, like 'She's not interested in boys, she'd rather play football with other girls', things like that.

> *She* has a boyfriend [*pointing*] that's why she doesn't always come Tuesdays . . . [*laughs*] She tells her mum she's at training though. She expects me to cover and she spends the subs [subscription fee] at McDonald's. Her mum'll ground her for months if she finds out.

Assertion of heterosexuality could be seen as conservatism, or the protection of a sexual self-image when participating in what has been seen as a male sport. It could also be a protection of the club and team from contention, or any combination of these. An openly homophobic point of view came from a male teacher and coach on a child protection course who initiated the conversation that girls' football was:

> A Full of lesbians using the Centres of Excellence to get close to girls to turn them.

Q Turn them?

A *You know* . . . into lesbians. They're very impressionable at that age. Fourteen is a funny age for girls and some of them look like boys, so boys don't find them attractive and then someone gives them attention . . .

It would appear that the insistence on heterosexuality was based on ideas of the respectability of the game as linked to the femininity of players. The disagreement was, in itself, evidence of the complications arising as players negotiate stereotypes.

On the one hand I wanted to view the information as reliable to the extent that it revealed ways about which women's football is discussed, whether or not the specific allegations were 'true'. On the other, the stereotype of the predatory lesbian figured large in my own experience as a teacher. Furthermore, the child protection literature suggested disbelief to be the key feature of abuse of vulnerable groups and individuals. Sports leadership is becoming slightly more self-regulating but remains a long way from the formal structures of other educational and professional practices. Most of note for this study is the correlation of increased female participation and child protection procedures, with the FA initiating training in 2000. The spectre of sexual harassment overshadows the basic form of abuse that many boys have been subject to for years by the nature of their engagement with the sport, namely parents who scream aggressive instructional comments from the sidelines.

On another level, for some women players in this project overtly macho behaviour was perceived as a tomboyish characteristic in which the participant was both representing their juvenile 'play' side and masculine traits. Especially with regard to tackles and discipline on the field, being like a man is used by some players to suggest their power and, by extension, the dominance of men in the sport. As one player put it, 'My nickname is Scud [as in the Scud missile], you can feel me but you won't hear me coming' and another, 'They call me Butch. I'm a strong player. I'm not scared of tackles'. This may not be masculine identification, however, but 'the fear of appearing female, or effeminate . . . unlike narcissism, femiphobia is a gender-negative construction, in being a barometer of what not to be' (Klein, 1993: 270). Acting out may be a feature of this. The 'ladette' and the 'she-bloke' attitude appeared to be both a liberation from perceived limits of femininity, in this case being frightened of being hurt, and a form of male emulation.

Few women indicated the English weather and exercising outdoors as demotivating factors, though there were numerous anecdotes relating to the playing and changing environments, from sharing pitches with grazing horses to serious injury caused by unseen broken glass. Rather, the challenge of facing the winter cold and mud led to feelings of being in control, identification with the body and pride in its achievements. Words such as 'capable', 'able', 'confidence' and 'challenge' appeared to signal strength rather than imperatives about exercise, body shape and weight. Training frequently enabled the players to see themselves as objectively working on the body as a machine to improve performance. The fact that much of this collective action was done outdoors in natural settings was part of the enjoyment of participating. In particular, training at night on floodlit grass or AstroTurf in a relatively safe group setting enables players to get fresh air while exercising and socialising. Many players extend this practice to go running together, for example, in preference to going to a gym or other indoor facility.

Two comments from elite players reflect a lack of awareness of the historical forces in women's football. In answer to the question 'How would you describe the history of the ban of the women's game?' the replies were:

> There never was a ban on the women's game, because there was no game to ban. The only restriction is that women cannot become professional footballers, but that wasn't a ban because women were never able to become professional footballers.

> It was okay before the industrial revolution when women were not expected to play sport. They were there just to watch. More women these days have a good physique compared to before.

The responses reflect a perception that the recent rise of interest is indicative of progress and is therefore a modern phenomenon. A significant number of elite and club players left this section blank, which suggests that women players' knowledge of previous generations is limited. Those who did complete the section usually used a single exclamatory 'disgusting' or 'typical' and this left me unsure whether the player had just learned of the ban or was expressing a considered view. The sense of a continuous tradition is the first element of community players lacked.[14] Nor were players and administrators necessarily curious about past events.

The players' views suggest that 'difference' is a pliable term. The question, 'Do you regard women's football as a separate sport to men's football, as a related sport or the same sport?' prompted responses including:

> It is the same sport but with different support.

> Separate, men's football has too much money involved now.

> Related due to the fact we are both playing football but there are so many different standards in facilities, kit and sponsorship.

> It's just the same only women's football is more competitive.

> Separate, because not many male teams actually come into contact with the women and don't do anything for the female game.

> I class it as the same game as it has the same rules. I think though men's and women's football is played in two different styles.

The range of views highlights the difficulty of defining the object of study in 'women's football' and demonstrates constant mediation with the term. Even where players feel it to be the same sport, some degree of differentiation is often part of the explanation. For example, many of the players disagreed with my ideas concerning mixed games at competitive level. This was frequently a defence of a female space, to encourage girls and other women to play whatever their ability. The question 'FA policy prevents girls and boys playing competitively together after age 12. Do you agree with this line, and is this the right age?' produced some highly personal and some more objective answers:

> I don't think boys and girls should play together. But training is a good idea as they learn from each other.

> Yes, because I know from karate competitions boys are physically a lot stronger, but in training the aggression can be controlled.

> I agree as boys are physically stronger than girls so it would be in the girls' and boys' interests. I think the age is right as well.

Mixed competitive football is resisted by some women within women's football as a protection of a female domain. They argue that mixed sport would inevitably be organised along the same lines as male football and then there would be no room for women or girls.[15] This topic will continue to be contentious and open to change as some women players play in mixed teams, often to improve the standard of the game. During the course of this study the Scottish FA has recently raised the age of mixed competition to 15. Some of the girls and women supported this idea in answer to the question posed above.

> I think it should be optional for people like me who, at age 10, would have liked to play for a team.

> I think girls and boys should be able to play competitively until senior level if they wanted to.

> I disagree. Some boys are better because they are given encouragement at a younger age. Boys and girls should be treated exactly the same.

> Disagree, because we are just as strong and good as boys/men.

More of the elite players disagreed with this question than agreed, and a few suggested age limits between 12 and 15, while another replied, 'If the girl is good enough, she should be able to stay in the boys' league as long as she can compete at the same level.'

In several instances coaches and players had opted for work that enabled them to have fixed, flexible working times in order to leave time free for training. This is only one public aspect of their lives affected because of their participation as players. Many would like to earn a full-time living in football but feel unable to gain access to any career opportunities. Interviews with relatives added to my impression that the players are often physically, emotionally, socially and financially invested in the sport. This began to answer my question about the worth of the game to the female player. Women travelling around the country to play football are experiencing sport tourism as part of the process of socialisation and, if my experience is typical, the level of hospitality ranges from warm mushy peas and pork pie in a Yorkshire pub, to tea and cakes in a tennis pavilion. At weekly games and special events, a fascinating expression of individual and group identity is on display; including fashion statements, such as headbands, bandannas and boots, the mix of ages and body types, the degree of serious preparation for competition, the presence of supporters and so forth. In these settings women's football as a subculture with its own codes and signs is clearly evident. In considering the construction of identity in such settings, women's agency and negotiation with commercialised aspects of the game are visually very prominent and I have tried to capture some of this on the page.

The difficulty of locating this work within a specific research context is one that other researchers who have taken a thematic approach to the study of women's football have negotiated: 'Is it "women's history", "sports history", "national history", or "local history"?' (Melling, 1999: 21). In considering the oral testimonies of the players against the background of other evidence, the history of women's football is an aspect of each of these other narratives. It also shows that, though this project was more of a departure than an arrival, research of women's sport has to be pursued within a social context and with political implications and this is something the next section develops. There may not be a sense of continuity or common destiny at the level of the sport in women's football but there is evidence of communal understanding in clubs and teams. This makes sense because teams have been created for diverse reasons, from participation to elite achievement. Less encouragingly, though ideas have been shown to be open to negotiation by players there have yet to be sufficient women playing to talk about a transformation in the conceptualisation of football.

With more time it would have been possible to extend the work done on oral history to consider oral tradition. That is, to go beyond questions about the knowledge and importance of cultural artefacts relating to the past for the players of today, to an analysis of the traditions and narratives of those past players over generations. For example, following her expulsion from Scottish women's football, Rose Reilly successfully played another ten years professionally in Italy and became the only player on the board of directors at Trani, earning around £1,000 a month plus sponsorship and free accommodation in 1984. It would be interesting to gather information about how that was viewed by the other players, by the board members and her relatives. Generations will have told the stories of the original players to others who may still be active in football today. One example is, Winnie Bourke, daughter of Alice Mills who emigrated to the United States in 1923 as mentioned previously. Winnie's own high school essay about women's football, the eulogy at her mother's funeral, *The Pawtucket Times* newspaper articles from the original Dick, Kerr tour provide examples of how the events have been handed down in the print and orally. Winnie is herself now 80 years old and has seven grandchildren, one of whom plays football. The émigré narrative of her mother's hard work, determination and success are a family tradition, in which football is an example of her mother's 'doing' nature and willingness to take an opportunity if offered. Unfortunately, my attempts to contact the relatives of players who remained in England from this era have been less successful.

Oral history and women's football in England

There has yet to be a systematic description of the clubs in the women's football from the 1880s to the present day. The historiography led me to test to what extent this was now possible given the basic administrative procedures of women's football and, at this stage, a great deal of research remains to be done before this map is complete. Nevertheless, the evidence that we do have sets an increased participation in football for women after the 1960s in context of the trend for sport development in Britain to be about numbers, targets and successive initiatives. The 1921 ban was successful in broad terms in spite of pockets of resistance, in ways that still affect the image of football today. Given the scope and pace of social and cultural change in English society during the period, the practice of containing football as a masculine preserve was not a straightforward economic, organisational or business practice. Common-sense ideas about football as a masculine-appropriate sport depend upon uncritically received assumptions about the way that this myth was fabricated. It is the invention of tradition of women as not interested in football that emerged as a contentious topic during this study in part because the lived experience of players is not widespread knowledge. During the process of research certain individuals have responded in an angry or perplexed manner to ideas about women playing. For some men and women it appears abnormal. The current use of slogans of a feminine future and increasingly common female participation are vaguely positive attempts to make women's football appear both natural and fashionable to the general public.

More than a decade on, it is difficult to share the optimism of Williams and Woodhouse writing in 1991.

> The establishment of the PFA/Football League 'Football and the Community' initiative at Football League clubs in 1985 brought with it a commitment to work with all sections of the community, including girls and women. As a consequence, coaching and playing opportunities for females increased substantially . . . the successful schemes involving women attracted local authority support and finance . . .

> where a commitment to equal opportunities came hand in hand with the promise of cash.
>
> (Williams and Woodhouse, 1991: 100)

A less supportive view of the financial and bureaucratic policies of the FA after 1993 could argue that while extracting the affiliation fees from women's leagues and players at recreational and competitive level, the association has belatedly begun to develop women's football at elite level. The lottery-funding framework, like Williams and Woodhouse, assumes the FA's expertise in developing the sport. Funding models have yet to address differences of opportunity to play, access to means of transport and the time to travel. This top-down cascade approach is clearly evident in the official memory and is reinforced by a concern with new initiatives: 'Our new targets are the Pro-League; International Development Centre; International developments and staff development; Increased Centres and Academies; Active Sports; New Girls' Football Campaign' (Kelly Simmons, FA Head of National Football Development, personal communication August 2001).

There is some evidence that schools have increasingly provided opportunities for girls to play but whether female football becomes an increasingly infantilised sport remains to be seen. In practice the transition from school-based sport to community clubs relies on the volunteers who are given least prestige and support by funding policies. It is these men and women who emerge from the privately held and local sources as the architects and engineers of women's football. Furthermore, the transfer from school to adult football is fraught with difficulty, ranging from individual transport and communication issues, to financial costs, to lifestyle choices and broader economic and cultural developments. As *Living in Britain* showed in 1996 and *Social Trends* indicated in 2001, there is a debatable relationship between school and adult participation generally, for women particularly and for female football specifically. The 1996 survey found that sport participation rates for adults excluding walking had fallen from 48 per cent in 1990 to 46 per cent, and 37 per cent of men took less than an hour's exercise compared with 60 per cent of women (Office for National Statistics, 2001: 136). In 1996 football, as the fifth most popular male sport, showed the greatest disparity between the sexes at a male to female ratio of less than ten to one (*Living in Britain*, 1996: 209). The 2001 study, though largely based on the 1996 figures, showed little difference for adult women, a smaller increase for female football in lessons than rounders and a male to female participant ratio of four to one (Office for National Statistics, 2001: 230; Office for National statistics, 2002: 62). However, the relative gains are small compared with newer individual sports, such as skateboarding for both sexes, with the increase for girls six times that of football.[1]

> Of the young people who said they had taken part in extra curricular sport, football continued to be the most popular and had the greatest increase in participation from 31% . . . in 1994 to 35% in 1999. In 1999 53% of boys and 12% of girls who did extra curricular sport took part in football.
>
> (Rowe and Champion, 2000: 17)

The paradox at the heart of the system is that increased participation by young women and girls has been facilitated by volunteers at competitive level whose continuing unpaid contribution is vital for the growth of the sport. The current policy to fund elite and school participation by lottery monies which local authorities can bid for *because* local teams exist to provide playing opportunities for post-school and pre-elite participants does little to consult or assist those most directly responsible for the development of women's football.

M. Ann Hall has made a notable addition to the work of Hargreaves and feminist analyses of sport by critiquing feminist theory and her own, originally positivist, work (Hall, 1996: 3). In particular she has borrowed from Birrell and Theberg the term 'leaky hegemony' and extended it to characterise the history of women in sport as cultural resistance.[2] The formal discriminations applied to women playing competitive football are by no means rational or inevitable. The entitlement currently extends to women to playing competitively only against women and this feminised form of the game is materially and ideologically significant. It places women's football is a faction and marginalises it at the same time as incorporating it into current stuctures. It is at once similar to men's football and different and therefore forms a 'structurally and functionally identical group which, by virtue of their similarity, compete for resources or positions of power or prestige, or both' (Brumfiel, 1989: 127). So the sex of participants is less important than the meanings given to gender difference by football administrations and wider society.

Finally it is crucial to place the rise of second-wave feminist writing alongside the rise of sport generally, football particularly, as a popular activity since the 1960s. Football has remained impervious to academic feminist appeals for change and for women it is still at the 'me too' stage.[3] Does the responsibility for this lie with football or feminism? The problem with current strategies of integration is that the initiative lies with men in giving up power. This is clearly a slow process. Football particularly and British sport generally have hardly been at the vanguard of what change has occurred. Football for women under the control of the NIWFA, LFAI, SWFA, FAW, WFA and the national associations is marked by conservatism. In addition, since the 1960s, women's attempts to enter football have corresponded with a new and emergent professionalism in the sport. The use of associations for various specialisms particularly and the process of patronage have served to include a few exceptional individuals at the expense of a critical mass of women in any aspect of the sport. Unless there is a more radical change, this looks set to continue.

Certain of the individuals interviewed for this study, although independent in terms of not being employed by the FA, are used by the association as speakers at conferences and in the media. Others are 'experts' in their chosen field but highly critical of FA policy. These individuals were most active as players in the 1970s and early 1980s and therefore have a particular view of the WFA and FA administration. There remains dispute about whether the majority of WFA material has also been taken into the archive. However, WFA administrators and volunteers often kept minutes of meetings and so some documented debates are traceable and we can develop our understanding of the process of assimilation by finding yet more. This contested control of the past and present image of women's football has been treated as a subject in itself, especially the relationship between marketing football to women as a fashionable activity and the dubious place of women's participation in social memory.

The trend of conspicuously not honouring women players continues to this day as individual players are largely still unknown to us, even at elite level. When England Captain Gill Coulthard joined the 100 club of international appearances she was awarded a small commemorative medal before the kick-off of an international game watched by 1,000 people. Unlike Mia Hamm of the United States (116 caps and rising) and Carolina Morace of Italy (108 caps when she retired) she is largely unknown as a media figure. Mia Hamm's honours include, for example, Nike naming the largest building on their corporate United States campus after her. No British woman is recognised in public memory as a great football player. Three women, Sylvia Gore, Sue Lopez and Kelly Simmons have been rewarded in the Queen's honours list for their contribution to football as coaches and administrators but they are hardly household names.

The problem of where to place women players in the public consciousness was reflected in a recent British Nike advertising campaign. The advertisement used Joan Whalley to evoke a tradition of women players. No contemporary English equivalent of Mia Hamm could be found to promote women's football so Joan was pictured in kit and wearing Lily Parr's boots.[4] Unfortunately, the stylist decided not to use photographs of the young player and groomed Joan beyond her normally casual look to fit the convention of a coiffed older lady. Tomlinson has usefully described the reservation of the male gaze in football for men as players and as symbols of the game itself as a form of 'male romance' (Tomlinson, 1999: 239). Heroic figures such as Bobby Moore and Pele are represented in advertisement after advertisement in prime physical shape.[5] When Mia Hamm is depicted as active, attractive and young, contemporary British women may not want to play 'like an old woman', as Joan was presented.

Where would memorabilia be located if it were to be collected? Some collectors wished to integrate their collections with a Football Association archive but others were vehement about keeping both the memory and memorabilia very separate. As one senior WFA administrator told me:

> There isn't any. I burned it. I was so angry when the WFA agreed to amalgamate with the FA, I had a big bonfire and I burned the lot . . . I know I shouldn't have done it now but I was so frustrated especially when they were so keen to get rid of the title WFA and changed it three or four times to the Women's Football Committee and even replaced the Women's FA Cup with the FA Cup for women.

The material that participants shared with me included programmes, advertisements, personal scrapbooks and correspondence. These compilations contradict the views of the editor of *She Kicks*, Jennifer O'Neill, currently working professionally in the production of a public image of women's football, who wrote in a 1999 press release, 'The older generation of women footballers have an inferiority complex about their achievements.' This kind of attitude helps to explain why there would be such anger from the volunteers.

The material in private collections, like the fixtures, fitted the players' own needs. An example is the evolution of the scrapbook from personal journal, to club magazine, to fanzine. It would be useful to extend this kind of investigation because the variety of playing identities is such that a comprehensive analysis is not possible in the space, but could include religion, ethnicity or sexuality as lines of future enquiry. There has been little work which compares various recreational, competitive and non-elite representative leagues, for example. So rather than describing women's football, it is possible to see that certain groups have created participatory cultures, and as such, the experiences of the majority of women players in England are, as yet, under-researched.

In some senses the interviews support this view as women's football is a voluntaristic initiative peopled by enthusiasts. One aspect contributing to maintenance and growth is this construction of a playing community beyond (usually preceding) extensive central bureaucratisation of the game. These distinctive forms of play are nevertheless highly organised and reflect a deep level of engagement, to the degree that participatory culture is the principal dimension of women's football in Britain today. However, as has been argued throughout, in order to assess the importance of the meanings that women players have made, the changes within the sport have to be set in a broader frame of reference. The interpretations of the players in this section stand against the overlapping and competing agendas for both women in sport and gender in football which Part II examines in the broader context of an international playing community.

Plate 1
'A fine all-round player' – an early example of the ways in which women's football passed into popular culture. Art and Humour Series 766, Fred Spurgin postcard *c*. 1920.

Source: Private collection of Peter Bridgett.

Plate 2 Baldwin's United Ladies' Football Team. This Chapman of Swansea postcard *c*. 1920 is an early example of the ways in which women's football passed into popular culture and their uniform contrasts with that in Plate 1 and the Stoke Ladies' team (Plate 8).

Source: Private collection of Jane Ebbage.

Plate 3 A Scottish women's team photograph *c*. World War I. Presumably the soldiers were home on leave. Note the children trying to get their faces into shot on the left. This photograph was bought at a car-boot sale by the collector, and the name of the team remains a mystery.

Source: Private collection of Jane Ebbage.

Plates 4, 5, and 6 *(right)* are postcards of women's football teams circa 1921–5. There are potentially many more images of this kind in the hands of postcard collectors. They show that munitions football was not the only form of women's participation in the early phase of interest and, women's work and leisure, rather than charitable fund-raising, influenced the formation of teams. The uniform has also become more standardised compared with the images here. The oldest postcards I was able to trace through David Williamson included images from 1895 in *Belles of the Ball*. Dick, Kerr's wore a recognisable football strip from the start of the club.

Plate 4 (left) 'Hey's Brewery (Bradford) Ladies' A.F.C., Champions of Yorkshire 1921–22'.

Plate 5 (right) Atalanta Ladies.

Plate 6 (below) 'The famous Dick, Kerr International Ladies' A.F.C., World's Champions 1917–25. Raised over £70,000 for ex-service men, hospitals and poor children.'

Plate 7 Greenwood and Batleys Ladies, Armley. Postcard *c.* 1918. The team are wearing boots and flannel-type shorts with woollen stockings and a variety of headgear.

Plate 8 Stoke Ladies' Football Team *c.* 1921–3. Arthur Bridgett stands on the rear right and E. Carroll, the coalman's daughter, is at the centre of the back row. Len Bridgett's wife and one of his daughters are on the left of the back row. The English Ladies' Football Cup trophy is displayed in the foreground.

Source: Private collection of Peter Bridgett.

Plate 9 England XI versus France XI, 1949. International competition was quickly revived after World War II. Several of the players pictured here, such as Lily Parr, had been involved in this kind of game for over twenty years. Many of the French and English women had longstanding friendships.

Source: Private collection of Gail Newsham.

Part II

The future is feminine

The rise of the women's game in a global and professional era

Part I alluded to international comparisons with the English form of football for women. Part II extends the correspondence by examining the perceived globalisation of football, during an era when issues surrounding professionalism have become increasingly complex. FIFA and national associations are rarely careful not to overstate the number of female participants and this tendency has been criticised earlier in this volume for deflecting attention from some of the more fundamental issues which continue to affect women's access to the sport. For example, in their recent survey, FIFA have estimated that approximately 20 million females play football worldwide, of which 8 million play in the United States (FIFA, 2001). The figures do not provide information about those who are excluded, for example by regional, cultural, racial, economic or other circumstances, though are meant to include unregistered players. Nor does an emphasis on numbers address why antiquated gender divisions should be accepted at either competitive or professional level. The ability of football to propose a differentiated vision for women is dealt with in Part II both from the point of view of legislation which affects women's access to sport and from the perspective of splintered female international participation. The degree of female player and administrative integration into any one national association can be quite distinct between members of the football family. In some instances, players and administrators speak about women's football as a different sport to male football and feel that in doing so, they are creating a space for women to play that is socially acceptable. Often this is overtly to counteract the view that women are trying to compete with men either in sport or for the resources necessary to play football. In some cases women's football is perceived as somehow feminised – simultaneously the same sport but played differently, perhaps with an emphasis on skill rather than physicality.[1]

Just as patterns of intensity and diffusion characterise women's football participation in Britain, there is considerable variety in the number of players and the forms of the game across the globe. Why would FIFA choose China to host the 2003 Women's World Cup for the second time in just over a decade if there was blanket support for female football across the community as a whole? The decision shows that when it comes to the value of women's participation to the international association, some countries are evidently more equal than others. As a guarantor of live audience support that, in turn, will help to sell the tournament as a media spectacle and with a medal-winning national female team who can help to promote the sport of football to Asia, China has clear advantages compared to other nations who sought to host the tournament, like Australia. So from the United States victory in the 1999 World Cup in Los Angeles, to the dominance of Scandinavian representation in international tournaments and late withdrawals of Namibia from international qualifiers in 1998, buoyant but irregular recreative and competitive participation within regions and varying degrees of professional preparation for elite competitions also indicate a complicated picture. The current relative strength of the US, Germany, Norway and Nigeria can be set against the decline of English international success since the mid-1980s. This illustrates how quickly the standard of play is changing as another aspect of an increasingly specialised approach in the female game. Therefore writing a global history of women's football would be a very large undertaking. As a starting point, there is room here for only two case studies, of the United States and Namibia respectively, in order to maintain the focus of the work as a whole and provide an international perspective on the speed and direction of change in women's football in England.

I wanted first of all to test the extent to which there is popular identification with elite representative players that Grant Jarvie identifies as an aspect of the relationship between sport and nationalism:[2]

> Sport itself often provides a form of symbolic action which states the case for the nation itself. The popular identification between athlete, team and nation or community has led to the suggestion that sporting struggles, and international triumphs and losses, are primary expressions of imagined communities.
>
> (Jarvie, 1993: 74–5)

In asking to what extent this applies to women's football, Part II asks what are the strengths and weaknesses of the English model of participation and elite development? How are elite English players viewed at home and abroad? What imaginary community, if any, do they represent?

The gap in public recognition of the male and female national team goes beyond a divide between amateur and professional sport. For example, in contrast to the recent Downing Street reception to mark a fairly successful World Cup campaign, excerpts from interviews with England women players show how little each asks in return for representing their nation. For instance, at week-long training camps, players are not paid but receive expenses of up to £15 a day and the regime was notoriously unpopular under Hope Powell's predecessor, Ted Copeland.

> But now there are different rules and none of the staff are allowed to drink, which I think is a good thing. You can go in the bar and you can have one night to have family or boyfriends or whatever come over . . . say for three hours, which again stops the boredom and makes you feel more at home. Anything to make you happy or want to be at England, [Hope Powell's] going to try to do, which is really good. Just three hours is a real boost to your spirits, which would never happen with Ted.
>
> The drinking thing . . . they used to all go into the bar and we had to go into our rooms and you were not supposed to go out again after 9 [p.m.]. Whereas Hope says they go in the bar but have to have orange or something and they allow us to do that if we want a drink of orange. This allows us to make use of the facilities as long as we are not too noisy.
>
> We weren't allowed to play cards with Ted because, he said, of the gambling aspect. But none of us gamble; we just play for fun, so, with Hope, she allowed us to play cards. She said, 'As long as you're not gambling.' Little home comforts she would let you have, which, you know . . . is more respectful of us as adults. The players really, really dreaded going to England in the past. We'd say we wished we could just train and play football and then be able to go home at the end of the day.
>
> [Hope Powell] was saying that she wanted to change it from people wanting to play for their country but not wanting to come here, to people wanting to play for their country and wanting to be here for a week or so. She definitely made a difference because we never had little things that showed they wanted to be decent to us. You know, they would drop a player in the bar and the young ones would maybe cry in front of a bar full of people on a conference or something . . . and [Ted Copeland] never did it himself. He got the female doctor to tell them.

If this community represents an imagined group, the players are the ones privileged to wear the England shirt and are consequently afforded rudimentary hospitality and asked to follow infantilised rules. The importance of the image of team representatives as respectable and worthy of wearing the three lions is far greater than rewarding these individuals financially or in terms of status. The profile of specific players is considerably lower than that of junior professional male players, as is the importance of the team as a whole. It therefore seemed that the idea of an imagined community, even one of credible amateurs, did not explain the status of the female national squad and Part II examines alternative perceptions of female elite players.

Another obvious theme for comparison is the role of equality of opportunity and equity laws to promote female participation, as British women's football has to be understood in context of British and European Union legislation. Additionally the role of women coaches and administrators in national and international associations as members of the workforce requires consideration. As with the examples proposed in the last section, patronage is the main form of sponsorship in international organisations of most influence in women's football. The attendant skills of diplomacy and tact are especially important in international sporting federations including the Olympic movement, and it is to this that the argument finally turns. This said, key individuals have changed and challenged ideas from insider positions, for example Julie Foudy had a pioneering and central role in forming the first female professional league in the United States, Women's United Soccer Association (WUSA). Overall, women's football has grown in popularity worldwide, albeit in pockets of interest, over the last forty years alongside the wider development of international women and sport activism. To this end, the key agencies in women's sport advocacy and their relationship with FIFA and the Olympic movement, the two international bodies most crucial to the development of women's football, are another aspect of the worldwide situation which impacts upon the English case.

Sport tourism pre-dates bureaucratisation at the national and international level and remains a key aspect of women's football. The most common forms are club competitions, either as representative team tours, or international tournaments for national sides. Enthusiasts in Scotland, for example, held trials (without SFA support) in 1966, 1967 and 1969 to form unofficial representative squads which played in international tournaments. While conventional wisdom is that the first home international officially took place in 1972, by this time Rose Reilly and Edna Nellis of Scotland plus England's Sue Lopez were already playing in Italy and touring other countries with club sides; in the latter case, for example, with Roma in the US in 1971. Both Scottish players received letters from the FA which told them women were no longer banned from playing football when they had already spent four years in Italy as professionals. A week after the ban was lifted north of the border in 1974, another letter invited them to play for their country. At club level, Stewarton and Thistle Ladies FC were created in May 1961 and played in tournaments such as the WFA Mitre Challenge Trophy in 1971 in England, the Scottish Cup and the Scottish Ladies Charity Shield.[3] So the European and international dimensions of female competitive networks at professional and participatory level are an area which has been virtually overlooked in academic treatments of football and women's sport. In assessing the place of elite competition again there is room for a limited overview and so Women's World Cup, Olympic competition and Women's USA have been given particular prominence here.

On an individual level, for those women who wish to be at the pinnacle of football, travel and preparation can involve considerable demands. The following is an excerpt from an interview with Canadian Sonia Denoncourt, the first woman to referee male professional football in Brazil, in which she describes her experience of tournaments such as the Olympic Games and Women's World Cup.

> A typical day at an international tournament would be seven o'clock training, nine o'clock breakfast, and 10 o'clock analysis of the previous day's game, working the day's game, going to bed very early . . . FIFA does not want you to smoke, drink, or socialise with players or journalists.
>
> (Sonia Denoncourt, Los Angeles, 1999)

Denoncourt insists on taking the tougher fitness tests for male referees so that she is eligible to officiate first-class football. A vegetarian who pays careful attention to her diet, she prepares by training six days a week all year, running and cycling in summer and playing ice hockey, lifting weights and riding a stationery bike in winter. Owning her own business enables the official to meet tournament and league commitments. So travel is not just an opportunity for Denoncourt, it entails considerable modification to her daily routine to facilitate an international profile. Analyses of time use and professional preparation by the elite female official, coach and player could therefore be extended in future research but there isn't really scope to cover them here.

In elite and participatory terms the number of unofficial and official tournaments available to women's teams is a dimension of international competition that is deserving of research in its own right, so only the key aspects will be alluded to at this point.[4] The 1980s were a time of rapid growth in international competition. The Asian Cup, for example, began in 1975, though it was by no means limited to Asian countries. The first Oceania Cup was held in 1983 and a UEFA-sponsored cup saw England runners-up in 1984 (rather unlike the early exit of England in the 2001 UEFA competition). Another important tournament pre-FIFA intervention was the World Women's Invitational in Taiwan in 1987, as the level of participation indicated strength in depth, sufficient to interest the international association. In contrast, FIFA-sponsored women's competition is a thing of the 1990s – the first Women's World Cup in 1991 in China and the second Women's World Cup in Sweden in 1995. This competition formed the qualifying route for the 1996 Olympics (where, for the first time, women's football was included as a full medal sport), and which is itself a peculiarity preventing England from participating in Olympic competition even when they do qualify via World Cup places. The complexities of the international governing bodies' view of women is worth covering in detail as a chapter in itself in this section as the Olympics is the second most significant tournament for women's football, maybe more meaningful in the United States than the Women's World Cup, whereas it is relatively unimportant to the male game compared with regionalised club tournaments.

A further remarkable element of international play useful for this study, is the number of individuals who travel abroad to play. Those elite players sufficiently talented and targeted for financial reward, either in the form of sponsored education or remuneration, could be studied to show how the limits of a given national infrastructure have been overcome by moving to other countries to play. Julie Murray of Australia, in a career spanning fifteen years at the elite level, is one such example. She made her first appearance at 15 in 1986 for the second Oceania Cup and debuted against the USA in 1987. From age 9 to 12 she lived in America and later played professionally for Fortuna Hjorring in Denmark. Dropped as captain of the Australian team following the 1995 Women's World Cup (to be recalled in 1997), in 2001 Murray scored two goals to put Bay Area Cyber Rays in the first ever Women's USA play-off. Tracing her career therefore indicates some of the prime areas of interest in women's football at international level.

The same is true of English women players. Though at the beginning of her career, Kelly Smith of England had a spectacularly successful college career at Seton Hall in the United States, including, in the 1999 season, twenty-one multiple-goal games, including ten where she scored three or more goals. She received Seton Hall's highest honour as her shirt number (6) was retired. Smith thereby became the first non-basketball athlete and the third woman to earn the distinction at the university.[5] The limits of development in certain nations has led to a migration in order to fulfil playing potential that has, in some cases, adversely affected national sides. There is now potential for this to change, as the United States professional league, Women's USA, has enabled players like Murray and Smith to develop playing expertise that translates back to national squads, but at the moment the foreign draft into the league is limited. The transfer of elite players, particularly of British players including Smith, Lopez, Reilly and Nellis and the sports tourism of non-elite players is therefore another area still to be fully treated as a topic.

Two international examples have been chosen to highlight the challenges faced by the English model of women's football. The intention in this approach is to question the idea of a globalised game in terms of geographical spread and to propose multiple scenarios with regard to female participation and development. Oceania, India and Asia are not considered in detail here though they undoubtedly constitute a market for professional football both in terms of Japan's *L* women's professional league sponsored by big business, and in terms of elite players and tournaments.[6] Another reason for not including the three continents is that they exemplify the need for study of each region as a subject in itself and FIFA has recently begun a research project of this kind in the latter in Asia. With an increasing media profile, Sun Wen of China, perhaps the most famous Asian woman player, recently achieved a world first in accomplishing candidature for the Asian player of the year award and was placed second in the FIFA World Women's Player of the year 2001. Another Chinese star, Liu Ailing, has been player of the week three times in the WUSA League. In contrast, in a relatively unknown country for women's football such as Nepal, Kalpana Sharma became a FIFA assistant referee as the result of a curtailed international playing career when the Nepalese FA discontinued women's football from 1992 to 1998. Lalita Shrestha, the national women's coach, and Rama Singh, the national captain, have both played while studying to Master's level. Even the brief details I have been able to track down so far indicate that the wider role of educational institutions in facilitating female play could be examined, as could the role of works teams such as the Nepal Police Women's team, and regions where women's teams are founded for representative football.[7]

It is also beneficial to supplement analysis of cross-cultural developments with examples of specific change. For example, Neriem Kerzabi, an academic working in Algiers, reports that, for the first time in 2000, women contested a national championship for football (Kerzabi, 1998a). Kerzabi's work provides a particular view of cultural influences on women and football over which the international community has chosen to have little influence (Kerzabi, 1998b). In the case of Brazil, as another example, the men's game has inhibited the development of women players until very recently. The third placing in the 1999 Women's World Cup is the most considerable improvement a women's national team has made in recent years over a relatively short space of time. However, a study by Myotin found that football and weightlifting were perceived to be the least appropriate sport for women amongst Brazilian girls aged 11–20 years (Myotin, 1996: 224). Elite success may not produce widespread participation or support if there is long-term antipathy to women players in a country which identifies itself as a football nation. As such this illustration is particularly pertinent to the English case but also calls into question the ways in which football is a mass female participation sport on any level.

Participant observation at women and sport conferences, international women's sport events and while playing has been crucial in compiling evidence. This was necessary because, unfortunately, my ability to speak other languages is worse than my capacity to kick a ball around and, risking a cliché, football became the common language I shared with some participants. The difficulty of reconciling feminist theory with practice in the lives of women was nowhere more evident than in the international sports development movement, which has grown exponentially since the 1960s and correlates with the quite separate rise of football as a mass mediated sport. Particularly, the competing views of activists which have been discussed and evaluated from Brighton in 1994 and Windhoek in 1998 to Toronto in 2002, proposed a sense of what women's sport campaigners hope and expect to achieve. This enabled me to consider the range of aims and tactics for the movement as a whole against which to gauge the current direction of women's football. On the one hand it is extremely encouraging to see a move towards looking at the outcomes of initiatives and policies rather than in vague terms at opportunity and yet, on the other, change is painfully slow and sometimes short-lived.

Also significant with regard to this study is the fact that academics have indicated that the process of codification in nineteenth-century sport was explicitly designed to include some groups and exclude others.[8] This is an enduring feature of women's relationship to football that goes beyond national boundaries. In context of sports in the twentieth century for women, at the European Women and Sport Conference in 2000, Margaret Talbot was still arguing:

> The most striking and universal difference between men and women in sport is in the organizations, bureaucracy and events management of sport, where men dominate positions of power, responsibility and decision making, except in traditionally all-female sports like netball, synchronized swimming and rhythmic gymnastics.
>
> (Talbot, 2000: 1)

Therefore the role of these bureaucracies in limiting women's access to decision-making elites in football at national and international level became a key focus as it has remarkable continuity over time and across cultures. However, in examining the issue of professionalism in football, the most remarkable and entire difference is the way that women's access to football as an occupational choice has been treated as unproblematic. The complexity of this issue, from the point of view of the woman player and coach alone, is treated in Chapter 4.

Since the 1960s there have been a number of national and international movements that have championed the contribution of sport to the well-being of women. For example, to discriminate against women in a sporting arena contravenes human rights agreements:

> The human rights of women and the girl-child are an inalienable, integral, and indivisible part of universal human rights. The full and equal participation of women in political, civil, economic, social, and cultural life, at the national, regional and international levels, and the eradication of all forms of discrimination on grounds of sex are priority objectives of the international community.
>
> (Vienna Declaration of Action, 1993: 2)

Nevertheless, even for those societies that actively support such covenants, equality is interpreted as equal but different, an approach which is fundamentally flawed as it takes no account of historical inequality in shaping future developments. Women's access to professional competition as a career, rather than as leisure, has been overlooked in part because of this international acceptance of gender-differentiated sport. What has not been debated widely enough is that this has had the effect of creating widely condoned protected labour markets for male players which in other areas of culture, society and the economy would be considered to be unacceptable and in need of change.

Because of this emphasis on equal but different provision, a key question in the promotion of women in sport at international level was the extent to which speakers were radical in their demands and strategies for change. The implied rights above are clearly not available to women at the level of fully equal participation in football in any country worldwide, nor has there been much debate about what that would entail. One dimension of this study, then, was to understand the mechanisms by which certain women have negotiated some access to power. For other women players and academics to whom I spoke, sport was unimportant given the difficulties certain women faced in areas of essential rights, such as overcoming poverty, ill health and lack of education, and I accept their view. Nonetheless, the economic, social, cultural and symbolic preference given to male forms of football by governing bodies internationally was overwhelming. From the contractual wrangles of the United States women players with US Soccer over the years, to the disappointments of women who had to choose between representing their nation or a club side, the imbalance was striking and broadly corresponded with the amateur–professional gender divide which requires attention if we are to examine the place of women's football in a professional era.

4 Bumbling along

The law and English women's football in a professional era[1]

In what ways can women become professionally involved in football in England?[2] As Part I outlined, the persistence of separate male and female spheres implied by the titles 'football' and 'women's football' continues to be a key factor in the way the game is played and perceived. This chapter explores the extent to which practices and policies based on the group intrude upon the rights of the individual woman football player. It then moves on to assess the impact of key legislation on aspects of professionalism for women players and then on to coaches. The argument begins with the confusion over football for girls, with the consequence that it has only very recently become a more widely accepted female sport within, for example, education.

There is very little that is 'natural' about the place of football in our culture and yet it continues to be constructed as a 'manly' sport. Arguments that girls generally could outperform boys in school-based forms of the sport or that women could have a place in the Premiership appear outlandish in the current climate. Interviewees offered contrasting ideas of both spontaneous and constructed elements of what is essentially female and inherently male. In the interview above, the school proposed a set of ideas about femininity negotiated by the character of the individual.

> Q Did you like hockey and netball?
> A I just didn't like the game [*sic*]. I'd rather be kicking, rather than, you know, it felt strange handling a ball?
> Q School was probably the first time that you can remember being discouraged from playing football?
> A I wouldn't say we were discouraged but we weren't encouraged. It just wasn't on the agenda so you just accepted that, because that's how it was.

For this player handling a ball felt unnatural whereas for many girls kicking is an alien skill. A second feature of this response is the stoical approach to behaviour reinforced as appropriate or 'ladylike'. The persistent and recurring theme to emerge in this chapter is tension between sporting practice as it impacts on ideas of femininity and masculinity, concepts of equality and personal freedom. The role of the professional athlete is one of the most visible occupations of our social structure. In the last forty years football has moved from the 'retain and transfer' system to an emergent profession with the concomitant benefits of high social rank, personal fulfilment and respect. The complexity of current employment legislation impacting on football was reflected in Michel Zen Ruffinen's appointment as FIFA General Secretary. His legal expertise was necessary, for example, because of difficult transfer negotiations still to be resolved with the European Union, which will result in a set of conditions that could be applied to football on a worldwide basis. What has been the direct and indirect effect of legislation on women's football?

The cultural norms around football which are reflected in the legislation are clearly a gendered issue, as became evident from secondary sources such as legal, educational and training texts. One of the earliest interviews with Pontuus Kamaark, a Swedish international then playing for Leicester City, alerted me to this. He suggested that, had he played as a schoolboy in England, he may not have continued to pursue a professional career. Kamaark described the tendency of English parents to shout at young boys as culturally alien, intimidating and aggressive.

> There is more shouting at children's games here than at home. It's more like they have to learn the hard way. I hear people shout at their children 'you stupid idiot' and this and that. That is not the way back home. They don't get punished at home if they don't do so well. I would have been scared to death if I was a kid here . . . being shouted at. I think it's very hard.

American soccer leagues and clubs have, in recent years, influenced amateur football in Britain by drawing up codes of conduct for supporters and players.[3] So masculinities in amateur and junior male football are a topic in need of considerable attention. Another participant in this project explained his co-option as a team coach, 'I don't play and I have no qualifications. I just see it as being part of my role as a supportive dad.' Since this police officer routinely changes shifts, plans training and leads the team at matches, male voluntary support for female sport could be further researched in wider terms in English sporting culture. The number of women involved in football necessarily means that their activity will involve men in supportive roles as assistants and helpers. How these co-operative relationships work and the ways in which the actors view their actions is another point in need of further attention.

Another way that this practical collaboration came across was my presence as the lone female at various events. At the pinnacle of the coaching pyramid is the Advanced Licence. There are three hundred men for every woman holding this qualification. While researching the way it is assessed with a view to improving the numbers of women coaches at the top level, it was necessary to play regularly against male and female players to see how they spoke about, and acted in, football-related environments. Following an all-women coaching course held in 1998, a second all-women course was arranged at the next level the following year. However, with two weeks to go it was cancelled and only two women took the next mixed course. As the group of twenty-four coaches was split into two in many coaching and playing situations, only one woman was in each group. On three further coaching courses I was the only woman. As a middle-aged and average club player my football was likely to confirm any prejudices that the male players might have about women players' (lack of) ability. Indeed those that were most dismissive were young ex-professionals recently out of contract, searching for non-playing roles within football. The majority of the attendees were helpful and supportive in what many admitted had been for them, until that time, an all-male grouping. Nevertheless, the organisation (coaching hearing impaired and differently abled candidates) and the variety of age, cultures and playing experience of the participants, meant that gender difference was one of many. This highlighted a gap between practice and policy which is explored in more detail in the section on coaching.

To place football in context, English equal opportunity policy making, and implementation specifically, remains far more conservative than in some of the countries well known for elite achievement, for example Norway. As an illustration, section 28 of the Local Government Act 1988 placed restrictions on the use of public money, particularly prohibiting the 'promotion' of homosexuality.[4] This insistence on characteristic forms of male and female behaviour influences sport in less than obvious ways. The persistent naming of many football clubs as 'ladies'' teams rather than 'women's' in the year 2001 is a conscious attempt to avoid a 'butch' tag and confirm the heterosexual image of the club. As an example, of the forty-five teams affiliated to the East Midlands League from 1998–2000, twenty-three used the term 'Ladies', eight 'Women' and fourteen androgynous names, often in reference to the village where the team is based. Kettering Amazons Ladies and Girls FC reflect this difficulty in placing women's football, as the athletic prowess of 'Amazon' is modified by the genteel and nostalgic 'ladies'.[5] Hence, section 28 is one dimension of a late twentieth-century emphasis on feminine- and masculine-appropriate roles which affects equity in education and beyond, to sport, as a form of sex discrimination.[6] In examining the relation of legislative controls to the women's game, two points emerge. First, the ways in which decisions made on behalf of women playing football have effects that are contrary to their interests. Second, there has been a lack of concerted and organised resistance on behalf of women players. This discussion begins by reviewing case law and statutes with regard to gender, education and football. It is more possible to find examples of anti-sexism, with its ontological vagueness, relative to debates of equality of opportunity and equity in this literature. In summary, a more robust and informed approach to policy formulation in equity in sport, and especially for football, is clearly overdue.

The stereotypical 'girls don't like football' has perhaps a grain of truth: why would they? For the mass of the female population, lack of interest in football is understandable as it offers little or no opportunity for social prestige, economic advancement or employment at the same time that women's participation has considerable social stigma. Equal but different sport development in school and beyond perpetuates not only playing inequalities for girls' football but also unequal employment opportunities for women. The ritualised, symbolic nature of sport appears to disseminate and reaffirm social values. Scraton in *Shaping up to Womanhood* (1992), for instance, has analysed the relationship between physical education and girls' role as future child-bearers. However, football remains a particularly contentious sport because girls and women are clearly physically able to execute the skills. In order to emphasise outcome rather than opportunity, the balance between ascribed and achieved status has to be a prime area of revision, in order to question what would equity in football, and by extension in sport, ideally achieve? Gender difference in football is rooted to some extent in biological narratives and to some extent in social and cultural imperatives and encouragingly these can be open to alteration. In order to move toward amendment the chapter demonstrates how views of femininities and masculinitities in football have been constructed. Two interviewees in Scraton's study expressed the nature of female participation as 'unfeminine' in the sense of being defective (as play) and rather ugly (as spectacle).

> I have yet to see an elegant woman footballer. Maybe I'm just prejudiced but they look just horrible . . .
>
> I've been to a woman's football match and there's nothing sorer to my feminine eyes than a big bust and a big behind and the attracted crowd and spectators.
>
> (Scraton, 1992: 49)

Just as ideas about the place of the feminine women in football appear to be rather muddled here, Mangan views manliness as a confused moral concept including 'success, aggression, and ruthlessness, yet victory within rules, courtesy in triumph, and compassion for the defeated' (Mangan, 1981: 135). Crosset views the distinction between the two, however arbitrary the definitions, as crucial. Masculinity is a 'primary ideological function and catalyst for the growth of early modern sport . . . [it] helped define male sexuality as distinct from female sexuality . . . thereby making sport part of a larger ideological battle' (Crossett, 1990: 46). It is therefore possible to see sport, and by implication football, as the demonstration and presentation of maleness which thereby provides a traditionalised sense of masculinity. Competition by and against women would disrupt the system of play in a dilution of manful behaviour. The real taboo of mixed competitive football from this perspective is not to defend the weaker sex but to defend the ideology of a stronger one.

To take the most contentious point first, the premise of the physical inferiority of girls and women relative to boys and men has been used to restrict female participation in football, particularly as an occupational activity. The apparently progressive attitude of FIFA, the English FA and English Schools FA in the last decade has done little to increase employment opportunities for women as players and coaches. Women's lack of access to professional League and Premiership football can therefore be treated as an employment issue. Equal but different treatment for male and female players is both vague as an aim and unrealisable as a tactic given the historical and contemporary situation outlined in this work: establishing a women's professional football league in England will be a lengthy and elaborate affair, likely to produce a less publicly supported sporting product. In this, football follows professional sport generally and contact sport particularly. A dramatic example of how violent the resistance to mixed professional contact sport can become comes from American Football. Patricia Palinkas became the first woman to play linebacker for the Orlando Panthers in the 1970 Atlantic Coast League. In her inaugural game she was deliberately and seriously injured by an opponent who felt that he was protecting his job and his masculinity, though not necessarily in that order. Paul Hoch quotes direct from the player in his study of racism, sexism and masculinity, 'I tried to break her neck. I don't know what she's trying to prove. I'm out here trying to make a living and she's out here prancing around making folly with a man's game' (Hoch, 1979: 65). The role of women has changed and is changing in the period of this study more quickly than the organisation of sport. What are the definitions of equality of opportunity used by the significant organisations in sport and football? Should all teams be open to males and females? What effect would this have on what we currently understand as women's football?

To take these issues in turn, the administrative policy excluding all women from competition with men depends upon policy decisions which are, in legal terms, over-broad in their application. This kind of overgeneralisation in administrative regulations prevails in sport generally and football particularly. This is not to say that women players would inevitably achieve a place on a male semi-professional or professional team if there were to be a change in legislation or that mixed teams should be the only avenue available to women or men in sport. However, the opportunity to participate at the highest competitive level should exist for male synchronised swimmers as for female footballers. Given the historical development of some sports as male- or female-appropriate in England there would inevitably be a transitional period should mixed teams eventually become the norm. Support for female-oriented programmes, with allowance for the gifted female to find her own level of performance by open selection would also then be a necessary part of this migration.

Allen Guttman makes the point that:

> The sports of older girls and adult women usually reveal more about culture and social structure than the games of young children do . . . [puberty is] the moment they begin in most times and places to diverge significantly from men's sports.
>
> (Guttman, 1991: 3)

Adult female fragility compared with the mythical average male is a motif in football particularly and sport generally. The most damaging legislation remains, paradoxically, the 1975 Sex Discrimination Act because it reinforces the principle that difference between the man and woman is biologically set. Furthermore, the legislation did not exempt all sports from mixed competition, for example horse racing, and so though the concept of a theoretically representative male or female is still widely used, each sport has to be taken in its own right. In football in England, puberty is the time at which a girl is confirmed as belonging to the weaker sex and requiring 'protection' from male competition. Men and women can train and play together, but not competitively under FA sanction after age 12. One instance of imprecise logic used to insist on a difference between the male and female player comes from coach education. The Football Association *Coaching Licence Course Pack Module 6* advised:

> Children of the same age may be up to four years apart in their physical development . . . Whilst boys and girls can, and do, play football with each other up to 11 years of age, this is not recommended in a competitive situation after 12 years of age. Boys develop a greater proportion of their body as bone and muscle so their bodies pack more weight than girls.
>
> (Football Association, 1998: 11)

However, bone structure and muscular development can be affected by heredity, nutrition, disease, hormones and function. For example bone strength also develops with use in competition and practice. This is not discussed as a variable in The Football Association *FA Coaching Licence Course Pack Module 8*, which insists on male–female dualism, rather than describing strength and its development as a continuum.

> Girls experience peak height velocity (PHV) at 11.8 years of age, peak weight velocity (PWV) at 12.5 years; boys' (PHV) occurs at 14.1, PWV at 14.4 years of age . . . After puberty, the gains made in strength, speed and endurance are greater for boys than girls.
>
> (Football Association, 1998: 8)

Maybe the age of 12, in being the average age of menarche, leads to the common-sense conclusion that this is when girls have less in common with boys of the same age and become young women. Extrapolating from a peak in bursts of growth as related to overall adult strength is especially inappropriate in sports requiring endurance, like football, as the anaerobic energy system that allows for sustained periods of exertion is beginning to develop during adolescence. Generalising from age categories that demonstrate four years of difference in maturity is also clearly questionable. The break between secondary and primary schooling as the point at which single-sex football for boys and girls is more appropriate is, in some respects, unique to the English case. Defining difference at age 12 therefore owes something to pragmatism, in that this is a clearly defined point of transition for most pupils but it also relates to a perception of participatory ethos at primary level and competition at secondary school. Finally, safeguarding girls from the competitive play of boys at this early age is a dubious line of reasoning when muscle mass could take years to develop. One world-class English female player experienced contrasting aspects of difference at age 15.

A I played for The School of Excellence, which is all boys again.
Q You actually got picked for the Boys' School of Excellence?
A Yeah, I played for a season, which was good.
Q Did you ever feel the odd one out?
A Sometimes, like when you had to get changed. I used to get changed after the refs, but apart from that they made me feel at home and treated me like one of the lads – it was ok.
Q What about at school?
A They made me play netball. They put it in a way like, you can either practice football and not play any games, or you can practice netball and play games. So I had to choose netball really. I still used to train with the lads but I played netball as well.

Lending legal weight to this separation is significant for the wider freedom of individual women and girls in football. Consequently, it is not in the formative years so much as in the later years that inequality has come to be taken for granted. This is not peculiar to the English or British case.

For example, the rapid development of athletic opportunities for women in the United States followed Title IX of the Education amendments of 1972, a federal statute which prohibited sex discrimination in the provision of goods, services and opportunities in high schools and colleges. Throughout the 1980s, however, a trend of setbacks besieged the women's movement, including the failure of the Equal Rights Amendment. Only more recently with the passage of the Civil Rights Restoration Act by Congress in 1988 and the settlement of entire programmatic sex equality complaints have the prospects for continued movement toward equality in athletics regained momentum.[7] Before the passage of Title IX women comprised only 5 per cent of the total number of athletic participants in high school and 15 per cent in college, compared with 35 per cent and 33 per cent in 1988 (Curtis and Grant, 2000: 5). Though this is a more general figure than football alone, the principle of increased participation is clear, whilst also suggesting the limits of the advances – for example, the comparatively greater increase in high school rather than collegiate participation and the creation of more female departments, which has had the unintended effect of disproportionately creating jobs for male head coaches. Title IX is also limited in scope because it affects educational provision only, not wider equity or employment rights. However, there has not been a similar treatment of educational provision in England, consequently the principles of anti-sexism, non-discrimination and equality of opportunity still prevail to less effect.

Sport, religion, single-sex club membership, hospital accommodation and some working practices are treated as exceptions to the original 1975 Sex Discrimination Act. The stated aim was to establish

> An Act to render unlawful certain kinds of sex discrimination and discrimination on the ground of marriage, and establish a Commission with the function of working towards the elimination of such discrimination and promoting equality of opportunity between men and women generally.
>
> (Sex Discrimination Act, 1975: 1)

Section 44 of the Act differentiates competitive from participative sport.

> Nothing in Parts II to IV shall, in relation to any sport, game or other activity of a competitive nature where the physical strength, stamina or physique of the average woman puts her at a disadvantage to the average man, render unlawful any act related to the participation of a person as a competitor in events involving that activity which are confined to competitors of one sex.
>
> (Sex Discrimination Act, 1975: 12)

This was applied expressly to women and football in the subsequent Appeal Court decision in 1978 by Lord Denning who ruled that Theresa Bennett, aged 12, was not entitled to play for her local boys' football team, even though she had been selected on merit. Lord Denning upheld the appeal of the FA against a decision by Newark County Court that the Association had discriminated against the girl on the grounds of her sex. Denning's interpretation is tautological, 'the law would be an ass and an idiot if it tried to make girls into boys so that they could join in all-boys' games' (Denning, 1978: 5).

The ruling contained two important elements for the future of women's football in England. The first was the point, as argued by Robert Johnson QC, that the English FA had to abide by the international rules which barred women players from male competition. The FIFA committee responsible for formulating the Laws of the Game on a worldwide basis still comprises today a representative each from England, Scotland, Ireland, Wales and four other FIFA officials. It is therefore highly likely that, historically, the regulations were formed to reflect the British hostility to women as players outlined in Part I of this work. It is also likely that this is why the issue has survived other amendments to the Laws. The idea of football as a young man's sports remains evident in the Laws of the Game, which allow an increased number of substitutions in the case of players under 16 years of age, women and veterans (over 35).[8] Furthermore, European states have argued repeatedly over the issue of mixed football and in some cases combined teams continue until late teens. In the Netherlands mixed football is acceptable until age 18 (Pauw, 1999: 2). As the National Women's Coach, Pauw has been influential in raising the age of mixed football in Scotland to 15.

The confusion in using gender as a means of differentiation can be shown in wider transnational terms. One of the players in the victorious United States squad of the Atlanta Games outlined some of the negotiations surrounding the 1996 Olympic rules which originally stipulated that matches for women should last eighty not ninety minutes. Women's squads were to have sixteen players as opposed to eighteen for men and the rest days between games was set at two. After appeals the ninety-minute match was introduced and the rest day was reduced to one, therefore making the schedule more onerous for the women players than the men. Rule changes to both the Laws and individual tournaments are not trivial and place women at a material disadvantage if they are enforced.

The second element from this case derives from the council's defence in the Bennett case that the title 'woman' does not apply to females under the age of 12. Sir David Cairns, in ruling, defined woman, for the purpose of the Act, as a female of any age and the FA's appeal was therefore allowed. This is quite clearly a nonsense.

> In my opinion, the expression 'average woman' does not mean a woman of the age which is the mean of all the ages of all the women in the country, nor a woman of the age which is the mean of all those who play football, nor an age which is a mean of all the ages of girls under 12. The words 'average woman' do not envisage any arithmetical average at all, but means something like 'the ordinary woman' and, in the context of sport, 'the ordinary woman of the sort of age and sort of physical characteristic who would be likely to engage in that sport'.
>
> (Equal Opportunities Commission, 1978: 2)

The vagueness of 'average' is deliberate, and cloudy phrases including 'the sort of age and sort of physical characteristic . . . likely to engage in that sport' abstract the legislation from real bodies. Consequently the Sex Discrimination Act, as it has been applied to football, allows for discrimination against girls and women because they are all defined as the 'average woman'. It is worth interrogating the argument that because, on average, girls would be unable to compete with boys for team positions equality of rights has not been abridged. It would follow that inherent biological difference is such an overwhelming factor at an early age of development that training and preparation could not bring women to compete with men. So if girls are to have a meaningful sports programme, it should be kept separate from the boys. It would seem that this view is unwilling for individual ability to demonstrate itself in favour of reinforcing gender distinction.

The Theresa Bennett case was not a prima facie case, as insufficient evidence was provided to prove the argument. However, it has served in the same way, in the first instance because Bennett's solicitor argued in favour of puberty as the defining moment of difference. But more so because Lord Denning established this sphere of women's experience as *de minimus non curat lex* by recording that he thought it extraordinary that a matter of such little importance should reach the Court of Appeal (Equal Opportunities Commission, 1978: 2). This effectively prevented further action in the courts for another three years and contributed to the idea of women's right to play as trivial. Denning's subsequent retraction of other controversial decisions made in relation to the Sex Discrimination Act, and specifically the case of Bennett, casts doubt on the value of this judgment.

Two subsequent cases from other sports did little to assist change. In 1981 the Employment Adjudication Tribunal held that section 44 applied only to provisions regulating those who take part in sport as competitors, in allowing Mrs B. Petty to referee men at national level in judo competitions. In 1982 a county court judgment rejected the argument that a woman's physique would place her at a disadvantage when playing snooker against men, brought by a pub landlord under section 44 of the Sex Discrimination Act. So until the section is altered is seems highly likely that cases will continue to be treated on an individual basis. However, there is little unanimity amongst women players about how desirable transformation is, as we have seen earlier. The main fear is that modification to allow more mixed football to later ages will lead to girls' teams being swamped by boy players and will not leave a separate domain for women to play against women. The issue is obviously a serious and understandable concern which would require temporary and more permanent management; however, as reasons for resisting change they are flawed.

At the highest levels it will only be exceptional men and women, by definition not the average, who are given the chance to play professionally. Pauw makes an intriguing point when discussing the approach of the Football Association of the Netherlands to mixed football.

> In the 16–18 age group some of the boys are stronger, faster, bigger and heavier than girls. However, it is remarkable in this age group that mixed football at lower levels becomes very popular and there is good integration of male and female players. At the top level only the best female players keep on playing in the mixed teams.
>
> (Pauw, 1999: 3)

The potential for socialising through mixed play has been underestimated relative to competition in Britain. In answer to the question for this study, 'Would you play mixed competitive football?', views conflicted.

> No, the game is different. You can't mix as the style of competition is not really about the sport so much as being different because of men's aggression.

> A lot of women could be as good as men but are they given the chance? You could have, say, a female goalkeeper as that position is about as involved in the game proper as a female ref would be.

> Yes, except women have a disadvantage as regards time to develop their game and so it's easier for me to be sure of a place on a women's football team. I play all the time with the guys from work and we have a female manager. It's a laugh though some of our opponents are a bit surprised.

> I'm unsure what the purpose of this would be, but there is no reason why not skill-wise, though men can't control their temper in competitions sometimes.

> Oh God! What's the big deal? I play in a mixed side every Thursday and it's just a group of us from the bar playing for a laugh . . . The blokes are sometimes too lazy or unfit or egotistical to get the ball and me and Zoe are pretty fit so what we lack in skill we make up for in speed.

There have been many girls since the Bennett appeal who have wanted to play mixed football either to compete at a given standard or because there isn't a local female team, but cases have only intermittently reached the courts and the original decision has been upheld. Most of these cases involve a female player picked on merit. For example, in 1981 the Bennett case was used to prevent Jo Hughes from playing for a youth football team on the grounds of her sex and this was criticised by David Pannick, QC, a leading consultant on sports law, in an articled entitled 'How the FA kicks girl footballers off the park' (Pannick, 1981).

Highly relevant here is the contrasting case of *Clinton v Nagy* (1974) in the US where 12-year-old Brenda Clinton wished to play American football (Berry and Wong, 1993: 292). Here again, the defence argued that exclusion of females from contact sports was 'necessary for their safety and welfare' and argued that boys are becoming faster and stronger than girls at age 12. Crucially, the defendants did not claim that Brenda did not meet the standards other than being female. The court rejected the argument and Clinton was successful because she did not bring the case as a class action (she wasn't seeking to represent all girls or all females) but as an individual seeking the opportunity to play. Moreover, the ruling did not require the coach to play Brenda Clinton but insisted that she not be discriminated against in selection procedures. This principle has been further reinforced in the United States in two cases of girls wishing to play association football, *Hoover v Meiklejohn* (1977) and *Libby v South Inter-Conference Association* (1990). In the former the US District Court expressly criticised the principle of protective and, supposedly, beneficial legislation:

> Those same laws applied to racial or ethnic minorities would readily be recognisable as invidious and impermissible . . . Any notion that young women are so inherently weak, delicate or physically inadequate that the State must protect them from the folly of participation in vigorous athletics is a cultural anachronism unrelated to reality.
>
> (Berry and Wong, 1993: 297)

However, in each case there was no female team and so this requires further development as the girls' right to participate is the principle which is protected, not the access to competitive opportunities.

In England the Pannick report of 1983 addressed these issues and developed the view that women could participate in mixed teams and, as a transitory measure, have single-sex competition.

> To give qualified women the opportunity to participate in sport at the level appropriate from their individual skills is far from ridiculous . . . sex discrimination is not a private concern. The injustice to individuals and the waste of society's resources justify the intervention of the state . . . it should remain lawful, as a form of 'compensatory opportunity' at least for the foreseeable future, to organise or provide separate facilities or opportunities for women from which men are excluded.
>
> (Pannick, 1983: 4–5)

A less convincing aspect of his argument is that the competitive disadvantage of women is analogous to the younger and lighter player in, for example, boxing. Whereas the older and heavier participants may not 'play down' a grade, the exceptional competitor may play up. This it seems to me requires further discussion as body shape and composition are more varied than this implies and the relationship of this to sporting prowess is another more complex issue altogether. Pannick terms this system 'affirmative action' to take account of past discrimination but also summarises prevailing reservations, 'our society may simply not yet be ready to take seriously mixed contact sports' (Pannick, 1983: 4–5). Most useful for this study, in terms of discussing English cultural attitudes to women and football, Pannick traces the parliamentary debates surrounding clause 39 which became section 44 of the 1975 Act as a 'football clause' which was drafted by one contributor at least to ensure that 'Leeds United can carry on' without women players (ibid. 10). Amending this outdated clause would not give women the right to resources and, consequently, even without section 44 females would have no *a priori* right to a place unless ability as a player merited it. The question of whether becoming a professional football player is a meritocratic process is another topic and one that should not deflect attention from the principle at hand. It is enough to give the example that, in spite of calling girls' Centres of Excellence and Academies by the same name as the male equivalent, the purpose of those units is inherently different. In the former case it is about an amateuristic leisure activity and in the latter a screening process and preparation for professional life as an athlete. Placing a structural ceiling on an individual's ability because of gender *is* a cultural anachronism which should become increasingly unrelated to reality.

Would the corollary effect of allowing girls to compete in boys' teams, lead to girls' teams being dominated by boys? There is little logic in suggesting that females would want to compete to the best of their ability if we did not suggest that boys and men would also want the same thing. It is therefore unlikely that boys would dominate female teams unless the competitive standard for girls were higher than for boys, in which case the boys' competitive opportunities would be enhanced. Beyond competition, reasons apart from physical ability, to do with economic, geographic, social and cultural factors, would also have a considerable influence on individual choice.[9] Another line of reasoning follows that mixed teams would offer tokenism for a few top female athletes rather than catering for the majority and may be used as the justification for not providing female teams at all as, theoretically, women can have trials for the men's team. This is a serious concern obviously because there has been a clear discrimination and a more far-reaching Title IX equivalent would need to be introduced. It is less convincing that, because of historical lack of support for women and sport, female teams would be additionally disadvantaged because they would lose their best athletes to male teams. In this rationale the exceptional participant is sacrificed for the good of the majority of women. The differences in funding, resources, status and employment opportunities are so evident in women's sport and particularly in football, that the separatist argument is unlikely to foster rapid or fundamental shifts either to the place of women in sport or to the structures of football itself precisely because the brightest and best cannot access the highest competitive opportunities available.

If selection for football is based on ability, as we tell ourselves, it ought to be competence which gets us onto the team. Separate but equal is clearly not equal in terms of outcome. Women may be very good players who wish to compete at the highest possible level. Furthermore separate teams are not equal because of benefits and opportunities. Fulham may have a professional women's team but the status and terms of those women is not the same as for the Fulham men. Moreover there is no suggestion that any club owes a duty to ensure that women's teams are provided with equal facilities, equality of reputation, tradition or prestige.

In order to ascertain exactly what 'competitive advantage' means it would be necessary to establish the mix of skills for each position on the field and this would vary with each game. The recent audit of injury by the FA is unlikely to lead to the separation of male players by size or weight, nor prevent smaller, lightweight professional players from returning to play once injured. The assumption that men have an advantage because they are men ignores examples where the ordinary male player is as unlikely to resemble his professional counterpart as the 'average woman'.

Two factors may, however, provide more optimism for the future of professional women players. The first is that there is a developing history of women who have earned a living from football in single-sex competition in other countries. So as the introduction to this section indicated, one area for further study is the migration of women footballers in order to explore and fulfil their playing potential as a professional. The attempts of the English FA to replicate the collegiate model as an aspect of the competitive community in women's football were evaluated in Chapter 2. However, suffice to say here that Kelly Smith, considered by some to be the most promising young English player, after completing her degree at Seton Hall University in 2000 joined the staff as a full-time assistant coach for the women's soccer programme. She is currently a star player for the Philadelphia Charge and has a national and international media profile unlike any other English player that includes hosting a monthly column for SoccerAmerica.com and having her own website. Others are likely to follow her example. In addition, Fulham's signing of Danish and Norwegian players implies a potential for attracting talent to English clubs and a degree of professional sponsorship of the women's game continues.

The second issue is the role of key individuals in bringing action against the authorities which demonstrates their interpretation of gender difference as a rationalising principle rather than a genuine disqualification. Players' agent Rachel Anderson was turned away twice from the Professional Footballers Association (PFA) dinners and later awarded £7,500 damages and costs of £210,000 because she was refused entry with her client. At the 2000 dinner thirty women associated with football were invited but the rules were changed to disqualify entry to Anderson.

There are opportunities for players through the present system but these are likely to be extremely limited and through the 'back door'. The establishment of a 'women's realm' in professional clubs has been adopted by the FA as the most desirable model and began with the establishment by Vic Akers at Arsenal of a women's Youth Training Scheme and subsequently an Academy. Regardless of arguments about how short-lived a male player's average career is, women in the scheme at Arsenal have, as adults, to divert to coaching or general sports development. Lou Waller, Rachel Yankey (now at Fulham) and others have derived some of the benefits from working with a professional male club, the former as a community coach and the latter as the face of women's soccer in Nike advertisements. However, the exceptional coach and the exceptional player would have to supplement their income from other sources if they were to equal their male counterparts' earnings. The next section of this chapter changes the focus to women who may want to become professional coaches to extend the point raised with regard to Rachel Anderson. Regardless of an apparent emphasis on equality of opportunity, football authorities continue to construct rules, formal and informal, which have the effect of preventing equity of outcome.

Football coaching at the highest level exceeds the financial status of the full professions whereas at lower levels it is little more than voluntary child-minding. The FA Coaches' Association (FACA) was formed in 1997. The Advanced Licence, as the highest qualification available, is only available by referral through a tutor-assessor at the successful completion of Part 2 since 1999. Previously, it was open to application. The cost has also trebled to over £3,000. At Academies in professional clubs the coach must hold, or be working toward, the UEFA B Part 2 qualification (known from 2001 as the 1st4Sport Level 3 Certificate in Coaching Football/UEFA B Certificate), which is more widely known as the Coaching Licence. The preliminary qualification is the UEFA B Part 1 Certificate (known from 2001 as the 1st4Sport Level 2 Certificate in Coaching Football) and the voluntary supervisory qualification is the Junior Team Manager Certificate (known from 2001 as the 1st4Sport Level 1 FA Club Coach qualification). To be considered eligible for work in professional football a coach must hold either the FA Advanced Coaching Licence/UEFA A Coaching Award or UEFA B Certificate and membership of FACA. In relation to professions and elites more generally we can begin to detect patterns in gender distribution between these levels of qualification that are not specific to football. A useful point of comparison is that the structure of most professions relies on sponsorship and access to career-building opportunities in order to reach the next stage. This, in turn, requires the support of colleagues and mentors. Sport, football and careers within it are seen as a meritocracy. If achievement alone is the main evaluative criterion, with the standards objective and even-handedly applied, why are women not more represented in non-playing professions?

With reference to Table 4.1, at Advanced Licence level a few women are doing outstandingly well but not the proportion that would have been predicted on the basis of comparison with their male counterparts. The extent to which women are able to talk of new career opportunities is, by extension, extremely limited. The three case studies of full A Licence 'badges' reflect the context in which change has occurred. Old patterns of resistance to women coaches and players persist and new patterns of opposition have developed. There is not just evidence of a gender bias though. The impediments for Asian players and coaches, for example, also remain pronounced. The number of black and Asian female coaches at all levels of football is therefore wildly disproportionate to the place of black and Asian women in the general population in England today.

Little research has focused on access to professional football employment for women. One approach taken in this part of the discussion is to examine the pool of talent at each level before also identifying barriers instrumental in preventing access to different strata. Table 4.1 is an indication of the pool of eligible coaches at each level. The first woman advanced or A Licence coach was appointed in the early 1980s and since that time women have, by and large, assimilated into professional structures rather than form their own unions or collectives. The three case studies show this tactic to be a double-edged sword. In an increasingly regulated profession, women coaches generally have tended to pool in the lower ranks. Nor is the overall situation improving, as more women held coaching qualifications overall before the system was changed in 1997 (Table 4.2, page 144), whereas increasing numbers now hold qualifications at the Junior Team Manager (threshold) level. Coaches who held qualifications under the previous regime had until June 2000 to convert to the revised system. In summary, the effect of the change has been to encourage fewer women generally to obtain a coaching qualification, to act as a disincentive to transfer to the new scheme and to make it extremely difficult for women to obtain qualifications at the highest level. A subsequent revision in 2002 looks set to make this pattern more pronounced.

Table 4.1 Numbers holding coaching qualifications in England, 2000

	Senior (Advanced Licence and International Diploma)	*Full (Intermediate Award, Coaching Licence, Coaching Certificate, International Certificate and Licence)*	*Associate (Junior Team Manager, Teaching Certificate, Basic, Intermediate and Diploma of Treatment of Injury)*
Male	1,105	5,806	2,319
Female	7	194	180
Total	1,112	6,000	2,499

Source: Football Association Coaches' Association *Membership Details*, 18 April 2000

In an analysis of women entering professions Carter suggested apropos women's access to certain foundation level positions:

> Though women may catch up with men rather rapidly in terms of proportionate representation on entry-level 'fast-track' positions, they will find it even more difficult than men to advance out of these positions into the sphere of high-status, high-paying work. Because such work is not expanding as rapidly as the sector as a whole (or as rapidly as the supply of highly educated workers!), we expect a constant pressure of excess supply.
>
> (Carter 1981: 480)

Applied to women's football, we could expect from this that growth at professional level will be smaller than expansion at recreation level and overall surplus has an unequal effect on female coaches. The figures bear this out, as the tiny apex of seven gives a relative proportion of one woman Advanced Licence coach for every twenty UEFA B Licence holders, whereas the ratio for male coaches is 1:5. Though the figure for the elementary level of qualification for women and the B Licence are similar, far fewer men hold the Junior Team Manager certificate. Whatever the reason for this, women are disproportionately represented at the threshold and progression is much less marked.

Women coaches tended to integrate into the existing structures of football rather than band together. There is no alliance of women either in informal or formal support groups. In the case of the three Advanced Licence case studies, the success of individuals can be attributed to extraordinary accomplishments, self-presentation and personal application as integral parts of their careers. In examining those who do earn a majority of their income and spend the bulk of their working time coaching, these case studies suggest possible career paths for women. There are also new avenues as the PFA has a fast-track scheme so the Fulham women will have the financial backing to undertake such courses.[10] Consideration of women as professional and semi-professional coaches does not include the majority of volunteers who run clubs, leagues and teams but an important and pace-setting minority who are willing to undergo formal tuition and assessment. Each woman has identified herself as willing to undertake the highest qualification available and made a considerable investment in a career as an FA Advanced Coaching Licence/UEFA A Coaching Award involves a minimum of three years' training for very strong candidates and, in most cases, double this. In the first two case studies below a change of career has been involved and so though the overall intention is to look at how some women have dealt with different stages in their work cycle, re-entry to football as a career is given special consideration.

The first woman was a professional player in the 1970s, an England international and is now a Director of a Centre of Excellence and an A

Licence tutor-assessor. As such she acts as a gatekeeper to the profession. She was the second woman to be awarded the Licence (the first woman Licence holder is not now active in coaching beyond her role as a PE teacher). This example mirrors the male ex-professional who wishes to maintain an active role in the sport once his playing career has finished. As the author of the most comprehensive book on the development of the women's game in recent years and an associate Lecturer of the Sir Norman Chester Centre for Football Research at Leicester, she has an academic as well as a technical interest. Her football coaching was supplemented for over a decade by work in education. In recent years she has been recognised by, amongst others, the *Sunday Times* Coach of the Year Award 1999, and she received an MBE for her services to sport in 2000. As such she has achieved national standing and an international reputation.

The second case is an ex-competitive player, without national honours, who moved into football as a career change in her mid-thirties and now holds a full A Licence. After coaching part time, including under-12 boys at a professional academy, she was a Director of a Centre of Excellence and is Academy Director at Loughborough. The combination of marriage and part-time employment is especially interesting because of the role of the family in supporting her decisions. A key theme to emerge at interview was the need for flexibility in long-term planning to achieve a satisfactory combination of paid career and family life:

> I attended every course going and you get to meet people so they were used to seeing me around . . . I'd save up and spend holidays at Lilleshall where the nationally arranged courses used to be held. I tried to absorb as much knowledge as I could and to meet with as many useful contacts but it took years. Eventually I was able to go part-time and that enabled me to really focus my energies on football.

Working alongside male coaches in a male academy, a professional setting, during evenings and vacations also enhanced confidence. However, in coaching the under-12 boys' team the interviewee felt that at age 13 the boys were increasingly prepared for a professional life and since this was beyond her experience she would feel it inappropriate to coach them. She did, however, feel able to coach the national female under-18 and under-16 squads. The financial and time commitments of attending courses meant that this individual's job subsidised her football career in its initial stages.

The age of these two coaches may indicate an area for further development of women sport leaders. Ward and Silverstone writing in 1980 suggested that:

> Women in the United Kingdom exhibit a pattern of work which is notably different from that in other countries of the EEC. Its distinguishing feature is the high proportion of women who return to work

> by the time they are forty years of age, having temporarily retired to care for young families. Although this pattern is of fairly recent origin, it is likely to be sustained.
>
> (Silverstone and Ward, 1980: 9)

In establishing the size of this phenomenon in the 1980s, more than half of the women in the UK worked outside the home and for those aged between 40 and 54 this proportion rose to two-thirds. They suggested that this is in contrast to other EEC countries and similar to the US and can be characterised as:

> An analogous bimodal or M-shaped pattern . . . a period of reduced participation in economic activity over the childbearing period is interposed between periods of higher employment activity. This has the effect of polarising the female workforce into two age groups – the young and the returners.
>
> (Ward and Silverstone, 1980: 10)

Though working arrangements across Britain as a whole have changed radically in the last twenty years, this concept does apply to the second case study and was written at the period when the individual chose to re-enter football as a career after the birth of her children. In football-specific terms, those who work in Academies are often part-time workers who combine that occupation with some other, be it playing, community development or external to the professional club. The third case study is a recently graduated teacher of Physical Education who is being mentored under the new FA regime to take her A Licence. She is Director of an Academy but her main occupation involves teaching leisure and recreation studies at a nearby local college. Her competitive career ended when she left college. The three examples combined suggest that the length of training in itself might deter women from choosing football as a career unless they can supplement their interest financially from other means.

Other elements of the decision to continue to a higher level qualification may not be related to gender. Several male and female coaches declared a preference for smaller-scale teams and an interest in the overall development of younger players – that is, to take on a group of young players and see their development through to adulthood. One women B Licence coach gave up a Centre of Excellence post to coach a small village side and several men suggested that their purpose in attending the course was to provide further assistance to their local team, not as career progression. Many of those who did not return for assessment indicated that they wanted to improve their football knowledge but were not so concerned with completing the qualification which would have made them more eligible to coach at a higher level:

> To be honest I don't enjoy coaching at this level . . . To me the main area that's neglected is the team of kids as they grow. It's great when my son's team play another where the manager will go to his players, 'Look you can't let them beat you, their coach is a woman' because my lot will get extra stuck in.

There are also coaches who have no intention of taking the qualification who are working in professional football. So long as they are registered to be 'working towards' the qualification and have not taken the assessment they can continue to coach in academies in professional clubs, therefore the older system of personal sponsorship is still prevalent.

The third female case study found girls at under the age of 14 to be less serious and committed than the boys of the same age she had coached and preferred the more professional approach of the academy. In this sense she was very positive about planning to ensure that she obtained the right kind of work experience. This candidate successfully secured a job in a further education context soon after qualifying as a PE teacher and then linked with the professional club to form the Academy and was able to offer vocational education and coaching expertise. This niche, within contexts that have clearly defined grading structures, can provide for future promotion in either or both settings. All three women denied ever having experienced discrimination in a football work setting and suggested it was a product of attitude of mind. They emphasised the critical aspect for career progression was to be given responsibility for a complete job in order to become familiar with all the processes. As Academy Directors, the women defended an area over which they had complete control to be judged by the outcome.

Coaching work in professional clubs with adults poses the most severe test because it is in this context that a woman is most alien:

> Managing players [in the male academy] requires a toughness and an ability to convince them that you know what you are talking about . . . I can't stand boyish looking girls and effeminate boys. I like the seriousness of the male academy rather than the silliness of some of the girls. In the professional game your session can always be improved and the players never perform 100 per cent but perfection is what you're after.

This woman's ability was helped by integration into an information network. A relationship with an FA Regional Director of Coach/Player Education meant that she knew key people, where to obtain particular information and generally what was going on. Practical success is only part of the key to a successful career and football, like many occupations, relies on informal processes of selection and sponsorship. On the basis of interviews and my observation of training and team selection there appeared to be little indication that women were more feelings-oriented than men. The three coaches shared a professional but detached concern for the players.

In examining the case studies combined it is possible to draw some conclusions before turning to look at the other tiers of coaching. Whether or not women are less likely to find suitable sponsors there are certainly relatively few females in senior positions to act as role models or to influence policy making within the profession. Women's absence from leadership positions sufficient to form a critical mass is a key aspect of development that requires attention. For men and women successful football careers are built on a combination of sponsorship, visibility and reciprocal respect. The type of team one coaches is a powerful sorting tool and tracking mechanism. In relation to this both the older women were able to indicate a turning point in their career, and mentoring schemes to foster the right kind of experience such as has been recently introduced could become valuable in this respect. Even with a high level of self-motivation all three women were relieved that things turned out so well. The first two in particular know they made choices with limited options. At Advanced Licence level women are trusted colleagues in male-dominated inner circles and groomed for leadership by powerful male sponsors. As role models, these exceptional women rarely challenge male domination directly by advancing other women or fighting for changes in social institutions. In this respect the mentoring system has also to revise the informal systems rather than merely finding and training more women. It remains to be seen whether women coaches will form groups to attain the social power to challenge their treatment as a category but it would seem highly unlikely.

The argument now moves on to examine the reserves of women available at B Licence, who could move to the FA Advanced Coaching Licence/UEFA A Coaching Award, to show how the informal systems of patronage impact upon the formal systems of assessment and training. Work on cross-national perspectives of women in elites proposes that they cluster at the bottom, are grouped in sex-role-appropriate activities as stereotypically areas of 'women's interest'. Epstein and Coser argue further that intervention has kept women out of elites, as they are blocked in the tracking process to the top because they do not have the same access to informal opportunities for advancement and even when they become members of elites women are consigned to specialities considered to be appropriate to women's concerns – 'The maintenance of systems, which require attention and input to keep them going, does not attract as much notice as the alteration of systems' (Epstein and Coser, 1981: 12).

This goes beyond sport but can equally be applied to football as it is clear that there are a large number of potential applicants to the A Licence course. Nevertheless, the insular attitude of those who deliver and run the courses means that both the formal and informal processes combine to limit women's achievement. The maintenance of this system and the subsequent reinforcement of an obviously discriminatory approach by the FA are particularly inglorious as episodes in the association's history and give the lie in practice to any claims for theoretical increases in equitable treatment for men and women.

As we've seen, despite the growing popularity of football among women, 1,105 men and seven women hold the Advanced Coaching Licence. The case of Vanessa Hardwick is crucial in showing how the current qualification system is neither meritocratic nor progressive. The PE teacher, then 32, tried to obtain the Advanced Licence to develop a career in football coaching but was given a fail grade on the final assessment on two occasions. In 1997 an Employment Tribunal held that she had been discriminated against.[11] The FA appealed and an Employment Appeal Tribunal ruling on 26 January 1999 agreed that the reasons for not granting the licence were not credible.[12] However, the recommendation by Equal Opportunities Commission that the Advanced Licence be granted within a month was declined by the FA, the association opting instead to pay an additional fine of £10,000 to the £16,000 compensation already awarded to Hardwick. She then accepted a job in the United States working with the female national team to avoid further difficulties in England and has recently returned to try once more for the qualification.[13]

Hardwick's legal advisers discovered that eight men on the second course had passed with worse marks and five had passed with the same mark. The FA claim that they did not award licences to course participants who did not meet the required standard was obviously inaccurate. Furthermore it was found that the decision to fail the candidate at her second attempt was taken before the final assessment staff meeting. Above and beyond the actual injustice, another aspect of the appeal judgment was that the settlement of the remedy payment was made before submissions. We might reasonably have expected Vanessa Hardwick's remedy payment to have been considerably more substantial given her age and the potential earnings available with the qualification. One of the successful candidates identified as a comparator in terms of grades now coaches with England youth teams, for example, five years after obtaining the qualification. This small financial compensation reflects a pattern in which both the FA and the law perceives women's involvement in football as a leisure activity rather than an employment issue. Georgina Christoforou attempted to become an Assistant Referee in 1995 and was prevented by South East Counties Football League on the grounds that there were no separate changing facilities for women. The settlement of £1,000 assumes that refereeing would remain a leisure interest. However, Mrs Elizabeth Forsdick, as the first female Class 1 referee in 1981 and the first to be appointed as an assistant referee in an FA Cup match, would have become eligible to referee Football League matches had she completed her non-league training.

The achievements and limitations of the Equal Opportunities Commission in achieving rights for women are highlighted by sport. Cases in sports employment have increased enormously in recent years. These include

Susan Thompson's application for membership of the Professional Pool Players organisation in 1992, Lisa Budd as the first female Master of Ceremonies and Jane Couch in obtaining a professional licence to box. Also significant for administration in sport is Beverly Davis' successful case against the Rugby Football Union for election to the national executive committee in 1995. The Commission doesn't just assist in bringing case actions. For example, a rather more unusual use of education and football is aimed at young men at Wolverhampton Wanderers FC, to give young men football facilities coupled with campaigns to improve their sexual health and counsel them on the risks of unprotected sex. The scheme, which will be launched with £250,000 funding from the Department of Health, will be aimed at young men at greatest risk from social exclusion or who have been in trouble with the police. However, given that the stated aim of the initiative is to reduce unwanted teenage pregnancy in the area it may be further evidence of welfare policies aimed disproportionately at young men rather than young women.[14]

Considering that much of the work in the area is, by nature, part-time and subject to a personal network of contacts, women may do well to concentrate their efforts elsewhere. The limited effectiveness of the Sex Discrimination Act and the effect of the judgments made to date with relation to women and football in themselves demonstrate limited recourse to the law. Although the Act was updated in 1988, sport was not considered at this time. Pannick concluded:

> In 1976–9 (inclusive), the EOC received 322 complaints/enquiries about sex discrimination in sports and competitions. In 1980 and 1981, there were in each year 21 such complaints/enquiries about sport. In 1982, the figure dropped to 12; the number of such complaints will no doubt continue to decline, as the limited effectiveness of the Sex Discrimination Act in this area becomes increasingly well known.
>
> (Pannick, 1983: 76)

The Equal Opportunities Commission policy of dealing direct with the company means that in the case of proven repeated discrimination, as has been the case with the FA, the subsequent follow-up is a private matter and not in the public domain. In employment terms this means that recommendations made publicly may be both publicly accepted and privately rejected, as was the case with Vanessa Hardwick. The theoretical commitment to an equal opportunities policy on the A Licence Course in no way mitigates the injury to Hardwick's career or the FA's shameful handling of the appeal.

Moreover, organisations such as the Women's Sport Foundation in England have tacitly taken the view that working with sports governing bodies is more productive than mounting campaigns for specific kinds of change. This is unlike the Women's Sport Foundation in the United States which has campaigned for class action and legislative change.[15] For example, the FA, the Women's Sports Foundation and the National Coaching Foundation introduced a combined elite female mentoring programme in 2001. The irony that Hope Powell, who was appointed without a senior coaching qualification, should launch an initiative to increase the number of qualified women coaches appears to be lost on the three partners. Hope Powell said at the launch of the programme:

> The FA are committed to providing opportunities for our top female coaches to develop as coaches at a pace and to a level which best suits their individual needs. The FA are delighted to be involved in this programme with key partners which will enable those coaches, under the guidance of Hope Powell (National Coach Women's Football), to benefit from the expertise and knowledge of specialists in this field. In the long term, the FA sees this scheme as an integral part of their coach mentoring programme for those women who will coach at the highest level of the women's game.

The first point is the objective of producing women coaches for the women's game which broadly fits with the amateur–professional divide which has been the subject of this chapter. The second, having attended a regional launch of this 'pacy' initiative in summer 2002 as a prospective A Licence candidate with the necessary recommendation, I have yet to be contacted six months later for my initial mentoring meeting. New developments in European law on women's rights could foster an era of change, though given the Hardwick case, it would be a real optimist who thinks that attempts to promote female coaching opportunities since 1999 are anything other than a public relations exercise.

The EU's current policy of mainstreaming represents a different conceptual base to equality of opportunity but is difficult to implement as the legal framework places considerable powers of interpretation in the hands of the courts.[16]

> The promotion of equality must not be confused with the simple objective of balancing the statistics: it is a question of promoting long-lasting changes in parental roles, family structures, institutional practices, the organization of work and time . . . it concerns men and the whole of society.
>
> (European Communities Commission, 1996: 5)

In English and European law the applicator must point to a comparator who does not have the 'protected characteristic' and who has been treated differently, usually to advantage. The choice of comparator is crucial. As Fredman puts it, this formal equality model reinforces liberal ideas of 'the primacy of the neutrality of law, the rights of the individual as individual, and the freedom of the market' (Fredman, 1997: 383). Mainstreaming conflicts with more substantive concepts of equality, which emphasise equality of outcomes or results. However, it has helped to hone new definitions of discrimination, described now as a distinction, which imposes burdens, obligations or disadvantages on an individual or group not imposed upon others. Applied to women's football in England, positive action and positive discrimination are vital because of the limited idea of equity that has informed the development of the sport to date. Not only are appointments demonstrably based on patronage but also the few women afforded senior positions are supporting the system that excludes the many. The 'protected characteristic' in Hardwick's case could only be shown because the FA were relatively careless with the paperwork of the comparators; however, as a distinction the material disadvantage of women's football and of individual women within football can be argued.

In football terms, the EU article 2 (4) of Directive 76/207 is particularly apposite. The Directive is intended to be applied 'without prejudice to measures which promote *equal opportunity* for men and women, in particular by removing existing inequalities which affect women's opportunities'. This was tested in the case of two park keepers who applied for promotion and, other factors being equal, the woman was given the job. However Kalanke, the man, questioned the Bremen law on positive discrimination which, in the case of a tie-break situation, gave priority to an equally qualified woman over a man, if women were under-represented. The 1995 Kalanke case ruled that if the woman (in this case Ms Glissman) had the same qualifications and experience, she *de facto* had equality of opportunity and so equality of result exceeds the scope of article 2 (4).[17] This ruling has been upheld on several successive occasions.

This ruling privileged the individual's right not to be discriminated against on grounds of sex over the rights of the disadvantaged group. In sum, in this case the court can either choose to worsen the situation of those more favoured or improve the situation of those less well favoured. In the Hardwick case, improving her situation would not have worsened the situation of the other candidates who would have passed anyway (even though eight perhaps ought not to have). As the law stands, a woman should have an equal right to compete for positions, not the right to obtain them. The Hardwick case reveals the limits of legislation, because it was only because her legal team was able to obtain information regarding the scores of the male participants that comparators could be offered and her case proven. Therefore, a pincer approach of legal changes and genuine mentoring arrangements are necessary to improve the formal and informal structures affecting women's place as coaches in football.

Referring to Table 4.1, page 133, whilst 0.6 per cent of the total of Advanced Licence coaches are women, 3 per cent of Full UEFA B equivalent coaches are women and 8 per cent of Associate qualifications are women. In deciding upon the pool available from associate to full member, specialisation of function is a factor. The figure may be enlarged because there are five qualifications, including auxiliary qualifications in the third category of coaches such as for the treatment of injury, and so it is my intention to concentrate on the second level. Before 1997 the qualification structure was dominated by the Preliminary Licence award. A survey completed by the FA by county is summarised in Table 4.2. After 1997 the Coaching Certificate could be updated to UEFA B Part One until June 2000 (see Table 4.2 overleaf).

Comparing Tables 4.1 and 4.2, overall the number of women with coaching qualifications has remained, at best, roughly level. However, when we see that the total of 365 in Table 4.2 represents those qualifying over three years, as opposed to the total number of women coaches and the figure of 381 from Table 4.1 includes women with first aid and coaching qualifications the situation is much worse. The combined effect of the new generation of coaching courses and the formation of a coaches association has severely limited the number of women coaches at B Licence Level. Whether women who hold the Junior Team Managers qualification are unwilling to join an association of coaches, and why fewer women are obtaining qualifications overall would be an avenue for further research and analysis.

In the English system, teams based in schools and colleges are a growth area but are not the main route for elite players to develop their ability or for national selection. As we've seen, the traditional women's teams such as Doncaster Belles, Premiership affiliated teams like Arsenal, and most recently, the semi-professional Fulham are the main providers of representative players. In addition, the place of educational establishments looks set to become a key area in the understanding of female football at participation and elite level. The idiosyncrasy of the English case and the rather different attributes of the US model suggest this topic to be in need of amplification. By extension, it would be useful to develop a view of the role of young elite, perhaps semi-professional, women players in defining their own involvement.

Alice Rossi calls 'the diminishing flow' the presence of women in inverse relation to rewards within a given occupation, that is, the higher the rank and prestige the smaller the number of women (Rossi, 1970: 37). Where the proportion of women is greater the deficiency of rewards, as compared with those of men, is higher. This concluding section applies the concept to women's football in England in accounting for the size of the available reserves of coaches. It would make little sense to stress the fact that there are so few women coaches without demonstrating how many women are engaged in football studies, nor to point to the low numbers of A Licence coaches if women hardly took part in other kinds of advanced physical education study. The oral evidence indicates that women who play also adopt ancillary roles in administration, coaching and officiating usually in conjunction with their participation, not as an alternative. Margaret Talbot has made the point with relation to sport's bureaucratic elites which the findings of this chapter support:

Table 4.2 Female Preliminary Licence award coaches, by county

County football associations	*1994*	*1995*	*1996 (–Aug)*	*Total*
North				*132*
Liverpool	15	10	1	26
West Riding	3	5	6	14
Lancashire	6	7	5	18
Manchester	2	3	2	7
Northumberland	3	1	1	5
North Riding	7	2	5	14
Sheffield/Hallamshire	6	10	4	20
Durham	0	1	6	7
East Riding	2	1	0	3
Cheshire	11	0	6	17
Cumberland	1	0	0	1
Midlands				*112*
Leicestershire	7	7	1	15
Bedfordshire	1	1	2	4
Cambridgeshire	3	2	0	5
Nottinghamshire	3	2	2	7
Staffordshire	4	1	2	7
Northamptonshire	2	4	1	7
Birmingham	16	3	22	41
Shropshire	2	1	1	4
Huntingdonshire	0	2	0	2
Derbyshire	5	2	2	9
Norfolk	5	0	2	7
Lincolnshire	1	0	1	2
Worcestershire	0	0	2	2
South				*121*
Army	2	0	0	2
Kent	1	3	1	5
Devon	2	1	3	6
Dorset	0	2	0	2
Oxfordshire	1	4	0	5
Sussex	2	3	2	7
Hampshire	4	2	3	9
Wiltshire	7	6	2	15
London	8	5	6	19
Somerset	3	4	2	9
Gloucestershire	3	9	2	14
Surrey	1	1	2	4
Hertfordshire	0	1	2	3
Middlesex	1	1	7	9
Essex	1	1	0	2
Berkshire/Buckinghamshire	9	0	1	10
Totals	*150*	*108*	*107*	*365*

Source: Kelly Simmons, The Football Association, Potters Bar 1998

> Sport remains one of the most conservative and inflexible areas of public life, lagging far behind other social structures. Distributional data has demonstrated that in Europe, despite more than a decade of strategies and actions to support progress towards gender equity in sports organisations, women are still under represented in executive and decision making positions.
>
> (Talbot, 2000: 1)

It is not only in England that football has promoted a form of equality for women while at the same time preserving rigid social distinctions. In the case of FA committee members in particular, it is necessary to accumulate wide-ranging experience as committee leader for advancement to senior and executive posts. This has produced the disturbing situation for women in the organisation that it is not in the formative years so much as the later years that inequality is conspicuous and hence very few women continue to make it through the pyramid of coaching qualifications to the top. In administrative terms, Josephine King makes this point about women leaders in international football administrations in the two following ways:

> One of the questions . . . is whether this increased participation has yet translated into significant advances in the number of women leaders in the sport of soccer and has it embraced all ethnic and disadvantaged groups . . . At the same time, it would be a mistake and dangerously limiting, to see the question as entirely one of women achieving and leading only in women's soccer.
>
> (King, 1999: 4)

This is an issue the next chapter discusses at an international scale as it replicates the creation of a women's football separate subcommittee within national associations, which has led to the integration of the women as provisional and partial, and much remains to be discussed on this issue. Women's football in England in its current form does not lend itself to mass spectatorship in the form of ticket-purchasing fans or a large audience and until this changes professionalisation is unlikely to occur to any significant degree. The consuming public must be interested, able and willing to pay. Current English plans to fund a women's professional league through satellite television are less than straightforward. The creation of a discrete identity for the possible English or European league or the extension of some form of the men's game will be instrumental in how the venture presents itself and so the exploration of the way that women players are mediated and represented is another area for further study which the following chapter begins to address. However, the development of an emergent international market implied by consumerist narratives and televised professional matches therefore should not obscure the regional diversity of communities within women's football culture and a considerable body of work has still to elaborate this.

The evidence from legal, educational and coaching material is that football remains a protected sphere for male workers at the highest level. From a European perspective the revised article 119(4) of the Treaty of Rome allows member states to adopt measures providing for specific advantages in order to make it easier for the under-represented sex to pursue a vocational activity or to prevent or compensate for disadvantages in their professional careers. Women-only coaching courses at all levels currently provide examples of just such an activity. Quotas would also assist in opening the full range of coaching opportunities. In terms of both players and coaches the football profession has been cautious about protecting its reputation and its monopoly on services by limiting the number of practitioners at elite level. Leaving overt discrimination aside, playing and coaching occupational communities exercise informal controls including exclusionary practices that limit membership. The strength of custom has institutionalised practice in delineating professional football as a unique territory of men. The most effective control of recruits has occurred at playing level. There are some women chief executives, marketing specialists, player's agents, journalists and coaches who have infiltrated the male game but they are notable as exceptions. The lack of recognition given to female performers is not merely a response to 'the world out there'. The construction of group identity by women players has been neither at the mercy of corporate production nor as necessarily outside of, and 'other' to, these influences. The structures and organisational aspects of English society discussed here consequently demonstrate contradictory perceptions of the women's football community.

An aspect of football that has altered immeasurably is the status of the sport itself following the removal of the maximum wage in 1961, the abolition of the 'retain and transfer' system in 1963 and the rise in transfer fees and wages since 1991.[18] In spite of the financial rewards of the male professional player, however, professionalism as it has manifested itself in women's football has been a mixed blessing, as we've seen from the 1970s players who had to choose between a professional career and representing their nation. As the issue of female professionalism in England becomes more pressing, women players will hopefully not have to make this choice, though, at the current time, some travel to the United States to follow a semi-professional career.

In summary, a key element in the development of the women's game is a consensus that increased commercialism and professionalism is desirable and bound to happen. This seems to be neither historically accurate nor inevitable in the near future. The widespread devaluation of women's sport, particularly of women football players, has impacted on the kind of policies and practices intended to achieve a limited integration. For example, Bury women players were shocked to find that in exchange for the kit and training facilities that had been 'donated', each player was obliged to steward at professional matches to save wages. So while there are ways in which the influence of male structures on women's football could be potentially beneficial, the ways in which the women's game is seen to be the ugly duckling to the swan raises fundamental questions about the nature and purpose of incorporating women into these frameworks. A desire for respectability and kudos, implied by commercial and professional agendas, has yet to translate into more forceful demands for increased control and recognition. This is an issue that the next chapter debates in reviewing the international situation.

5 Women's football

An international comparison

This chapter pursues some international comparisons to ask what are the strengths and weaknesses of the English model of dispersed voluntary recreational and competitive participation and centralised elite development? Along with growth in the interest in women's football, women's sport advocacy organisations continue to increase in number: WomenSport International, the International Association of Physical Education and Sport for Girls and Women (IAPESGW), the Commonwealth Games Women and Sport Committee, The Arab Women and Sport Group, the Islamic Countries Women's Sports Solidarity Council, Asia Women and Sport, The European Women and Sport Group, and the African Women and Sport Association are examples of organisations which have evolved into regional and global networks. The increasing representation of female sports initiatives can be extended to women's football to ask two critical questions. Is there sufficient common purpose in these multiple initiatives to provide a coherent vision of the future or are women's sports activists more united by a common past of exclusion, than in agreement about where it is they want to arrive at? How do such initiatives as the Brighton Declaration, the FIFA Declaration of Women's Football and the Olympic Declaration of Women affect the opportunities of a competitive woman football player in a regional league in England today?

International women's sports associations have a relatively moderate approach to the representation of women in sport compared with other aspects of the women's movement. For example, the Olympic movement's use of targets takes the historical under-representation of women as its basis, with the request that '10% of all offices in all decision making structures (in particular all legislative or executive agencies) be held by women and that such percentage reach at least 20% by 31 December 2005' (International Olympic Committee, 2000a: 15). Perhaps the most thoughtful use of quotas came from the Canadian Association for the Advancement of Women in Sport (CAAWS) which advocated that no more than 40 per cent of committee members should belong to the same sex for all sports.[1] In contrast, a third view, that gender representation targets should be set within sports by their governing bodies, with different targets for different sports, is a more liberal approach than the Olympic view.[2] Therefore agreement about the aims of, and tactics for, progress are contested in the international arena. The Olympic Committee's use of a 20 per cent target appears on the one hand to be a collaborative and moderate proposal and has been met with broad approval. As an appeal, rather than as an enforceable requirement a superficial move towards compliance is a risk, as is a very gradualist approach to reform. The 40 per cent rule appears on the surface to be both a response to archaic inequity and a means of making male and female sport the province of men and women. This would require a wholesale shift in sports culture that is not implied by the third solution. As the case of football has so far indicated, governing bodies have shown themselves to be conservative and reactionary in accommodating women participants and so asking these associations to set sports-specific objectives place too much faith in their desire for rapid or essential alteration to current systems. The need for a comprehensive change within football is a point that has been made repeatedly and so without quotas, and fairly ambitious ones at that, there is unlikely to be a critical mass of women in leadership positions within the sport and national or international level. However, there remains considerable ambivalence within the women's sport movement about the speed and direction that change ought to take.

As a cynical attendee at the Second Olympic Congress on Women's Sport summed up the programme, 'The speeches will all be the same, we've come a long way, and we're doing well. We're moving forwards but there's still a lot to do.' Whether this was conference fatigue or world-weariness, it did indicate the unfocused nature of some of the good news that I was being asked to applaud. As proclamation has followed affirmation after the 1994 Brighton Declaration, there have been many governments and sports federations who have 'committed' to the women in sport movement, particularly to increasing female participation in physical activities. At Windhoek in 1998 and Toronto in 2002 the number of national and international partners continues to grow and this *is* encouraging. It is also shocking to realise at these global gatherings and other regional events how much has yet to be achieved while another generation of young women and men grow up without fundamental change in sight. So though I'd like to, I cannot share the view of some of my contemporaries that the undertakings are, in themselves, the paradigm shift. While not yet as bitter as the delegate above, my impatience makes me question the nature of the commitment to Brighton and so forth. In some cases, it can appear about as satisfying as getting married on the Internet: too much about the hypothetical expression of good intention and very little about attentively fulfilling the promise. Brighton, and the fashion for visionary statements of intention, have served a purpose in the last twelve years by allowing recalcitrant bureaucracies, sporting and otherwise, to make a grand gesture. The international women's sports movement needs to move on the next stage of the process, which is to institutionalise further progress within those organisations that have given a pledge. Using football as an example, the FA have commended themselves to Brighton and FIFA's own Los Angeles Declaration, and to capitalise on this we should not be distracted by messages of goodwill or good intention and should be more rigorous in asking that undertakings guarantee consigned resources, allocation of roles and responsibilities and the appointment of key individuals to effect energetic and measurable transformation. In an era of performance targets, talk of public accountability and added value, in England at least, the topic of women's sports should be more politicised in order to make transparent what is behind opaque slogans about female participation.

Jennifer Hargreaves has explored the issue of globalisation and women's sport and makes two points that are particularly useful for women's football.

> International sports organizations have been in place since the late nineteenth century, at which time the nation state was the primary unit of understanding and analysis . . . But the further growth of international, supranational and transnational organizations, institutions and movements implies a shift away from 'society' and 'nation state' to 'world society'.
>
> (Hargreaves, 2000: 217)

Traditional values of feminine appropriacy continue to affect the international development of women's football at the same time as female sport is allied to ideas of progress and modernity: 'Women's football is evolving a distinctive style of women's play . . . it will succeed in attracting women players because of its own beauty and grace, not because of its potential to mimic men players' (Blatter, 1995: Editorial). 'Difference' is still the key to acceptance of women's football at international level: the future of women's football *must be* feminine. This difference is not the term as used by feminists to indicate the multiplicity of shifting identities of women but a convenient cul-de-sac in which female participation is located as distinct and not mainstream. FIFA and the Olympic movement, like the national football associations, possess mechanisms that provide channels of mobility for members of in-groups and close them to others. As a class and as individuals, certain women are tolerated to the extent that their participation is not immediately threatening as a source of competition to either those in power or to the pool of eligible individuals who may achieve power.

There is a recent worrying trend within women's sport advocacy circles to argue the case for women's increased role in sport as consumer of products. Economic arguments are not based on equivalence of facilities and support, but on women's right to expend their income in return for sporting experience. As a relatively crude criterion for defining a potential 'new' market these claims are problematic in terms of interpreting women's value in sport as related to the ability to purchase wares. In this way research centred on women, as opposed to what M. Ann Hall and others have called women-centred research, may distort the variety of women's experiences in relation to sport (Hall, 1996: 8).

The significance of women as a market in the development of women's sport can be seen from the profile afforded to Maria Steffan, the Vice President of Global Business Development of the Sporting Goods Manufacturers Association by the Olympic movement at a recent conference (Steffan, 2000). Steffan is also a member of the board of trustees of the United States Women's Sports Foundation, Chair of the Development Committee of the World Federation of the Sporting Goods Industry and a member of the Education Committee of the US Olympic Association and her expertise is undoubtedly crucial in awakening the business world to the potential of women as part of the sporting public. What is most disturbing about this consumerist narrative is its link with discussions of equality in international women's sport circles, for example Steffan's paper on 'Financing women's sport' directly followed the presentation by Dr Elizabeth Ferris, *Promoting Women Sports Leaders: Are quotas the way forward?* (Ferris, 2000). Alliances of commercial and proponent interest tell us less about what women participants bring to sport than what they are perceived to stand for.

The concern to develop women's football by wealthy, high-status sports administrations is often presented as altruistic. Of course football is not alone in constantly needing to sell its brand of sport to successive generations of players. Nor is it unusual that women's sport should have achieved some measure of success as entertainment at the same time as facing considerable challenge. However, football for women as a globally popular game belies the patchy and controversial development that are still the most enduring feature of the sport from the days of the 1921 ban in England to the current development of the inaugural FIFA Under 19s Women's World Cup. The development of an emergent international market therefore should not obscure the regional diversity within nations or across cultures and a considerable body of work has still to elaborate this.

In the International Council of Sport Science and Physical Education (ICSSPE) Bulletin of November 1998, Fasting *et al.* drew the conclusion, 'There would appear to be a female soccer culture that cuts across nation state boundaries' (Fasting *et al.*, 1998: 39). There is a women's football culture in England that the previous chapters have begun to describe and so is there evidence of a corresponding international construct and, if so, what is England's contribution to it? Whilst the United States won the World Cup in 1991 and 1999 and the Olympic Games in 1996, Norway took top honours in 1995 in Sweden and the Olympics of 2000. Any discussion of a cosmopolitan culture for women's football would have to begin with Scandinavia, albeit the brief coverage given here. There are useful counterpoints regarding matters of equity, athletic regulations and access to leadership in administrative and decision-making roles. Europe, particularly

Scandinavia, has been at the forefront of championing women's football since the 1960s.

With a population 1.6 per cent that of the US, per capita Norway is the most successful women's football nation in the world. The participation rate at senior level (16 and over) was 22,000 in 1995, a little more than half of the under-16 players (Espelund, 1995: 1). The conventional wisdom of a mass of players at the base of a playing pyramid from which a few elite athletes emerge, doesn't fully explain the relationship between participation and elite success in Norway as handball, not football, is the most popular female sport. Though it was 1976 before the Norwegian Soccer Federation officially recognised the women's game, this was relatively early compared with other associations and it was Norway's Ellen Wille that proposed that FIFA promote women's football a decade later in 1986. The nature of the integration of women's football has been more developed than in other associations, for instance, male and female national coaches have long worked from the same office at Norwegian HQ and watch both sets of matches. The league system highlights talent regionally and this leads to national selection. In addition Norway are the forerunners of a professional approach to preparation for large tournaments as their 1995 World Cup victory, and Olympic triumph in 2000, suggests. The relative underachievement of fourth place in the 1999 Women's World Cup was not a standard they were prepared to accept and the intense heat in the Rosebowl was probably a factor in this result.

This tournament-grooming has been extended by other nations like China and the United States so that the national squad have increasingly operated as a full-time unit and the calendar of fixtures against opponents devised to ensure peak performance at the two top trophy-winning events in women's football. Meanwhile, it has taken until 1999 for the English FA to emulate the Norwegian and Swedish elite representative systems by forming under-20 and under-16 squads coached by men and women as well as having a female National Team coach. Several England Internationals play semi-professionally in Sweden and Norway to improve their game. These countries have been had considerable influence on the growth of women's football, which there isn't space to elaborate on here. However, though women's football is a more popular spectator- or media-supported event in both Sweden and Norway, the female game in Europe is placed at a disadvantage by the interest in male professional competition. For instance, the Second Women's World Cup in Sweden was a considerable departure from the standard format as it involved sharing four venues with another major event: the World Athletics Championship in Gothenburg. The Women's World Cup in Los Angeles learned from the experiment as the crowds in Sweden were a big disappointment. The athletics competed with women's football for audience and media attention, rather than helping to create a multi-sport spectacle.

In spite of this considerable success and archetypal influence, the views of the highest-ranking Norwegian women and men are not always treated with the respect they deserve at international level. At the 1995 UEFA conference Karen Espelund, who was elected Vice President of the Norwegian FA in 1996 with special responsibility for elite programmes, spoke of the need to dispense with the prefix of men's and women's and to speak of football. Of the seven areas of development Espelund suggested, very few have been implemented internationally, across Europe or in England. She called for total female integration into the association, identical rules and regulations for males and females, the need for female leaders at all levels, the use of elite players as role models and continuity of personnel within bureaucracies (Espelund, 1995: 2). So the 'ripple in the pond' effect for overall standards which is so clear in the Norwegian example has yet to be given the acclaim it merits.

Norway, Sweden and Denmark have historically had the greatest concentration of elite players, and if we include Russia, Germany and Italy, Europe has been the largest contributor of top women athletes to international competition.[3] Since 1995 a different pattern is beginning to emerge. See for example the 'Hundreds Club' in Tables 5.1 and 5.2 below.

At this time England's Gill Coulthard stood at equal 22nd on 111 caps. So the operation of the US team as a virtual national club produces impressive statistics as the opportunities for national appearances and goals are increased in a relatively short space of time. As the statistics become updated and embellished, inter- and intra-national comparison will develop into an aspect of further study. With the newly introduced UEFA club championship for women under trial, the balance of professional league, tournament and club competition for elite women players is also likely to be subject to revision.

The patronage by FIFA and the Olympic movement has been a crucial part of the mediatisation of women's football and has given it a platform.

Table 5.1 Hundreds Club tally 1994

Rank	*Name*	*Country*	*Caps*
1	Carolina Morace	Italy	119
	Heidi Stoere	Norway	119
3	Pia Sundhage	Sweden	114
4	Elisabetta Vignotto	Italy	110
	Gunn Nyborg	Norway	110
6	Elisabeth Leidinge	Sweden	101
7	Maura Furlotti	Italy	93
8	Lena Lidekull	Sweden	90
9	Sylvia Neid	Germany	89
10	Feriana Ferraguzzi	Italy	84

Source: Figures adapted from *FIFA News* September 1994

Table 5.2 Hundreds Club tally 1999

Rank	*Name*	*Country*	*Caps*
1	Kristine Lilly	USA	175
2	Mia Hamm	USA	169
3	Heidi Stoere	Norway	151*
4	Carolina Morace	Italy	150*
	Julie Foudy	USA	150
6	Pia Sundhage	Sweden	146*
7	Linda Medalen	Norway	143
8	Carla Overbeck	USA	140
9	Joy Fawcett	USA	138
10	Michelle Akers	USA	137

Source: Figures adapted from *FIFA News* May 1999

Note: *Those asterisked are no longer active international players.

Barbara Allen, the outgoing Chief Executive of Women's USA, describes the cultivation of a television audience as crucial to Women's USA as a professional league in an entertainment market:

> The most significant achievement was the fan attendance and satisfaction ratings. The attendance throughout the season was above the planned projections. The satisfaction ratings from fans in exit interviews were extremely positive and reinforced our view that the fan experience was excellent . . . We fell short in convincing fans to tune in to the television broadcasts, there were lower ratings than we would have hoped for on a national basis and in the team cities with a few exceptions
>
> (Barbara Allen, personal communication 5 October 2001)

Five large media partners own the Women's USA professional league and consequently all games are televised, as are advertisements between times for individual teams and the league as a whole.[4] The English FA plans to launch a professional league in this country on the back of satellite television interest. The majority of women players surveyed in England understood that television and implied commercialism was imperative to the spread of the game. In answer to the question, 'Please suggest two or three things which you think would encourage girls and women to play football on a wider basis', the responses included:

> More media coverage of women's football (and on a more local level on regional TV and radio) to improve the social status of ladies' teams . . . Whole teams and individual interviews should be shown on TV a lot more, on radio, and in the paper.

> There should be better and more TV coverage of league games and internationals. Women's World Cup [1999] looked great but I haven't seen anything since then.

> More coverage on TV will lead to more clubs being set up. The FA should advertise it more and televise English women's football instead of men's Italian football.

However, one of the major challenges to women's football in England and internationally is the establishment of this TV audience if it is to become, in any sense of the word, a global game. As Lauren Gregg commented during WUSA's inaugural year:

> TV viewership remains a challenge for soccer in this country. Although not bad, we want to improve our numbers there . . . I think we have provided a welcomed addition to the professional sports market. We are family oriented, affordable, entertaining and very integrated into our communities – all critical ingredients to sustaining the league over time. Clearly, you need fans to create a truly professional environment. We accomplished that and intend to work to build upon it. The relationship between a live audience and a TV audience is less defined to me. However, the appeal of the game is often tied into the atmosphere surrounding the event itself. Our fans contributed to that, making the TV product very exciting and inviting.
>
> (Lauren Gregg, personal communication 31 October 2000)

The pattern of live audience support providing televised sporting spectacle has been at the heart of FIFA's plans for the female game since FIFA President Joao Havelange accepted the need to begin international development. Havelange listened to proposals for the first Women's World Cup at the 1986 Congress in Mexico City. It was trialled in 1988 and eventually held in 1991 in China. At the first symposium on women's football in 1992 the conclusions were rather elementary and cautious, 'Every association was requested to assess the current level of play in each age category. Depending on the outcome, further competitions may perhaps be set up at national and international level' (FIFA, 1992). Seven years later targets began to emerge in the Los Angeles Declaration on Women's Football which stipulated 'An increase of at least 10% in the number of registered women football players in competitions organised by the national associations over the next four years' (FIFA, 1999a). In spite of this greater certainty in FIFA's commitment to the women's game, problems with targets like those above remain. Associations that do not run women's competitions, for example, are neatly excluded. On the other hand the move toward more international competition, such as the Under-19 Championship, is encouraging, if belated.[5]

During this time some women have been active in the flow of information within the international association but overall the extent of their power is limited. One reason for this is that modern administrative systems depend on large numbers of committees in the process of making and executing policy. Recruitment to committees in FIFA is based on organisational membership, position in the public hierarchies and successful appointment by the leadership. Women in higher positions are usually found in the centre, and in advisory roles rather than the decision-making bodies. The subordination of equitable gender distribution to geographical representation is the major obstacle preventing a growth in the number of women.

In *FIFA and the Contest for World Football: Who Rules the People's Game?* Sugden and Tomlinson analysed the role of gatekeepers effective in maintaining existing hierarchies at FIFA (Sugden and Tomlinson, 1998). The maintenance of systems of patronage endures but more notice is taken of the relatively small alterations to include women. For example, in 1994 the decision by the FIFA executive committee to double the number of members on the Women's Football Committee from seven to fourteen was not in the spirit of increased gender representation, but to include national associations without representation on the committee, including three from South America. This is further complicated by the multifaceted nature of large sports organisations as women are more evident as administrative appointees than elected representatives.

However, in brand terms, an important component of contemporary legitimisation is representativeness. As major brands, as well as large international organisations, sports conglomerates are under pressure to make concessions to women. The system of patronage within FIFA, like other large organisations, is demonstrably not meritocratic. It is a tracking process and in order for people to move from one level to the next, they must gain in rank, status and acceptability as they go. One example is Donna De Varona, the Chair of the organising committee of Women's World Cup 1999. Though her elite experience was as a swimmer, her high media profile with the Women's Sport Foundation gave her sufficient status to head the tournament in the United States. However, her appointment was for a fixed term. Within FIFA women are noticeable by their absence on the most influential boards.

Michelle Akers has been invited to join the players' technical committee, but in most cases it is necessary to accumulate wide-ranging experience as deputy or leader to gain advancement to senior and executive posts. Even within the circumscribed province of women's football, females have been committee members rather than leaders. From 1996–8 Dr Viacheslav Koloskov was chair and Carlos Coello deputy of the Women's Committee. Minutes of meeting number 10 of the Committee for Women's Football held in Zurich on Tuesday 18 February 1997 suggest that, of the fourteen members present, four were women. Per Ravn Omdal of Norway has also held the Chair and Worawi Makudi acted as Deputy Chair. Omdal's other responsibilities within FIFA have included Chair of Marketing and Television Advisory Board and Deputy Chair of the Confederations Cup Committee and the Club World Championship Committee. He is a member of the Security Matters Committee and of the Executive Committee.[6] In contrast, among the seven out of fourteen Women's Committee members who are female, none currently holds a position of responsibility on any other board. Hannelore Ratzeburg, the lone female on the Women's Committee at its inception in 1990 and who took part in the organising committee for the first Women's World Cup in China, then held similar status to Omdal in also being a member, but still holds no other rank in spite of having twenty years' experience with the German Soccer Federation and UEFA.[7]

In contrast, Josephine King is the only woman to hold office as one of six Confederation General Secretaries. King's career is evidence that women can move outside the protected sphere of 'women's football' to mainstream administration. She is a past member of the FIFA Women's Committee and currently a member of the Player Status Committee. In addition to working at men's and women's world cups, organising international tournaments and courses, she is also a FIFA FUTURO course instructor. So the self-protecting nature of the organisation sits a few women in elite positions alongside the established fraternity.

Similarly, though it is encouraging that the next highest representation of women is on the Technical Advisory and Coaching Committee, none are graded as technical advisers; Elizabeth Loisel, Vera Pauw, Gunilla Paijkull, and Sylvie Beliveau are listed as instructors (FIFA, 2000). In the most influential committees, the financial and executive, and in the most prestigious competitions, for example the 2002 World Cup Organising Body, there are no women, and there was only one for the Sydney 2000 competition (FIFA, 2000). FIFA therefore falls short of its own sloganeering regarding a female-focus to the future but is moving gradually in the right direction. Like other sporting federations comprising member countries, FIFA must accommodate a range of cultures and its stated policies and ideologies reflect compromise. It is not only in England that football has promoted a form of equality for women while at the same time preserving rigid social distinctions. On an international stage, as yet, elite administration posts are not, by and large, afforded to women.

In moving from FIFA as an administrative entity in its own right, to a body responsible for developing women's football, the tension between facilitating international competition and the development of mass participation is the major challenge for the federation as it continues to invest disproportionately in male football. The motif in wealthy countries like the United States and in developing countries like Namibia is that the actual resource available to a national association matters less than the perception that there is not enough to fund women's football equally at elite or at participation levels. As with the case of England, equity is not perceived to entail equivalence because the female form of the sport is seen to be in its infancy.

Reacting to the relative gains in the popularity of basketball, FIFA are, like the English Association, keen to present football as the globally popular team sport for males and females. The next section analyses the FIFA surveys of associations to examine the accuracy of that description. In the 1992 and 1997 FIFA surveys of women's football around the world, thirteen countries reported that they did not have women's teams. Some of the European examples, like Andorra and San Marino, are extremely small, though as the case for Norway has made clear, there is not always a direct correlation between the size of the population and women's participation.

Table 5.3 FIFA survey of women's football around the world 1992

Region	*No. of national associations*	*No. of national associations with women's football*
CONMEBOL[1]	10	4
UEFA[2]	35	28
OFC[3]	8	3
CAF[4]	48	8
AFC[5]	33	8
CONCACAF[6]	27	5[7]

Source: Adapted from the FIFA Evaluation of the questionnaire on women's football as at 30 July 1997, Zurich, 2 March 1998

Notes: 1 Confederación Sudamericana de Fútbol (South American Football Confederation)
2 Union of European Football Associations
3 Oceania Football Confederation
4 Confédération Africaine de Football (African Football Confederation)
5 Asian Football Confederation
6 Confederation of North, Central American and Caribbean Association Football
7 Two indicated no women's football

Table 5.4 FIFA survey of women's football around the world 1997

Region	*No. of national associations*	*No. of national associations with women's football*
CONMEBOL[1]	10	9
UEFA[2]	53	43
OFC[3]	10	5
CAF[4]	51	25
AFC[5]	43	17
CONCACAF[6]	33	8

Source: Adapted from the FIFA Evaluation of the questionnaire on women's football as at 30 July 1997, Zurich, 2 March 1998

Notes: 1 Confederación Sudamericana de Fútbol (South American Football Confederation
2 Union of European Football Associations
3 Oceania Football Confederation
4 Confédération Africaine de Football (African Football Confederation)
5 Asian Football Confederation
6 Confederation of North, Central American and Caribbean Association Football

In 1992, of a possible 161 associations, 56 answered (34.7 per cent), 13 of which did not have women's football. In 1997 out of a total of 200 associations, 107 answered (53 per cent). This in itself could cautiously be said to indicate wider acceptance of women playing football. The thirteen associations in both which indicated that they did not have women's football were: Andorra, Armenia, Bahrain, Cyprus, Kuwait, Macedonia, Malawi, Maldives, Niger, Qatar, San Marino, Turkmenistan and United Arab Emirates. This would seem to indicate that countries with cultures which place a premium on female modesty, including predominantly Muslim societies, have tended not to develop women's football to the same degree. However, as with the case of Algeria mentioned earlier, each culture varies in the extent to which it is prepared to tolerate and sponsor women players and a non-return may reflect antipathy at the level of the national association rather than being an accurate summary of women's participation. In Egypt, for example, a fatwa prevented women from playing football but Sahar El-Hawary began by developing an indoor league in which players covered their legs to avoid criticism. From this an eleven-a-side Egyptian representative team was formed and school and rural initiatives began. El-Hawary is the first African, Egyptian Arabic woman on the FIFA Women's Committee.[8] The examples of El-Hawary, Kerzabi, Ratzeburg and King reinforce the point that rather than there being a combined or concerted effort, the sum total of the achievements of individual women has produced uneven effects.

In addition to the poor rate of response, it would be unwise to extrapolate overall trends from these surveys, though there does appear to be an increased willingness on behalf of national associations to provide an umbrella for women's football. Additional qualitative responses provided in response to the surveys indicate considerable variance in regional development. In the Oceania Football Confederation, for example, the New Zealand association suggests that football at school and junior level is socially acceptable, but for adult women it is not (FIFA, 1998: 4) In contrast, for Tahiti (where Evelyn Whitman is President of the Football Federation) and the smaller islands, travel and funding difficulties inhibit development (FIFA, 1998: 3). Whereas Australia has recently hosted the Olympic competition and lobbied unsuccessfully to host the 2003 Women's World Cup. In the CONMEBOL confederation Paraguay has no activity apart from indoor football, Chile reported poorer than expected development and Argentina and Brazil report 'favourable' growth (FIFA, 1998: 5).

These details give a flavour of the range of engagement but, again, are limited as they portray the culture of women's football from the national associations' point of view. As has been suggested in earlier chapters, the impetus for competition has only latterly come from such organisations. For example, Brazil has had a national women's competition since 1983 but it was only with a disappointing ninth place finish in the Women's World Cup in Sweden that the association took the women's game more seriously.[9] The development of women's football is more often at the instigation of individuals and interested parties, as is the case with Namibia which is discussed in more detail later. Before looking at FIFA's use of Women's World Cup 1999, it is useful then to consider football in a multi-sport, multi-national arena which provides the second largest showcase of international competition.

The development of football as an Olympic sport, and the place of women as athletes from the turn of the century have, in turn, affected the acceptance of women's football.[10] Women made their Olympic debut as athletes in 1900 in Paris but it took until 1996 for women's football to be included as an Olympic sport.[11] As FIFA grew in power during the nineteenth century, and the World Cup became increasingly mediated, the importance of the Olympics to international football competition has decreased, at the same time as its importance to women's sport has increased. A notable exception to this is the United States, where football has yet to establish itself against American football, basketball, baseball and hockey. Since the 1970s the women's Olympic programme has been enlarged in co-operation with the respective international sports federations and the Organising Committee. The global status of the 'world's most popular team sport' logically depended upon inclusion, as President Havelange, a long-serving member of the IOC, was aware. This has been further reinforced by the decision that all sports seeking inclusion to the Games must include women's events. FIFA's characteristic caution in developing women's competition meant that football lagged behind basketball, handball and volleyball by at least four years in becoming a full medal sport. The 1994 Congress of Unity stipulated the inclusion into the Olympic Charter of an explicit reference to the promotion of women's advancement in sport at all levels:

> The IOC strongly encourages, by appropriate means, the promotion of women in sport at all levels and in all structures, particularly in the executive bodies of national and international sports organisations with a view to the strict application of the principle of equality between men and women.
>
> (International Olympic Committee, 1998: 3)

There remain statistical imbalances in participation as well as administrative inequities, for example in the Sydney 2000 Games women competed in twenty-five sports and comprised roughly 38 per cent of 10,382 athletes.[12]

The relationship between the Women's World Cup and the Olympic Games is further connected by the fact that the former tournament serves as the qualification for the latter. In this way the Olympics provides international competition between the quadrennial World Cup tournaments. The seven quarter-finalists of the 1999 tournament and the host country in 2000, Australia, were guaranteed a place, whereas the male Olympic tournament is for sixteen teams. The female squad's minimum age is 16, whilst men may not be more than 23, with three exceptions. In spite of these, and other, rule changes the Olympics benefits women's football in terms of creating an international television and live audience. Until such time as confederation and club championships for women are developed, Olympic competition continues to be a key element in international women's football culture at elite level. The success of the Women's World Cup in 1999 followed the 1996 Olympic final which had created the largest live audience for a women-only event.[13] Considered in this light, the men's World Cup of 1994, the Atlanta Games in 1996 and the Women's World Cup in 1999 are key moments in the continuing attempt by FIFA to sell the world's most popular sport to ever-increasing markets. In short, the Women's World Cup re-presented soccer as a spectator sport to the United States in the third significant tournament in five years. Consequently the Women's World Cup was a collaboration by a variety of stakeholders, interested in making this a landmark event and a breakthrough for women's sport in areas of marketing and publicity. The implications for the international culture of women's football are potentially considerable.

The Women's World Cup 1999 drew on the failure of the 1995 tournament to capture live audiences with an ambitiously planned single-sex, single-sport event. It built on the Olympic tradition in the United States by making the live and televised event sensational and it adroitly disseminated the opportunity to spectate as a family friendly activity. The timing was particularly significant for women's sports generally and for association football for women particularly. The implications of Women's World Cup 1999 for the international profile of women's football, therefore, go beyond women as consumers and producers of soccer in the United States. Sugden and Tomlinson's *Hosts and Champions* used an image of the Statue of Liberty holding aloft the Jules Rimet trophy in her right hand and balancing a football in her left and argued:

> It has been convincingly argued that not only is soccer in the USA the sport of minority ethnic communities, of the middle-class educational institutions – but it is the sport, at its most spectacularly successful level, of women. This has caused great problems for the game in gaining acceptance in the still so-macho and nativist sports culture.
>
> (Tomlinson and Sugden, 1994: 4)

This is both an advantage for women who wish to play and a problem in marketing the sport to the American public. The current elite women are, in the main, young, well-educated college students or graduates. This is unlike Major League Soccer, especially the male European stars who are, by comparison, often seen to be extending their career in sunny climes. Julie Foudy, for example, is a veteran of three Women's World Cups and gave up a graduate career in medicine at Stanford to concentrate on soccer. Lothar

Matthaeus signed to the Major League Soccer (MLS) Metrostars team at 38. He joined Stoichkov and Anders Limpar (both 34), Carlos Valderama (38) and Paul Caligiuri (37). These examples are not mean to imply that MLS is a veteran's league but that issues of developing young players are at a relatively unsettled stage.[14] The two most consequential trends for women's soccer in the United States are the constantly growing base of active women players and flourishing elite achievement in international competition. The lower profile of the male team on the international stage makes the national women's team success all the more conspicuous.

Perhaps mindful of the 'so-macho' and nativist elements, Women's World Cup 1999 promotional material used the metaphor of family throughout. This mirrors four key issues in marketing women's sport in the United States suggested by Maria Steffan:

> Taking women's sports to the next level requires an expanded fan base . . . the spectator pool for women's sports is a separate market than the spectator pool for men's sports . . . the sports feminism of 'Dads' with athletic daughters is also inexorably tied to the battle for sports resources . . . New ventures tend to be judged and graded against 'perfection' – we forget a successful National Football League took nine tries.
>
> (Steffan, 2000: 4)

The commercial affiliates reflected this familial atmosphere but also the aspirations of FIFA, the Women's Sports Foundation and US Soccer. They included large multi-national companies such as Adidas, Bud Light, Coca-Cola, Fujifilm, JVC, Gillette, Hewlett-Packard, MasterCard and McDonald's. The marketing partners included Allstate, Sybase and *Sports Illustrated for Women*. The media partners included the *Boston Globe*, *Chicago Tribune* and the *New York Times* plus Lifetime Television, although some games and especially highlights were shown on sports channels. This group of mainstream official sponsors therefore mitigated the 'newness factor' of a tournament dedicated to teams of women athletes. From discrete merchandise to strategic co-option of key personnel the Women's World Cup attempted to increase the market for women's sport, women's football, football itself and to non-sports fans. For example, the commodities included items for non-players, players, women players and supporters, from World Cup Barbie to the 'Icon', the first ball specifically produced for a women's event.[15] The TV scheduling was equally shrewd, with over sixty-four hours of televised coverage on ABC/ESPN over three weekends, one of which was a Fourth of July national holiday.

Alan Rothberg, Chairman of the Board, made the point that investors and sponsors are offered a wider spectrum of potential consumer by such strategies, one that is 'higher-educated, higher-income, more families, more females . . . a lot of companies who are not traditional sponsors of men's sports open their eyes widely when they see the opportunity to sponsor women's sports' (Rothberg, 1999). The role of US Soccer was also critical as the US Soccer Foundation, set up to administer the profits from the 1994 World Cup tournament, granted a $2.5 million loan to the Women's World Cup Organising Committee in 1997.[16] Five of the eight Women's World Cup Board of Directors had positions with US Soccer, and one with the international Olympic committee. Marla Messing, President of the Women's World Cup 1999 Organising Committee, outlined the benefits of this strategic co-operation:

> This is the largest commercial market in the world and this is the largest commercial market for women's soccer. People will come out for the big events, and they'll come out to see the pinnacle event in virtually every sport. While we won't have the Olympic name attached to us, we will have the World Cup name attached and that's just as important and meaningful to the American public . . . In '94, because the tickets were sold so fast, a lot of those soccer players . . . never had the opportunity to purchase tickets . . . it's important for them to be part of this World Cup . . . to connect with the youth . . .
>
> (Messing, 1999)

The organisers had a particular view of the slice of the American public who would be attracted to the event. For example, a grassroots Development Director was appointed to tap into a potentially under-exploited demographic pool to translate the fan base to stadium and television consumers.

So as a specifically domestic, youth market Women's World Cup 1999 used the success of the US women's team to attract audiences perhaps excluded by previous premier events. Of course the traditional sports fan may not have been interested in a women's competition even if the 'World Cup' title was meaningful to them. The competition involved sixteen teams compared with thirty-two in France 1998, in an attempt to keep the playing standard as high as possible. More importantly, the athletes of the American team acted as eloquent ambassadors and media spokespersons for the tournament. Each player received a reward for these duties and a win bonus. The main point of contrast with the English context is that advocates of women's sports, the national and international associations, media and marketing partners each felt they benefited from the success of the tournament which used mainstream venues and averaged crowds of 60,000. This potential advantage is as yet unharnessed in England or anywhere else in the world to the same extent and while commercialism should not be the only face of women's football, the event demonstrates the ability of a women-only event to harness and direct several competing interests.

Nor were commercial affiliates and soccer authorities the only ones to use the tournament to reach wider audiences. Politicians were eager to speak on behalf of the Women's World Cup and to use it as a platform for public relations. The celebration of sport as part of healthy living, for example, was overt in the anti-smoking messages of the build-up – 'U.S. women rule with fire not with smoke . . . Smoke defenders not cigarettes . . . Keep your engine running clean!' (FIFA, 1999b: 44). Donna Shalala, US Secretary of Health and Human Services, stressed the clean-living images of the players and the honour that participation brought to the individual, her family, town and country. The support of the White House for the US team featured in daily newspapers, the President and First Lady acted as Honourary Co-Chairs of the competition, included a message of support in the Final Programme and appeared in person to support the championship. Nevertheless, following the Lewinsky affair this joint public support for a women's event was not uncontested by the families that flocked to the Rose Bowl finale. Clinton did not leave the press box after being jeered. The final itself was an expression of the patriotism of both the US team and the wider audience. In a particularly gendered expression of allegiance players painted their nails and hair in red, white and blue. The anthems were followed, and overshadowed, by the release of balloons and streamers and a Vulcan Bomber fly-over. The tournament, as a demonstration of the home team's ability to win to the US public, was an accomplished cultivator of nationalist sentiment.

Until the final, the team and family were key metaphors in press coverage but the image changed at the point of victory. Brandi Chastain's pride in her body had already been demonstrated by her posing naked for a *Gear* men's magazine shoot. Whether taking off her shirt after the last kick was a spontaneous expression of joy, an advertisement for a brand of sports bra or self-promotion, the tendency to define herself against both her US team-mates and rivals was clear. In doing so, in some media she eclipsed Briana Scurry, the black goalkeeper, who saved the penalty to win the tournament. Chastain did little in this solitary act to alter the deeply masculine nature of the nation's sporting imagery.[17]

Whether the young supporters continue their interest as spectators remains to be seen post-Sydney and at the Women's World Cup in China. Even so, it is hard to imagine a similar enthusiasm on behalf of the English or European public, were national teams to qualify for a future World Cup. This point was highlighted during the UEFA 2001 competition. England struggled to draw with Russia and lost to Sweden and Germany by three and four goals respectively in games supported by, at best, a few thousand. This said, the influence of the competition on the international configuration of women's football is likely to be far-reaching. Certainly the scale and success of Women's World Cup 1999 has contributed to the impetus for a professional women's league which has drawn on some of the marketing techniques that proved so successful in Los Angeles. However, the difference between a tournament as a discrete moment in the sport and a league means that sponsors and supporters who dipped a toe in the water in 1999 face a rather more stamina-sapping experience after April 2001 with

Women's USA. Nevertheless, lessons have not only come from within the sport.

The increase in the number of professional leagues for women's sport in the United States has been a crucial development of the late 1990s. The inaugural season of the Women's National Basketball Association (WNBA) in 1997 was preceded by a hundred years of women's basketball and several failed professional leagues. The organisers opted for a clear break with the past in the official slogan 'We Got Next' and Women's World Cup 1999 opted for a similar theme; 'This Is My Game. This Is My Future. Watch Me Play.' The success of WNBA and particularly its links to and differentiation from NBA indicates some of the modifications required for professional women's team sport to become established. WNBA was launched as a summer extension to basketball's traditional season, held in large auditoria in urban centres and with television-friendly draping to disguise the smaller crowds. Women's USA organisers, in selecting venues and targeting support, have not followed the WNBA model. This raises the possibility of an alternative professional model for women's sport. It also means that women's football enters a transitory period in the United States to incorporate a professional league populated by national team drafts and foreign players.

In this movement, there is some unwelcome continuity across cultures that remains stubbornly difficult to overcome. It is not, for example, a recent development that the women's team receives different support from the men, in spite of their obvious success. After winning the 1991 Women's World Cup, US Soccer spent little on the team for a year. The reason given was a lack of funding which meant the focus of attention had to be on the male World Cup of 1994.[18] Also at national level the appointment of Lauren Gregg as the first woman full-time National Coach to the under-20 team and Assistant Coach of the Women's National Team, and April Heinrich's selection as National Team Coach for Under-16 Girls appeared to be positive examples of mentoring. However, Heinrichs' subsequent appointment as National Team Coach, without having applied for the position, caused consternation in American women's soccer participatory culture. The furore in magazines such as *Women's Soccer World* demonstrate a willingness to contest such decisions, which contrasts sharply with the lack of public debate surrounding Hope Powell's appointment in England.[19] Nevertheless the principle of patronage in both appointments is clearly evident. Gregg has risen above this episode to become Head of Player Personnel for Women's USA and her foreign draft negotiations of two players from around the world per team have proven to be exceptionally good, both in enabling gifted athletes to compete at the highest level, and for the league.

This section of the chapter, in outlining a United States model of women's football, begins with the newly launched professional league, then on to collegiate soccer before examining two examples of the use of women's participation football. Susan Birrell has used Charles Schulz's *Peanuts* depiction of women athletes in the United States to give an analysis of 'Peppermint Patty, tomboy and serious athlete . . . often referred to as "Sir" . . . Marci, straight-haired, buck-toothed, bespectacled, neophyte intellectual . . . in between Lucy Van Pelt, everywoman-in-training . . . her failure in sports is inconsequential and excusable because she's a girl' (Birrell, 1994: 143). If, in some key respects, WUSA has chosen an alternate course to WNBA the characterisation of the players in the media in both leagues steers a path between Patty on the field or court of play and Lucy off it. The image combines female athletic aggression in the sport and more traditional roles of mother and carer outside that arena. The players of the WNBA and WUSA are diplomatic, polite and courteous to fans. This has led Sarah Banet-Wiser to suggest:

> Despite the rhetoric of equality, conventional narratives of femininity are precisely what gives the WNBA its cultural legitimation as an all-female team sport. The WNBA, as a cultural arena, is clearly about normative femininity, heterosexuality, maternity, and perhaps most importantly, respectability.
>
> (Barnet-Wiser, 1999: 404)

The portrayal of women athletes as altruistic emphasises players as less individually athletic, showing more team commitment and generally worthy, rather than the fiercely competitive individuals in male team sport, and this is as much the case for WUSA as the WNBA. Though not necessarily about normative femininity or heterosexuality, this consideration also has the potential to affect the broader image of professional sport, and in particular football, for the better.

WUSA is not the first attempt to begin a professional soccer league for women in America. For example, in July 1999 the National Soccer Alliance was unsuccessful in its attempt to get approval from the US Soccer Federation (USSF) for a professional league. The decision to draft US Women's National Team players into one of the eight squads in Women's USA is intended to improve the United States' preparation for big tournaments, as they will play against elite women competitors more frequently, as well as providing a competitive spectacle. Players' negotiation with WUSA is more individualistic than has been the case for the national squad. For example, the Chinese player Sun Wen has agreed a deal which sees no transfer fee for her old team, Shanghai TV, but guarantees the cost of her medical bills for the surgery that she underwent before she began her one-year contract. Sara Whalen of the New York Power has a personal deal with Kodak and Tommy Hilfiger to lead their promotion to end youth violence. Additional duties also contribute to the air of caring and respect, such as Shannon MacMillan acting as celebrity chaperone to Special Olympics participants. Having said that, there is a degree of co-operation in the history of the women's national team that continues in the league. Undoubtedly a collective spirit informs individual player salaries, with an $825,000 salary cap for a twenty-player squad and Mia Hamm agreeing to the league maximum of $85,000, the same as other Women's World Cup players receive.

It is worth outlining the conditions that the full-time amateur women accepted before the advent of the professional league. Before June 1991 elite US players spent so much time travelling that many were fired or had to leave jobs. Unlike the men's team, the financial assistance was based on team bonuses and equal player compensation rather than individual performance. The trial format was $1,000 per month to each player regardless of the number of tours or training camps; $30 a day compensation during tours and camps plus a further $10–15 per day per person expenses and health insurance coverage. Each player then earned shares of the total amount by participation, to reward those who had put in the most hours, and a win bonus for each game won. This was a decision supported by the players as a collective, although there has not been a women players' union as such.

Some comments about the organisation of the league will serve to highlight aspects that could be translated across cultures if other professional women's football leagues were to be created. The names of franchises, like those of Major League Soccer, evoke speed, power and excitement with abstractions like Charge (Philadelphia), Freedom (Washington), Spirit (San Diego), Power (New York) and Beat (Atlanta). The Bay Area Cyber Rays, the Carolina Tempest and the Boston Breakers tie the teams more closely with geographical features of the franchise. The stadia differ in size and affiliation to a degree that is a departure from the use of large mainstream auditoria, as in WNBA and Women's World Cup 1999. Atlanta's use of the Bobby Dodd Stadium, which has a capacity of 46,000 and originally opened in 1913, contrasted with Boston's use of three potential sites for home games ranging from the 6,000 seat Zimman Field, the campus of Tufts University, Medford or Foxboro Stadium. The Bay Area Cyber Rays share Spartan Stadium (26,000) with the newly formed male team, the San Jose Earthquakes. It is a university-based field, as is the Tempest's University of North Carolina Fetzer Field with a capacity of 5,700.

The expectation is that the Carolina franchise, for example, will move in 2003 to a football-only complex and the aim of the whole league is to eventually play in soccer-specific arenas. The April start runs concurrently with Major League Soccer, so college-based spectators for women's teams are a primary market, though it also allows for double header games. Television fans are also sought in alternative ways; for example, the Women's Soccer Challenge tour of six-a-side teams to promote the new league was sponsored by and aired on Discovery Health Channel. The burden of helping to create sports specific arenas for display is not one that the WNBA had to face but remains an issue for women's professional leagues around the world. WUSA has not only to establish itself but also to ensure that it is sufficiently installed to create new sites for the sport in the United States. Whether the relatively small numbers of regular live supporters can become a critical mass of fans year on year remains to be seen. Women's football in England and Europe has the opposite problem to soccer in the United States because the men's game is so ubiquitous. Any proposed professional league would have to negotiate a path between the WNBA line of presenting a feminised version of a mainstream male sport and the WUSA strategy of tapping into alternative live support and a mainstream televised audience.

One aspect of professionalism that the organisers of WUSA have really pioneered is that the success of any sport on the professional level depends on its ability to generate revenues from gate receipts and television rights. Women's football in England in its current form does not lend itself to mass spectatorship in the form of ticket purchasing fans or a large audience, and until this changes professionalisation is unlikely to occur to any significant degree. The consuming public must be interested, able and willing to pay. Current English plans to fund a women's professional league through satellite television are less than straightforward. This has been the crux in moving from launch to establishment in WUSA's second year of operation. The creation of a discrete identity for the possible English or European league or the extension of some form of the men's game will be instrumental in how the venture presents itself.

Following the success of Women's World Cup 1999 Julie Foudy and the US national team players insisted on not integrating with the men of MLS but instead forming their own league.[20] The owners are uniquely a group of cable companies including Time Warner, Cox and Com Cast and the players sign a contract with the franchise, not a particular team. Rather than forming a league and selling it to television, the companies own the league and so every minute of every match is televised, in addition to screening promotional advertisements. From February to April 2001 Cox Communications ran 4,500 thirty-second promotional advertisements for its team, the San Diego Spirit. The combination of investors has the advantage of regional and national coverage. However, the national cable rating for the inaugural match, even with Mia Hamm playing, was a disappointing 0.5 per cent. Dan Novak of Cox has said, 'We all realise that this is bigger than just sports. This isn't just another new sports league. It has culture changing potential' (Zeigler, 2001). While the investors expect to lose money for four years, the challenge of the wholesome image of WUSA in defining a niche for itself in live support and on television remains considerable. Nevertheless there are signs that the league is of benefit to the wider women's football community at elite level; for instance, after the first four games of WUSA 2001 all the goals had been scored by foreign-draft players. Whether it contributes to US tournament success will be shown in China 2003.

Having explored the role of the United States university campuses as sites for the professional league, the collegiate system offers a unique example for women to play sport that may lead to a professional career. Professional leagues have been pioneered in Italy since the early 1970s and in Japan since the early 1990s, and players in a variety of countries have earned a living as semi-professionals from the sport. Only in the United States can the decision to pursue an education to graduate level and to develop one's playing capacity to elite level be reconciled. Such is the popularity of this route that three of the current England senior women's squad hold, or have completed, scholarships in America: Kelly Smith at Seton Hall, Rachel Brown at Alabama and Danielle Murphy at Florida. Kelly Smith, having graduated, is now assistant coach, plays for WUSA at a salary of $45,000 and appeared in the World All Star team to promote the new league. Compared with Gill Coulthard and Sue Smith (also a World All Star player before the 1999 World Cup) who both made a conscious decision not to go to the United States, Kelly Smith's potential future professional career as a player, coach and media personality could be derived solely from football. The move across the Atlantic by talented female players is tacitly accepted as offering the most scope, even by elite players who decide not to go:

> I've had three or four offers from various universities and I have thought about it because it is a big thing over there, but I just feel that the Americans are stealing our players which I don't like. But it is a great opportunity – it's a tough one. If you look at their prospectuses compared to ours it's unbelievable.

However, the US collegiate scheme has been described as an expensive, institutionalised system dominated by male champions in major sport. In establishing and maintaining organised youth programmes the college model is often justified by the participation opportunities provided for the youngsters. M. Ann Hall has critiqued this view:

> The less able see the team may win if they do not play . . . Professionalizing sport down to the high school level is one of the greatest enemies of general health and fitness that we have.
>
> (Hall, 1996: 3)

Intercollegiate sport is itself a diversified phenomenon. However, progress has been patchy. The increase in funding stipulated by Title IX saw a dramatic rise in male head coaches for women's programmes and this is mirrored in the new professional league, with Marcia McDermott of the Carolina Courage as the only female Head Coach. Acosta and Carpenter's longitudinal study regarding the effect of Title IX on women's athletic programmes in the US found that in 1972, 90 per cent of women's athletic programmes run by female administrators compared with 15.9 per cent in

1990. While the average number of administrators of athletics per institution in 1990 was 2.35 the average number of women was 0.76 (Acosta and Carpenter, 1994: 4–6). This is unlikely to indicate limited experience on behalf of women in the coaching ranks as the rise in opportunity for male coaches in women's sport is a clear trend in England and the United States. It would be useful to examine how far-reaching this tendency is across other nations.

The growth in female participation in soccer at collegiate level appears to be accelerating. In 1979 there were seventeen women's collegiate programmes for soccer, but 387 teams and 8,226 players were reported in 1992–3. This rose to 515 teams and 10,909 players in 1994–5, with a rise of over a hundred teams the following season (620) and an increase of players in the region of 20 per cent to 13,277. Given that the overall numbers of women athletes increased from 99,859 in 1992 to 123,832 in 1996 soccer is growing at a faster rate than most other women's collegiate sport. Basketball, for example, increased from 827 to 962 teams during the same period and volleyball from 784 to 910 (Curtis and Grant, 2000: 8–12). The growth is not mirrored in men's collegiate soccer, because the lure of an MLS career might tempt a male player possibly to terminate his college career. However, collegiate opportunity provides the best route for elite women players in the US and this looks likely to continue. This is unlike the English system where teams based in schools and colleges are also a growth area but are not the main route for elite players to develop their ability or for national selection. The traditional women's teams such as Doncaster Belles, Premiership affiliated teams such as Arsenal and, most recently, the semi-professional Fulham playing in the English Women's Premiership are the main providers of representative players. The place of educational establishments in an international culture of women's football is critical to an understanding of female football at participation and elite level. The idiosyncrasy of the English case and the rather different attributes of the US model suggest this topic to be in need of amplification, particularly the role of players in defining their own involvement.

In the question of participation as opposed to elite development, the National Soccer Participation Survey reported that in 1994 there were 16.4 million individuals playing soccer at least once a year, up 8 per cent from 1992 (Soccer Line, 1994: 6–8). This includes 12.2 million children (under the age of 18) who play. The total increase in female participation was the largest at 16 per cent to 6.7 million, predominantly from the under-18 age group as adult participation totalled 4.2 million (Soccer Line, 1994: 6). In moving on to look at how certain groups have created participatory cultures, the majority of women's participation in the US is as yet under-researched. There has been little inquiry made which compiles the diversity of recreational, competitive and non-elite representative leagues in the US and so the examples can do no more than scratch the surface of a broader issue.

The variety of playing identities is such that a comprehensive analysis is not possible in the space, but includes as possible categories religious competition (for example the Maccabi games), or ethnicity (the Native American games), or sexuality (the Gay Games) and combinations of identity. Analyses of the correlation between sport participation and academic achievement for certain groups have begun. For example, 39 per cent of Hispanic girl athletes scored in the top quartile of a standardised academic test compared with 23 per cent of non-athletes, and rural Hispanic girls athletes were found to have lower drop-out rates and were more likely to go to a four-year college than non-athletes. However, the same study found that black girls who cease to participate in sports are more likely to have problems with transportation or inadequate funds.[21] It would be useful to extend this kind of investigation to see who has, and who does not have, access to recreative and participant women's football in the United States and in other countries. As a voluntaristic initiative peopled by enthusiasts, one aspect contributing to international growth is this construction of a playing community beyond (usually preceding) centrally administered and bureaucratised manifestations of the game. Though specialised, *La Opinion* is probably the most powerful Spanish language publication in the US and its associate publisher served on the Women's World Cup advisory board. In spite of a bias in favour of the Latin community and men's teams in a number of articles, the assignation of reporters familiar with coaches and players was well ahead of English language newspapers' coverage of women's football, particularly Rigoberto Cervantez's analytical, highly technical analysis. The distinctive forms of play are highly organised and reflect a deep level of engagement, to the degree that participatory culture is the principal dimension of women's football.

Certain groups have created involvement that also features a high level of competition. The Nike-sponsored W-League, known also as the Swizzle, fills the post-collegiate gap. The two-month summer league includes college players and enables ex-elite players to disseminate their expertise of the game to younger team-mates. In contrast to the centralised media, another aspect of football's popularity is as a celebration of gay women by, for example, *Roxxie*. Originally begun as an underground magazine along the lines of other fanzines, *Girljock* has become so popular that the production values have improved and books compiled of previous articles and stories released. The style is a pastiche of male sports magazines, by its own description 'the joy to be had when sports meets humour meets libido' (*Roxxie*, 1998: cover blurb). Brian Pronger has characterised similar initiatives as a Euro-American phenomenon:

> In most European and American cities, lesbian and gay sports groups are the largest community organisations . . . Gay community competitive sports are essentially the same as masters' sports, or ethnic and other sports where participation is a high priority.
>
> (Pronger, 1999: 375)

The lesbian sports movement as the 'product of old time gay/lesbian bar leagues . . . and the newer Gay Games movement: both coupled with the gay/lesbian visibility/rights movements' (Pronger, 1999: 376) is another aspect of the sport that has to be addressed internationally through research. In theoretical terms academics call upon women athletes to resist discrimination against lesbian women.[22] A San Francisco football tournament, 'The Festival of the Babes', looks set to move in the right direction as it is advertised as being open to lesbians and 'those willing to be mistaken for lesbians' so this community and participatory ethos looks likely to be extended. For example, the Gay and Lesbian World Cup was first held in 1995 between teams from Europe and North America and now includes teams from outside the West. Certainly more progressive attitudes by governing bodies, in school and in the media, would help but given the persistence of terms such as 'family values' there is a considerable way to go before this occurs.

In spite of these positive elements the persistence of inequality is an enduring feature of women's sport, including football, in the United States as in the rest of the world. In addition to the financial, educational and media privilege given to men, this inequality is due to types of argument used in American law. The Fifth Amendment of the US Constitution guarantees equal protection of the law to all persons found within the United States. However, sex is not deemed to be a class in the same way that race and national origin are. Nor is sport a fundamental right; consequently, women may be excluded from athletic participation upon the showing of the 'separate but equal' policy common elsewhere. When separate teams do not exist, however, both sexes may have an opportunity to try out and players can meet the necessary physical requirements on an individual basis. The disputes between the women's national team and US Soccer show clearly that women's lower pay is not a matter of equality but of segregated labour markets and the under-evaluation of women's work. In spite of the continuity of demonstrably unequal treatment, it is significant that the US team are sufficiently successful to be able to dispute their terms with the governing body in their country. The English national team players are in no such position and are heavily reliant on the patronage and continued sponsorship of the FA. Also important in this regard are women's organisations, which are more sophisticated activists than in Europe, contacting US Soccer in relation to disputes but also targeting US Soccer's sponsors.[23]

The US also shares with other nations the tiny proportion of women in decision-making bodies of both national and international football federations and players' unions. Concerted action by women sports performers and football players particularly could improve both information and bargaining power. Though extremely modest in any national association's budget, the subscriptions paid by players and, more importantly, funding drawn down on their behalf are resources over which women could contest in order to improve opportunities. On an international level, new forms of communication are another resource that could be utilised to form communities of women players to initiate action. Consideration of the Namibian case provides further points of comparison with England. The women interviewed for this study valued a sense of fair play and the enhancement of physical fitness and used words like 'team', 'co-operation' and 'play'. However, the Namibian women also experienced sport as a male competitive activity that takes place in a privatised space. In spite of a lack of formal enclosure on many playing fields, women were prevented from playing on marked-out pitches because of taboos related to their sex. Another internationally consistent feature of women's right to play is the gendered use of geographical space. In addition, issues were also raised about access to transport and problems of competition over large distances; that is, questions beyond the sport itself affecting participation, which also affect women everywhere but more acutely in large countries with developing communications infrastructures.[24]

Namibia has been concerned to develop a positive sense of nationalism post-independence, and since the percentage of Namibian women playing and administering football remains extremely small this case study provides a useful counterpoint to European and American understandings of women's sport, and football, particularly. Women's rights to education and health have been throughout the world a question of debate and struggle. How realistic might it be to talk about a woman's human right to participation in sport is a key theme of the chapter as a whole. Hence the reason for choosing Namibia in 1998, as with other cases the theoretical right to participation is difficult to enforce in practice. Another point of comparison is the interaction of governmental and FA departments. Although Namibia held trials for World Cup qualifying matches sponsored by the Ministry for Youth and Sport at the instigation of the first female Minister for Sport, Penduke Ivanthana, the team was prevented at the last minute from representing its country when the national association withdrew its support in early 1998. This was the case in eight other African national associations. The $1 million due from FIFA in 2000 made football associations fairly wealthy and the influence of equity programmes was further limited by the refusal of FIFA to stipulate the proportion of money to be spent on women's participation.

Global organisations link women's sport with other advances in human rights, particularly educational progress:

> Increasingly, in the development literature, education for females is being recognised as crucial to development, not just of women and girls, but for the social and economic development of whole cultures and nations: 'Girls' education correlates positively with several important national and international goals, including universal primary education, economic productivity, social development, social equity and sustainability of development efforts.' UNICEF 1992.
>
> (Talbot, 1998: 1)

The difficulty of this approach is that health and education are often provided as services by governments and a rights approach is therefore viable. In contrast, women's rights with regard to sport are often rhetorical rather than legally enforceable and where sport is provided by independent organisations of different codes, some of the most blatant discrimination in access and resources is evident. There are also competing definitions of physical education, sport and leisure activity that someone from a non-African background has to appreciate. In 1998 Elizabeth Chitika, Deputy Minister of Sport, Youth and Child Development of Zambia gave as the theme of her speech to the Second World Conference on Women and Sport, 'Educate a man and you educate an individual, educate a woman and you educate a nation'. She summed up three main aims in sport development: physical education in schools, sport for all, including community-based and township programmes, and investment in coaching and sports leaders. Her highest ambition was that 'it will not be long before the Football Association of Zambia is headed by a lady' (Chitika, 1998). The aims and objectives appear familiar but the context very different. There is continuity in that, as Margaret Talbot has indicated,

> Physical Education has not yet managed to persuade parents or policy makers that it is actually an important vocational area. It is worth remembering that in the EU, sport and recreation accounts for around 1.5% GNP; and offers more jobs in the UK than the car industry, agriculture, fisheries and food combined!
>
> (Talbot, 1998: 2)

However, in Africa several nations have overlapping developmental concerns but with different priorities. The representative from Swaziland highlighted leadership and training, participation and excellence as economic and social barriers, related to the traditional role of women, particularly the high rate of teenage pregnancy, which inhibit girls with potential from becoming elite athletes. Ideas of leisure time can also differ as girls use free time to cook, sew and complete household tasks. The wider remit for sporting development is also as a means of reaching out to youth at risk of drugs, Aids, teenage pregnancy and criminal activities. In football particularly this is a key theme for engaging young people in safe activities, and not just in Namibia. For example, the Mathare Youth Sport Association operates separate soccer leagues for girls and boys in the townships of Nairobi where winning teams are awarded three points in league standings, but teams who help to clean the environment are awarded six points (Commonwealth Games Association of Canada, 1998: 3). Also under the same scheme, Beauty Nyoni is a blind goalkeeping coach who took a qualification in sports leadership and travels to rural areas to assist with disabled youth sport development. Initiatives like this are funded by the Commonwealth Sport Development Programme and are relatively low-cost activities; the UK Sport Council committed £25,000 for 1997–8 (Commonwealth Games Association of Canada, 1998: 3).

The Namibian Director General of Women's Affairs situated sport in the immense pressures facing African women:

> It is recorded that about 50% of African women are married by the age of eighteen. In many rural areas women spend up to 50 hours per week on domestic work and subsistence food production . . . studies have shown that women work 12–13 hours a week more than men . . . Cuts in social sector spending have moved substantial costs from the state to the household. The unpaid workload of caring for the young, aged and sick (especially HIV sufferers) has increased.
>
> (Nandi-Ndaitwah 1998: 2–3)

In some rural areas, such as Okavango, the population is predominantly young; women, the majority of whom are under 20 years of age, head many households. Additionally the high number of widows is an important factor, as 50 per cent of all households and 80 per cent of female-headed households are below the subsistence line and half of those are considered to be in abject poverty (Voluntary Services Overseas 1997a: 14). This region has one of the fastest growing populations and constituted almost 10 per cent of the total population of Namibia as at 1994. In a country which is 40 per cent desert, 70 per cent of black Namibians live in the north and are mainly engaged in subsistence agriculture (Bergmar, 1997: 3). Western ideas of leisure, for example walking as a popular activity, are not directly applicable as many of the women involved in subsistence agriculture and labour intensive household chores routinely walk several miles a day in the course of these duties. In contrast to western sedentary lifestyles the use of leisure to recuperate and rest was seen as essential by some Namibian women. Nevertheless a German coach working in Namibia in 1994 reported up to 160 girls, some prepared to walk several miles, at her training sessions, 'Many of the girls I met were very talented, but there were several among them who, given appropriate regular training, would have no problem holding their own in one of the top German teams.'

In Namibia 1994 saw the development of a Ministry for Youth and Sport which, by 1995 presented the first Namibia Sports Bill, creating a syllabus for physical education. The importance given to football, netball and volleyball as relatively cheap team games in schools where the majority of learners are boarders means that there are pools of players in one place and games are an alternative to less healthy uses of time (Voluntary Service Overseas 1997a: 10). Consequently schools and the university team are potentially vital to the development of the sport outside of the capital and Otjiwarango in central Namibia.[25] However, as with other nations, the relative control by government authorities and sports administrations is contested, with consequences that do little to help women sports participants generally and women who wish to take part in organised football particularly.

The 1995 Sports Act introduced by the Ministry of Youth and Sport was formulated to counteract haphazard and inequitable sporting practices. Previously, funding had been dependent upon the number of political regions the code was practised in and how many registered participants it had. The effects of apartheid, wherein small numbers of participants in urban areas, usually white, claimed for support from government at the expense of mass participatory black codes, have tended to linger. The Namibian Schools Sports Union (NSSU), used this to emphasise a need for elite competition in a very few codes. For this reason the use of educational establishments to develop women's football has been limited so far.

> It is virtually impossible for any schools sport union in Southern Africa to meet international standards in all disciplines. Strategic choices must be made as to which areas and activities are likely to produce the greatest development benefits for NSSU. The choice thus, is whether to increase the number of codes or rather to focus on identified and prioritised disciplines.
>
> (Gertze, 1997: 13)

The relative control and power of the NSSU and the Ministry was further complicated by the role of the football association. An initial problem was that soccer was funded directly by the Ministry of Youth and Sport, but then the funding was given over to the Football Association. This both weakened the commission and exempted soccer from the general ethos of sports for all initiated by the ministry. The importance of football to national identity in Namibia has grown at the same time as the power relations between the ministry and other stakeholders, including the NSSU, the football association and women's rights movements, have disputed their right to control resources. The Brave Warriors, the national men's team, lost 2-1 in their first friendly international against Saudi Arabia and this led to a call for proper structures for talent development and administration with many players gaining valuable experience by playing in South African professional leagues.

> Namibia, as the politically, economically and socially youngest African country, qualified amongst the best 16 of the African continent. Currently, Namibia is ranked 80 in the World and 20 in Africa. However, this ranking will change following the excellent performance in Mozambique and Gabon respectively.
>
> (Gertze, 1997: 19)

Post-independence, the Brave Warriors have become an important vehicle for Namibian nationalism following the retirement of Frank Fredericks and

Monica Dahl. The knock-on effect of this for women's football is that the national association has the choice of whether to spend the funds it has on developing the game for all as a participatory and competitive activity or to fund the Brave Warriors to achieve international victory.

Julien Garises, the President of the Women's Soccer Association, launched in 1992, suggests that 95 per cent of female players are school age or college students. Pauline Yemm, a sports development officer for the Voluntary Service Overseas (VSO) programme supports this picture.[26] But women's football is not entirely a youth sport. The majority of potential players still live in the rural areas designated as communal areas or Bantusans by the South African administration before 1992. Noticeable in the press cuttings from *The Namibian* and from my own visit is that football for women is predominantly a non-white sport.[27] The biggest financial supporter in women's football to date has been the government. However, the major contribution has been on behalf of the women themselves.

On 21 June 1997 ten teams participated in the selection process for the national squad. With the trials following a national tournament in Windhoek there was considerable enthusiasm. The geographical problems facing possible players are evident from the Kavango region team who began to travel to the trials on the previous day at 4 a.m. One of the first teams to be established, City Girls, is perhaps unsurprisingly based in Windhoek, but in other regions the existence of further education establishments provide a focus for women's teams such as Luderitz and Rundu. International influence is evident in the Otjiwarongo Manchester XI. As in other countries, occupational teams also have a presence, such as Houmoed FC, the Namibian Police team. All ten teams competed for selection on one day and so games began at 6 a.m. on 21 June to avoid the heat, and were played until after dark under floodlights. The decision of the Namibian Football Association to withdraw the entry of the team at the last minute from the first African Women's Football Championship in the Democratic Republic of Congo in April 1998 due to lack of funds therefore looks especially harsh given the efforts to select a squad. More so since the decision came only three days before the team were due to fly out to Burkina Faso to play the Kabila Queens for the first round of the tournament.

Following the trials selected players were invited to attend a training camp before the COSAFA tournament, at which they were also invited to complete their high school examinations. The success of the initiative in a short space of time was achievable because of existing patterns of provision, such as educational and university buildings. The use of VSO initiatives is one way in which sport, including football, in Africa, Asia and the Caribbean could be developed. A Namibian VSO post was supported with help from the Sports Council and in response to the Commonwealth Heads of Government communiqué in 1993. Recognising the role of sport in development is itself a change in the view of the VSO from:

> The feeling that 'real' development had more to do with doctors, engineers and the like – and that sport belonged more to the good things in life . . . it is undeniably true that there is a great deal more to the human development process than is met solely by work in these sectors.[28]

Including football as one of several women's sports was a departure for the programme traditionally concerned with public, usually reproductive, health since it began as a fill-in year for public schoolboys between A levels and a degree, and now covers 1,700 volunteers in fifty-five countries. At some schools there are no physical education teachers available and the subject is not taught. As at 1996, 5 per cent of the total number of teachers trained in this field and 90 per cent of those worked in Windhoek and Swamkomund, with two of the seven educational regions having people in post as regional level subject advisors so voluntary work is crucial to development within schools as well as beyond (Voluntary Service Overseas: 10).

Since the withdrawal of the national team in 1998, women's football has improved steadily in Namibia, in large part because of the determination of Julian Garises, another in the long line of individuals promoting women's football. However educational establishments continue to be an underdeveloped resource. Also the pattern of progression has not been steady or the result of an enlightened view by the football administration. The importance of football as a code in Southern Africa, and the need for independent financial support, are indicated when one team, the Soweto Ladies, received R50,000 from Pasta Romagna for 1993 alone. In that year the Namibia Pilchards Women's Soccer Tournament (the most prestigious competition) had sponsorship for N$10,000. In contrast, the central association only supported the Namibian Women's Soccer Association Challenge Cup 1995 to the tune of N$1,000 (Angula, 1995). The N$10,000 sponsorship of the preview tournament to national team trials by J.R. Watkins Cosmetics in April 1997 was consequently a major development, with the winning team, City FC, benefiting by N$3,000. Beyond this, economic support was shown to be fragile when matches against an invitational South African side, Tsakane, left the Women's Association practically bankrupt at the same time as the Namibian side won against their more experienced rivals.

Tournaments with other African nations will be valuable to future development. The Swaziland All Women Soccer Tournament for example brings together South Africa, Mozambique, Lesotho, Botswana, Namibia and Zimbabwe. There is also increased bureaucratic representation with the formation of the Confederation of Southern African Football Associations of a women's desk to provide an initial point of contact and subsequently an executive committee. Namibia was elected as chair of the committee to draft a constitution. However, the extent of the withdrawal of women's teams in Africa from the first round of the Women's World Cup in 1998 suggests more than financial decisions to be operating. The decisions by

Angola, Botswana, Malawai, Zambia and Zimbabwe not to compete in the qualifying tournament were taken without the knowledge of the women who head the women's football section, as their complaints to a FIFA representative made clear in May of that year.[29] Since for the first time Africa had two places in the 1999 Women's World Cup, Namibia, Congo, Lesotho, Mozambique, Swaziland and South Africa had a chance of progressing to the tournament. The eventual chance for Egypt to compete came as a result of the withdrawal of several nations. Since each of those above had decided to enter a team which was then withdrawn at the last moment it remains to be seen whether at future World Cups African women are permitted to take part in competition. Perhaps touring teams, such as a German Universities side in 1994, could be used to build performance, to encourage further international co-operation and to provide competition.

FIFA's decision not to stipulate the level of funding for female development programmes leaves each women's section in national football associations to fight its corner in relative isolation. For example, in Nigeria, Africa's top female side, Islamic sharia law has been imposed in the North West State of Zamfara, where women's football has been pronounced un-Islamic. At the same time, the Nigerian team won the CAF 2000 women's tournament, competed in Sydney 2000 and their midfield player 'Marvellous' Mercy Aikide is the only African foreign draft in the Women's USA league.[30] Women's football in Namibia, in Africa and on the international stage is likely to remain contested and diverse within nations as well as between societies. As yet, there is no forum for women within the sport to express their shared experience and their difference in authoring the future of their sport. As this chapter has repeatedly shown, significant individuals are advocates of women's football. Whether some form of coalition would replicate the problems found in women's sport movements and international associations raised in this chapter remains to be seen. It is likely, though, that without a definition from those within women's football about how they perceive the sport, the local, national and international identity will continue to be controlled by men.

This chapter has gone some way toward extending the argument that women's football is a regionally widespread game with a cross-class, cross-race following and an identity which is not necessarily urban. It is not, in the passive sense, a reflection of development programmes of centralised administrations. Similarly the view of a relatively non-interacting regional population of players is too restrictive. Considerable intra-national and international competition is taking place and the increase in speed of growth of these tournaments is notable. However, it would go too far to say that women's football is a globally popular game either with participants, administrations or spectators.

Calls to improve the image of women's and girls' football, for better media coverage and for more women representatives on administrative committees in the bureaucracy of football are continuities across the international community. The involvement of ex-players is a key growth area, as is the need for co-ordination of school-based sport into adult participative cultures. More controversially, the possible age limit of mixed teams could be raised and genuine vocational opportunities provided to female players and coaches. At the same time Women's World Cup 1999 and the inauguration of Women's USA are likely to be of considerable significance for women's sport generally and football particularly, not just in the US. In summary, the women who played football who agreed to speak to me felt their perception of capability to be an important factor in sport participation. Volunteers, players and administrators invest an enormous amount of time and energy in women's football-related activity. By making plain the value of participation, perhaps the sport could move toward a redefinition of its current status. It seems peculiarly inappropriate to use static models of football and 'women's football' in sport in a world that has become more culturally plural. It would be most encouraging to think that we had begun to move to an era where these kinds of constructs become redundant as the complexity of players' experience of sport, including football, is developed.

Conclusions

A female future for a man's game?

In looking at issues of professionalism in women's football, the starting point was to ask what purposes does the conceptualisation of gender difference serve? The beliefs discussed in Chapter 4 are inherently conservative and should be disentangled, subject to critical enquiry and directly addressed. It is so normal, everyday and accepted to separate women and men, boys and girls in football though that it has been virtually ignored as an academic topic. Little is known about the variety of ways that players make meaning in everyday ways in their sport, and the legislation that affects women's access to competitive sport indicates the danger of defining people as collections. On the basis of respectful engagement, there are important commonalitites as well as differences between the individuals, groups and communities of football players and analysis of the collective enterprise of the creation, maintenance and repair of group culture and personal identity could be made much more widespread.

Individual cases regarding women players and coaches are examples of the continuing struggle to make a difference in women's status in football. The investment in gender difference by ruling bodies and in the principle of female amateurism provides a certain kind of control over this. We clearly need to invest in new forms of meaning to change the conditions of football as authentically male.

Women's football has been contested only twice at Olympic level and has had some success with spectators in the Atlanta Games but less with international TV audiences. The message of the Olympic movement for the future of women's sport is mixed. On the one hand, other recently accepted sports, such a beach volleyball, have stipulated that women players wear sports uniforms that are very revealing.[1] It is possible that the televisual success of the latter could influence other sports governing bodies to tailor women's sports uniforms for greater erotic effect. In WUSA this has not yet happened but the topic was debated in WNBA with seven possible kinds of uniform suggested. At the present time the soccer uniform for women and men is remarkably similar but this could change if football becomes more like other women's sports in order to appeal, at elite level, to a television audience. Alternatively, if we overlook the kinds of participation made likely by the move to professionalism and look at increased participation *per se* then FIFA's involvement with the Olympics could produce gains for players and administrators that are not currently forthcoming from within the International Federation's own structures

It is possible to describe an international dimension to women's football but it is debatable whether the interests of those participants are represented in the preoccupations of FIFA or the Olympic movement. Several kinds of elite communities were present at the Women's World Cup 1999 in the United States, but very different ideas of collectivism were operating in Namibia in the April of 1998 as women travelled twelve hours to take part in national trials. It would be possible to conduct international comparisons by looking at, for example the year national football associations assume control of women's football, the league structure in each country, the number of teams, the number of players, the national team structure, the number of women officials, sponsorship arrangements, television coverage and the status of mixed football, to suggest a few themes. However, without examining how women engage in producerly activity with regard to football, the nuts and bolts of female participation, the picture will be incomplete. As a cultural activity the process of making play is a source of empowerment, though privilege and value are accorded to only a few elite athletes. Though the demographic profile of the female player may radically differ along with distinctive interpretations of the game, organisational aspects and so on, women are creating, performing and distributing knowledge about football in cultures of production.

Though there has been evidence of a shift in the perception of football as an appropriate game for women worldwide, there is still a tendency to devalue female participation in international football. Domestic and international strategies for expanding the numbers of women playing football in very recent years have correlated with the partial integration of female sections into long-existing administrative structures. Women appear to have joined the family of football as uninvited late arrivals and are currently attempting to ingratiate themselves with paternalists who have extended a lukewarm welcome. In this sense, the English Football Association policy of presenting female players to the public as belonging to a different branch of the family is representative of other national and international sports organisations.

Increased participation and elite success are crucial elements of the development of football for women in this era, according to football authorities. However, players suggest that enjoyment of a personal and collective hobby is the main reason for their engagement. One aspect of the study has been to examine how shared ideas and opinions emerge in the community and how these mutual understandings shape strategic choices. For instance, women's football has moved away from what could be called its traditional focal point of spectator-supported leisure but elements of this remain. By the end of the 1990s it had consolidated its place in international multi-event entertainment, such as the Olympic Games, and in its own right with Women's World Cup matches broadcast around the globe. In this decade, women's football has developed a public relations profile with FIFA leading the way in licensed products and sponsorship, now extended by the Women's USA franchise. These initiatives have been underpinned by a radical change in tactics by the leaders of football administration who, until the 1980s, did not want to include women in the football community. As the privately held material has shown, the financial and bureaucratic patronage of these associations has been overstated as a catalyst for increased participation and the localised enthusiasm of collectives of players underestimated. Yet much remains to be known about the factors that contributed to the emergence of these new ideas in the bureaucracies. Even less defined is the relationship between the mass of players and the tiny pinnacle presented to the public in mediated forms of the sport.

In some key respects the widespread adoption of female play by national associations and by professional sports organisations remains partial and disputed. Women's football in England has yet to gain a positive high profile and remains a distinctly unglamorous sport, especially when compared with the United States. The techniques employed by sport to enter public and corporate markets, including the use of new technologies, have influenced women's football to the extent that long-term objectives to establish professional leagues necessarily involve sponsorship and patronage by valued media partners, television in particular. So if cable television companies have provided an opportunity for a professional league in the United States, independent of the tradition of male teams and franchises on the one hand, on the other, the belief in gender-segregated sport emerges as a defining feature of the institutionalisation of women's football. At the same time, the absence of a public memory of a history of women's football contributes to the idea of participation as recently fashionable and Chapter 1 illustrated how this view had come to be the academic and popular consensus. The issue of how to present the female player, live or televised, to a fee-paying public is one current issue affected by this interpretation of difference.

The vast majority of English women will not play football during their lifetime. To date there is no English women's professional league. Instead there are a handful of semi-professional players and thousands of amateur women and girls whose play is watched by a smattering of spectators. In the home of football, women's football has no home, in a local or national sense. Chapter 2 outlined how there has been an unbroken tradition of communities of teams, clubs and leagues, playing in periods of concentrated and more interrupted, distributed participation. The increase in the number of women participants since the 1960s has largely come about as the result of a loose alliance of devotees that accordingly demonstrates continuity from an earlier model. This has influenced the quality and quantity of playing opportunities at key moments, for better and for worse. Encouragingly, in 2002 the mass of female participation in England still relies on the voluntarism that played such a major role in the early stages of women's football and this has endured in a diffuse and flexible way. In this sense, at the level of organising play, women control their own sport.

Less positively, the tradition of over seventy years of spectator-supported entertainment is much less in evidence in contemporary women's play. This seems to be one of the strong indicators that one could not ignore the relationship between participation and politics, even if the players wanted to see football in an insular way. A paradoxical gentlemanly political correctness operates otherwise, whereby equal but different sports policy discriminates against women, sometimes unintentionally, because they are seen as an essentially dissimilar cohort of players to men and therefore deserving of discrete treatment. The nature of equality is therefore twisted to mean something like protecting women from male play, which in practice defends and privileges masculinity.

For most of the period under question in England women's football as an organised competitive activity has been the confine of adults. This is remarkable in itself and to develop our understanding of this Chapter 3 looked at the public and private memory of this. It goes beyond a change in British society since the 1960s where women have tended to participate in activities virtually reserved for men. For example, the current debates about whether women should be deployed as combat troops or in peace-keeping roles is another case where individuals are subject to legislation based on the classification of women as a group. In this sense the taboos that surround women's access to football are evident in other traditionally male occupations. In this way mixed competitive football remains inconceivable for the majority of male and female participants and the general public. Football is not as serious as life and death and yet for a woman to compete in a formally sanctioned leisure activity against men is unimaginable. The constructedness of this cultural practice incorporates numerous minor conflicts and the various kinds of memory in women's football suggests the need for a transformation of our understanding of the female player but also of sporting custom and English social history. Players therefore describe aspects of female-based leisure as offering social and sporting experience which is absorbing and stimulating. This enjoyment is carefully protected as appealing but not part of wider activism or a feminist persona. The distance between the practical demonstration of support for other women and a theoretical reflection on women's rights is one that requires more attention.

In suggesting the need for a revision of gender in Chapter 4 the dominant structures and discourses are shown to be exclusionary by design. Difference is used in another way throughout the thesis, to include both multiplicity and similarity in women's experiences of football. Practically and conceptually, the way we think about gender in football should be subject to revision and change because it is not just in the increased bureaucratisation of the sport itself that these practices have been institutionalised but also in wider social and cultural systems. The liberal reformism implied by a fast-growing sport can be questioned in favour of a more controversial radicalism to argue that protected employment opportunities for male players and coaches have been depoliticised and need to be challenged. Increased participation has yet to lead to a critical mass of female play and if we are to accelerate change then these wider imbalances require revision through targeted advocacy and revision of legislation and practice.

For the majority of girls in the survey football meant informal mixed games and a kick about until puberty, and school-based feminine appropriate team games after adolescence. By the time that the Women's Football Association was formed in 1969, the seeds of change for the status of the male player were sown. Early attempts to formalise alliances to develop and administer women's football were characterised by limited resources and disagreements about the future direction of the sport. Rapid increases in the number of players in the mid-1980s reflected the strength and the weakness of voluntary efforts of the administrators who had limited time but ensured continuity through their long-term commitment. Recent interest and recognition in academic circles has coincided with the patronage of football authorities in the 1990s. In contrast, the determined women players have such a varied and complex history that much remains to be found and presented. The images shown to me by the players suggest an illusive glimpse of football as part of the daily round for women players and the variety of clothing is alone enough to prompt further inquiry. The work has attempted to begin to explore the noticeable gap between theory and practice in women's sport, particularly in football, by attempting to link the material conditions of women's play with academic knowledge of some female experiences of that leisure.

A key question for the sport and the players remains the extent to which women are playing their own game. The difference in status accorded men's and women's elite football is immense, as we could expect. So profound has the effect of the 1921 ban been on the legitimacy of women's involvement that it is difficult to talk about female mass participation in this country in the near future. In and around football, changes in attitude are becoming more evident. The media's role is largely conspicuous by its absence in the history of women's football. Apart from some national and local newspapers and Channel 4 television in the 1980s, coverage has been sporadic and women players share more with other female athletes in this regard than with male footballers in having considerable and substantive ground to make up. So a clear vision of woman as footballer was difficult to determine from these sources, whereas women players offered often celebratory definitions of their playing persona and the ethos of the team. One of the ways our understanding of the term 'player' can develop from this is to focus on those individual practices and actions that form a sense of agency.

There is an international insistence on the feminine nature of women's football. The control, like the definition, of football for women depends upon the patronage of the sport's authorities who, in turn, are keen to differentiate between men and women players. The social and cultural expectations of women's behaviour have changed during the period of this study but women's opportunities as players are confined to those achieved by women's football, not football as such. The inaugural season of the first professional league in the United States, the third in the world after Italian and Japanese business-sponsored leagues, has been partially successful. Bright and beautiful players who are idolised by spectators create the wholesome image of the league. This is mutually beneficial as the league and the players are becoming valuable commodities. Given the dominance of masculine sports in the United States there remains some way to go to establish the league but in England there is discussion of using satellite companies to promote a professional women's league, and a European Cup (now in its second year) could form another potential route to professionalisation. The transferability of the model of ownership by television companies will be complicated in both models by the absence of a favourable image for the sport, the lack of a fan base at spectator level and the obvious difference in male and female playing standards at elite level in Europe.

Nevertheless the women's version of the game has its own fragile memory that reflects the players, aspects of community and beyond. We can observe recent changes to this construct as education-based football for females represents a shift in the balance of participation but also in bureaucratic relations. At elite level, central administrators are increasingly intent on mirroring male professional systems. The current English tactic of locating Centres of Excellence in local Football League clubs and elite Academies in educational settings is a new moment in the problematic placement of the sport. Women's relationship to football has made a social and cultural impact. There are obvious parallels with other women's sports, with amateur football and other minority pursuits. In other respects football, as a high-profile national team sport tied to the 'English disease' of violence, is a very specific example. So, while locating the revival of women's football after the 1960s in the wider sweep of women's history and football history this century, some markers have been placed to trace the construction and maintenance of a playing community.

At key moments, there has been rapid expansion of participation followed by retrenchment or consolidation. Arguments for a recent and rapid rise in players are at best partially accurate. The parochial and voluntaristic culture of local clubs has been very successful in organising play but less effective in transmitting ideas of community amongst players and the general public. This is a feature of the sport that could be explored further. The competitive interdependency of teams and clubs *is* the identity of women's football rather than evidence of a national community. In this way, most women's football is not very different in 2001 to what it was in 1971 or

1921. In other ways the Football Association is backing projects aimed at sustainable development because there appears to be an inevitability about professionalism.

Given the divisive framework of the development of sport for men and women it is not surprising that every new proposal for women's football tends to degenerate into a rehearsal of the same old questions. Women's weakness, inexperience and lack of achievement relative to men appear all too visible in football. In a world grown complicated and prone to rapid innovation, the order to be found in the explanation that men are essentially better at football is a simple answer to a number of complex questions. The organisation of the work has been influenced by these cyclical debates in examining the persistent themes of women's participation. Free market economics have been pursued in England to the extent that there is almost unbridled belief in competition, as we can see from the current education system. In this environment, the system-building of the football authorities is clearly of its time in terms of successive initiatives, inputs, outputs and number crunching. Against this background it is illogical to have a vision of the future which regulates women's disadvantage as its fundamental proposition.

Women football players, from Windhoek to New York, made a case for protecting gender-segregated sport as a way of defending women's participation. It is difficult to propose a future for mixed elite sport given football's place in the global entertainment economy today. By extension, it is also presumptuous to herald a new dawn when present trends forecast a feminine era in football to be a distant possibility. However, the findings indicated that women playing football for pleasure, health, association, independence and personal achievement are principal elements of that evolving future. The oral history of women football players changes the debate because data about the number of players tells us a rather dull story on its own. The values that women bring to bear in sport are more elusive but also more compelling. Drawn by the vision of my informants, this history has been composed by a large variety of themes not always evidently or logically connected with football in the academic treatments undertaken so far.

The place of women in English football presents some fragments that are essential to understand the place of this sport in our current culture and society. Not only will we pay a high price for a target-driven success if those volunteer practitioners at the heart of sports' development are not consulted. The derision of women in sport, football particularly, does little to normalise physical activity for females and also ignores some of the positive sporting values including mutual respect, engagement and collaboration. A comprehensive portrait of the complex realities of contemporary football and women's place in English society would have to acknowledge these and other aspects of female ownership of football. Hopefully we are moving in a direction when the experience described by the first informant below belongs to the distant past and we can begin to appreciate the view proposed by the second:

> They call me dirty . . . 'Oh, look at those dykes – lesbian!' . . . Men laugh and comment like it's a joke . . . 'Women can't play football' . . . 'It's a man's game' . . . 'All women footballers are gay, aren't they?' . . . When I played in boys' teams I usually had to deal with insulting remarks and comments.

> Cause it was us that were a unit . . . and it really . . . 1982–83 was the best time because we did everything together. We trained twice a week, we'd play on a Sunday, we'd socialise. It was a really, really special time and when I talk to the people who played then we all felt the same . . . it really was special.

Notes

Introduction

1 FIFA had published a number of articles before this but they were generally more neutral in tone, reflecting the experimental nature of the adoption of the female game and its staging; see, for example, *FIFA Report, Women's World Cup, China*, Zurich 1991.

2 Tony Mason *Association Football and English Society 1863–1915* Brighton: Harvester 1981 outlines the formation of the Football Association and wider social history; Charles Korr *West Ham United: The Making of a Football Club* London: Duckworth 1986 explores the role of the club in the local area. See also James Walvin *Football and the Decline of Britain* Basingstoke: Macmillan 1986; Nicholas Fishwick *English Football and Society 1910–1950* Manchester: Manchester University Press 1989.

3 Tom Reilly 'Physiology and the Female Football Player' *Insight: The FA Coaches Association Journal* Issue 3 Volume 4 Summer 2001 pp. 26–9 is representative of this approach. Reilly devotes a third of the article to detailing the menstrual cycle as a possible factor in affecting female sports performance generally and football particularly.

4 The Football Association 'Developing Asian Girls' Football' *On the Ball* May 2001 p. 6.

5 Women's football has been covered by a number of treatments: David Williamson *Belles of the Ball* Devon: R & D Associates 1991 gives an account of the early development of women's football; Sue Lopez *Women on the Ball* London: Scarlet 1997 details developments in the last three decades both nationally and internationally; Gail Newsham *In a League of their Own* London: Scarlet Press 1998 focuses on Dick, Kerr Ladies, later Preston, one of the most enduring and successful women's clubs between 1917 and 1964 and Alethea Melling *Ladies' Football: Gender and the Socialisation of Women Football Players in Lancashire 1916–1960* Unpublished Ph.D. Thesis University of Central Lancashire November 1999.

6 Alyson Rudd *Astroturf Blonde (It's a Man's Game – Sometimes)* London: Headline 1998 and the paperback version of the same text *Astroturf Blonde: Up Front and Onside in a Man's Game* London: Headline 1999 for a park player's experience, including her criticism, and subsequent rejection of, women's football.

7 Interviewees were selected for a spread of age, geographical origin, geographical present location, race, international playing experience, family circumstance and occupation. At club level, additional considerations were a balance of those drawn from urban and rural areas and noteworthy examples, such as the army

and other service teams. There were three important strands to the interviews: the factual reporting of personal details; comments on personal identity in relation to control of a responsive body; and team play and the perceived local and international effects of the dominant discourse on women players.

8 Donna Woodhouse *The Post War Development of Football for Females: A Cross Cultural and Comparative Study of England, the USA and Norway* Unpublished Ph.D. Thesis University of Leicester 2001 – in this recent, FA-commissioned, project at the Sir Norman Chester Centre for Football Research certain findings need to be treated with caution. Surveys in 1998 found that Lou Waller was the most popular player amongst fans of women's football. One of the two grounds surveyed was Millwall and Lou is a community coach in local schools in that area. Given that entry to the match at which the survey was distributed was free to children, who constituted three-quarters of the crowd, this possibly meant a disproportionate number of local youngsters were represented in those sampled.

9 K. Fasting *et al.* 'Women Playing Soccer – Experiences from Europe' ICSSPE Bulletin No. 25 Berlin involves Kari Fasting (Norweigan University of Sport, Oslo), Sheila Scraton (Leeds Metropolitan University), Gertrud Pfister (Frei University, Berlin) and Anna Bunuel (Institute of Madrid); Alethea Melling *Ladies' Football: Gender and the Socialisation of Women Football Players in Lancashire 1926–1960* Unpublished Ph.D. Thesis University of Central Lancashire November 1999 compares French and English women footballers pre-1960; Donna Woodhouse *The Post War Development of Football for Females: A Cross Cultural and Comparative Study of England, the USA and Norway* Unpublished Ph.D. Thesis University of Leicester October 2001 examines Norway and the USA.

Part-title page

1 Oscar Wilde's apocryphal observation 'Football is all very well a good game for rough girls, but is quite unsuitable for delicate boys' has become sufficiently part of football popular culture for it to appear on T-shirts printed by Philosophy Football Shirts of London.

Serious fun

1 Alice Kell, Dick, Kerr's captain and goalkeeper *Stoke Ladies versus Dick, Kerr's Ladies 22 September 1923 Souvenir Programme* Horsfield Ground, Colne.

2 Tony Mason *Association Football and English Society 1863–1915* Brighton: Harvester 1981 has eighteen references to women but mainly in the context of wives. He is cautious, for example, in describing shareholders of Woolwich Arsenal in 1893, 'There were also 54 married women . . . this is an intriguing piece of information although what it signifies I do not know' (56, n. 91); James Walvin *The People's Game: The History of Football Revisited* London, Edinburgh: Mainstream 1994 covers the period of this study in addition to pre-industrial football but, even with the revised content, has no indexed reference to women and mentions them most frequently in domestic settings (pp. 165–6).

3 The Football Association http://www.the-fa.org/reference (accessed 3 October 2001). Note the difference between this figure and the figure of 35,000 given by the Football Association at http:www.the-fa.org.womens on the same date.

4 Cissie Charlton and Vince Gladhill *Cissie: Football's Most Famous Mother* Morpeth: Bridge Studio 1988 is only one text where women's relationship with professional footballers is described. See, for example, very different treatments of the 'football wife' in the biography of Beattie Fry by Ronald Morris *The Captain's Lady* London: Chatto and Windus 1985 and Penny Watson *My Dear*

Watson: The Story of a Football Marriage London: Arthur Barker 1981; the personal assistant's point of view in Jane Nottage *Paul Gascoigne: The Inside Story* London: Collins Willow 1993; and the daughter's perspective of a family including four brother professionals in Phil Jackson *Liverpool's Sporting Pages* Bromborough: Lechlade Press 1991.

5 Brian Glanville referring to Dr Johnson's comments about women preaching, 'A Woman's preaching is like a dog's walking on his hinder legs. It is not done well but you are surprised to find it done at all' in Boswell *Life* Vol. 1 cited in Sue Lopez *Women on the Ball* London: Scarlet 1997 p. 210.

1 A brief history of women's football

1 Commentaries in *The Scottish Referee, The Scottish Sport, The Scottish Umpire* from 1895.

2 David Williamson *Belles of the Ball* pp. 2–3 includes examples at Brighton High School for Girls, Girton College and Roedean.

3 Sheila Fletcher *Women First: The Female Tradition in English Physical Education 1880–1980* London: Athlone p. 26 also gives a reference to schoolgirl football passing into popular culture in Angela Brazil's *The Fortunes of Phillippa* (1906).

4 I am indebted for the information on the ESFA to Chief Executive John Read who provided information from ESFA files, 16 July 2001.

5 In a letter to the ESFA dated 17 March 1988, for example, Goodger and Auden suggest 'It does occur to me, that there must be in existence an English Schools Football Association for schoolgirls, and I wonder if they are a registered charity' Buckingham: Open University Press 1992.

6 Sheila Scraton *Shaping up to Womanhood: Gender and Girls' Physical Education* p. 65 describes some of the problems around the theoretical and practical participation of girls in mixed football teams.

7 See, for example, the Imperial War Museum, Women's Work Collection (IWM, WWC) MUN 24/6; MUN 24/15; 24/17.

8 This is not specific to Britain; for instance, in the United States collegiate and social teams are often part of multi-sport ventures. In Scandinavia sports clubs may be multi-sport for both sexes. In Africa, though there is less of a problem with the containment of sports grounds, there are taboos specifically concerning women's presence on pitches used by men.

9 Alison Walker *et al. Living In Britain: Results from the 2000 General Household Survey* London: HMSO *c.* 2001 p. 213 figure 13E indicates that, even given the loose definition of sport, other leisure activities, such as watching television and listening to music, were at least eight times as popular as football for men and at least eighty times as popular as football for women.

10 Ross McKibbin *The Ideologies of Class: Social Relations in Britain, 1880–1950* Oxford: Clarendon Press 1990 p. 164 describes hobbies as giving pleasure through privacy and solitude in working-class life that was otherwise overwhelmingly collective.

11 The patronage of the middle and upper classes was key to the early formation of women's associations, as the role of Florence Dixie suggests. Other women's sports associations were formed during the 1920s but with mixed success. Like football, women's cricket has a long history. The White Heather Club began with a collection of eight noblewomen in 1887 and in four years had a membership of fifty. The Women's Cricket Association (WCA) was formed in 1926 and integrated with the England and Wales Cricket Board in 1998. However, cricket has never reached the popularity amongst British women that football has in spite of having an association and elite sponsorship. For example in the 1970s the number

of women's football clubs in England grew fivefold in a decade, whereas the number of women's cricket clubs remained at fifty (John Bale *Sport and Place: A Geography of Sport in England, Scotland and Wales* London: Hurst 1982 p. 51).

12 John Bale *Sport and Place* p. 3 refers to Lawson and Morford's model of commercial–consumer and participatory–recreational sport which is too rigid to describe the nature of women's football before the 1960s. Some aspects of both 'ideal types' apply in that it was both spectator-driven and organised by a fixture list, rather than a league.

13 However, this was short-lived and the WFA was forced to field only a senior squad in international competition due to financial difficulties in 1980. It was not until 1997 that a junior squad was again assembled for representative competition.

14 Sue Lopez *Women on the Ball* p. 71 'it is obvious that their greater resources and expertise could help the game considerably'; Kelly Simmons, The Football Association Women's Development Officer, 'Women's football is developing at a dramatic rate and we have many new policies and programmes', personal communication, 29 June 2001.

15 The FA restated its position on women in 1946 and 1962, and the Football League, via county FAs, repeatedly warned against staging women's matches. Mixed matches are still banned; for example, in 1994 Hayle were fined by the FA for allowing BBC Radio Cornwall to play two women in a charity match against Hayle on their home ground.

16 FIFA preamble to *The Laws of the Game* Zurich 1999 states, 'Laws may be modified for matches for players of under 16 years of age, for women footballers and for veteran footballers over 35 years of age. Any or all of the following modifications are permissible: size of the field of play; size, weight and material of the ball; width of goalposts and height of crossbar from the ground; the duration of the periods of play; substitutions.'

17 Combinations of the Women's Premier League, Women's Premier League Cup and Women's FA Cup.

2 Competition and community in English women's football

1 I am indebted to PB, son of Arthur Bridgett, for this information.

2 Estra Henry is believed to have been an American benefactor. The Edinburgh Dynamo team appear in programmes from 1952, 1962 and 1963 sent to me by an ex-player whose father is said to have founded the team.

3 Rachel Brown is at the University of Pittsburgh, Danielle Murphy is at the University of Florida and Kelly Smith is with the Philadelphia Charge and a coach (formerly a student) at Seton Hall.

3 Memory and English women's football

1 Sheila Fletcher *Women First: The Female Tradition in English Physical Education 1880–1980* London: Athlone 1984; Sheila Scraton *Shaping up to Womanhood: Gender and Girls' Physical Education* Buckingham: Open University Press 1992; Jennifer Hargreaves *Sporting Females: Critical Issues in the History and Sociology of Women's Sport* London: Routledge 1994; Jennifer Hargreaves *Heroines of Sport: The Politics of Difference and Identity* London: Routledge 2000.

2 See, for example, Sheila Scraton 'Images of Femininity and the Teaching of Girls' Physical Education' in J. Evans (ed.) *Physical Education, Sport and Schooling: Studies in the Sociology of Physical Education* London: Falmer 1986 pp. 44–66.

3 Jo Boaler 'When do Girls Prefer Football to Fashion? An Analysis of Female Underachievement in Relation to "realistic" Mathematic Contexts' *British*

Educational Research Journal Vol. 20 No. 5 pp. 551–65 1994 played on contemporary stereotypes; for example this quotation, 'When do girls prefer football to fashion, the answer I believe, is in a mathematics examination . . . the world of football is still perceived by many girls as almost exclusively male and this alone is good enough reason not to connect football with mathematics. The issue of context and "reality" in mathematics education is, however, extremely complex' (p. 551).

4 *Daily Express* 31 October 1978 p. 14; *Evening Post* 19 September 1984 p. 6; *Sportsnews* 12 October 1990 p. 11; *Guardian Sport* 10 December 1990 p. 7.
5 'Dolly Led Stoke (Ladies) to Victory in Cup' *Stoke Evening Sentinel* 21 January 1955; '1922 Cup Victory for Stoke Ladies' *Stoke Evening Sentinel* 10 February 1968; 'They Were The Champions' *Stoke Evening Sentinel* 12 March 1976; 'Survivor Recalls Famous Team' *Stoke Evening Sentinel* 18 April 1992.
6 See Peter Seddon *A Football Compendium* Wetherby: The British Library 1995 p. 321 for a comprehensive list of authors who wrote about women's football for *The Football and Sports Library* (published by Amalgamated Press 1921–3); Alethea Melling ' "Ray of the Rovers": The Working Class Heroine in Popular Football Fiction 1915–25' *The International Journal of the History of Sport* Vol. 16 No. 1 April 1998 pp. 97–122.
7 *Football Today*, May 1985 to June 1986.
8 Unknown producer, *Haslingden Carnival 9 September 1950*, the North West Film Archive, Manchester: Manchester Metropolitan University, accession number 578; unknown producer, *Garden Party and Pensioners' Picnic 1960*, the North West Film Archive, Manchester: Manchester Metropolitan University, accession number 1228; Manchester Film and Video Workshop and Salford Council for Voluntary Service, *Salford Festival 1980*, the North West Film Archive, Manchester: Manchester Metropolitan University, accession number 1735.
9 Manchester Film and Video Workshop and Salford Council for Voluntary Service, *Salford Festival 1980*, Trim 1, accession number 1736, Trim 2, accession number 1737, Trim 3, accession number 1754 and Trim 4, accession number 1763.
10 Ronald Frankland, *Dick, Kerr Ladies' Football and TA Volunteers Circa 1945–1955*, The North West Film Archive, Manchester: Manchester Metropolitan University, accession number 3441.
11 *WFA News* November 1985 p. 1; *WFA News* July 1986 p. 1; *WFA News* November 1986 p. 1.
12 *Sunday Kicks: The Magazine for Women's Football* London: Grafex Print Copy Centre No. 1 April 1995 to No. 15 July 1996.
13 Jere Longman *The Girls of Summer: The US Women's Soccer Team and How it Changed the World* New York: HarperCollins 2000; Marla Miller and Zachery Bryan *All American Girls: The US National Women's Team* Los Angeles: Archway 1999; Mia Hamm and Aaron Heifetz *Go for the Goal: A Champion's Guide to Winning in Soccer and Life* San Francisco: Quill 2000; Michelle Akers and Greg Lewis *The Game and the Glory* New York: Zandervan Books 2000.
14 Grant Jarvie 'Sport, Nationalism and Cultural Identity' in Lincoln Allison (ed.) *The Changing Politics of Sport* Manchester: Manchester University Press 1993 p. 76 suggested three components of a shared experience leading to a collective identity. The first is a sense of continuity, the second is shared memories of specific turning points, and third is a sense of common destiny.
15 An argument used by the WFA in supporting the ruling against Theresa Bennett, who wished to play in a mixed team. Reported in 1978 *WFA News* November 1978 p. 4 and referred to in more detail in Part II (page 126ff.).

Oral history and women's football in England

1. Nick Rowe and Ross Champion *Young People and Sport National Survey 1999* London: Sport England Research 2000 p. 14: skateboarding increased from 0 in 1994 to 28 per cent in 1999 compared with football's increase from 13 per cent to 18 per cent for girls (Figure 15). Another individual sport, swimming, was the most popular at 54 per cent.
2. Susan Birrell and Nancy Theberg 'Feminist Resistance and Transformation in Sport' in D. Costa and S. Guthrie (eds) *Women and Sport: Interdisciplinary Perspectives* Champaign, Ill: Human Kinetics 1994 p. 263.
3. Sheila Fletcher *Women First: The Female Tradition in English Physical Education 1880–1980* London: Athlone 1984 p. 5; the phrase is originally attributed to Eleanor Rathbone in 1938.
4. Lily Parr, not to be confused with Lily from Parr, is a personal heroine and deserves a book in her own right, both because of her football prowess and her eccentricities. She played for Dick, Kerr Ladies for thirty-one years.
5. For example the 2003 *Kick it Out* promotional material distributed by the Football Supporters' Association.

The rise of the women's game in a global and professional era

1. Netball is still the most popular team sport for school-age females in England, with school-age participation at least double that of football. Volleyball is not as popular in the UK as in some European countries and the Americas. Both netball and volleyball as female team sports emphasise manual dexterity and minimise contact. Whilst girls may dance, it does seem to be a common international theme that they are not suited to kicking or making contact. Those commentators who ridicule women's football, such as Brian Glanville, assert that female inability to kick forcefully would make watching a professional women's football league beyond boring and 'like watching dry paint' (Radio 5 Live interview in response to the FA pledge to launch a professional women's league within three years, July 2000).
2. Sport and nationalism as expressions of 'imagined communities' had previously been discussed by Anderson in 1983. For the revised edition of this work see B. Anderson *Imagined Communities*, rev. ed. New York: Verso 1991.
3. I am indebted to Elsie Cook for excerpts from her scrapbook, letters dated 2 and 10 September 1974 respectively, Mitre Challenge Tournament Programme 1971 and photographs of trials.
4. The Society, of Sports Statisticians Foundation's website, http://www.rsssf.com/women (accessed 19 October 2001) provides a good source of reference for tournaments and the results for individual nations, which gives some sense of the variety and scope of international competition.
5. For more information on Smith's career and increasing media profile see http://www.wusaleague.com/kellysmith and http://kellysmithsoccer.com (accessed 20 September 2001).
6. I am indebted for information on the L League to Akiko Takahashi of the Women's Sports Foundation, Japan (personal communication, 28 October 2000).
7. I am indebted for information to the Women's Football Association of Nepal representative, and leaflet *Women's Football*, at the European Women and Sport Conference Helsinki, Finland 7 June 2000.
8. See for example Jennifer Hargreaves 'Victorian Familism and the Formative Years of Female Sport' in J.A. Mangan and Roberta Park (eds) *From 'Fair Sex' to Feminism: Sport and the Socialization of Women in the Industrial and Post-Industrial Eras* London: Frank Cass 1987 pp. 130–44.

4 Bumbling along

1 Lord Denning *Theresa Bennett v. The Football Association Limited and Nottinghamshire Football Association* unreported transcript of judgment 28 July 1978 p. 5: 'It is plain as can be . . . that football is not within the Sex Discrimination Act . . . if the law should bring football within it, it would be exposing itself to absurdity. Everyone would say with Mr Bumble "If the law supposes that, the law is an ass – an idiot".'

2 Fulham has the first women's professional team in England; however, at the moment, the players are classed as semi-professionals by the PFA and have been given associate rather than full membership.

3 Many junior leagues now have a Code of Conduct covering players, spectators and referees; for example, http://www.gcis.net/saynorth/codeconduct (accessed 24 May 2000).

4 Local Government Act 1988 (*c.* 9) HMSO 2A: 'A local authority shall not intentionally promote homosexuality or publish material with the intention of promoting homosexuality; [or] promote the teaching in any maintained school of the acceptability of homosexuality as a pretended family relationship.'

5 *East Midlands Women's League Directory* 1998 and 1999; the figure forty-five is taken before the withdrawal of some teams during both seasons.

6 See also A. Koppelman 'Why Discrimination Against Lesbians and Gay Men is Sex Discrimination' *New York University Law Review* Vol. 69 No. 2 pp. 197–287 1994.

7 Against Temple University, Washington State University and the Montana High School Association for example.

8 See http://fifa2.com/Preface/Modifications (accessed 12 April 2000). The modifications that already existed for these three groups were any or all of the size of the field of play; size, weight and material of the ball; width between the goalposts and height of the crossbar from the ground; and the duration of the periods of play.

9 See for example Jas Bains and Sanjiev Johal *Corner Flags and Corner Shops: The Asian Football Player's Experience* London: Victor Gollancz 1998.

10 I am indebted to Gordon Taylor, Head of the PFA, for this information.

11 The case was jointly funded by the Equal Opportunities Commission and the National Association of Schoolmasters and Union of Women Teachers.

12 Within the wider field of employment, ideas of physical 'fitness' for certain jobs are currently under review. For example, the fire service is undergoing an examination of its militaristic trappings and its employment practices after a survey in March 1998 found that of 33,597 uniformed staff and 14,483 retained staff only 513 people were from black and ethnic minorities and 436 were women (HM Fire Service Inspectorate 31 March 1998). Similarly contested is the notion of 'combat effectiveness' which the Equal Opportunities Commission estimates to limit 30 per cent of jobs in the armed forces to male-only recruitment. The recent case of Angela Sidar, a cook with the Marines, has caused the European Court of Justice to review the exclusion of women from such posts (Equal Opportunities Commission 26 December 1999).

13 For further details see *Vanessa Hardwick v. the Football Association* Equal Opportunities Commission Employment Appeal Tribunal Transcript 30 April 1999.

14 For further details see Equal Opportunities Commission *Valuing Women: A Report* London: Equal Opportunities Commission 28 May 2000.

15 See the list of issues and ongoing action at www.womensportfoundation.org/issues (accessed 25 April 2002).

16 For a detailed discussion see European Commission *Incorporating Equal Opportunities for Women and Men into all Community Policies and Activities* European Commission Communication 1996 Section 67.

17 For a more in-depth analysis see Janice Richards and Ralph Sandland *Feminist Perspectives on Law and Theory* London: Cavendish 2000 p. 52.
18 Tony Mason *Sport in Britain* Cambridge: Cambridge University Press 1989 pp. 162–3. Mason's figures for the 1985–6 season show that 4.4 per cent of the 1,950 registered players earned £50,000 per annum and 40 per cent less than £10,000.

5 Women's football

1 The debates over the use of quotas can be followed at the CAAWS web-page on *Equity and Leadership* www.caaws.com (accessed 3 April 2000).
2 Given at the Second Olympic Congress as a verbal opinion from the floor, Paris 8 March 2000.
3 Women's World Cup 1999 – six of the sixteen teams were from Europe.
4 The five partners in 2001 were Discovery Enterprises; Comcast Corporation; Time Warner Corporation; Advance Newhouse Communications; Cox Communications.
5 Kevan Pipe 'The Development of Women's Football Programmes' 2nd Symposium on Women's Football Los Angeles 8 July 1999 p. 5 provocatively suggested international youth competition to be crucial to the development of women's football and ended the paper with the question, 'Does this indeed represent FIFA's next steps in future programming decisions?' Pipe is Chief Operating Officer of the Canadian Soccer Association; the 2002 Under 19 Chamionships in Canada are FIFA's reply to the question.
6 For more information on the gender and representative background of FIFA Committees see http://www.fifa.com/committees (accessed 23 June 2000).
7 For more information on women's football in Germany see Hannelore Razteburg 'Women's Football in the Next Millennium' 2nd Symposium on Women's Football Los Angeles 8 July 1999 pp. 1–4.
8 For more details see Sahar El-Hawary, Head of Women's Football in Egypt and FIFA Women's Committee member, Los Angeles 8 July 1999.
9 See for example FIFA *Evaluation of the Questionnaire on Women's Football as at 30.7.97* Zurich 2 March 1998 p. 6: 'We have a huge reservoir of talent,' explains the Brazilian FA's Carlos Alberto Pinheiro, 'we just have to start getting properly organised'.
10 After the creation of FIFA in 1904 the idea of having a major international competition remained unrealised until the tournament that took place within the context of the Olympic Games in London in 1908. Problems arose, which were still unsolved when the 1912 games took place in Stockholm. This modern, unfamiliar sport was seen by the Olympic Committee as a show and not as competition, as it was a team event.
11 International Olympic Committee, *The Promotion of Women in the Olympic Movement* Lausanne: IOC Department of International Co-operation February 2000 p. 5. Historians do not agree on the number of women participants in 1900 or the number of sports but it is agreed that fewer than two dozen women took part and they competed in fewer than five sports.
12 International Olympic Committee, *Women in the Olympic Movement* Lausanne: IOC p. 8 compared with twenty-eight sports for men.
13 Mario Rimati *Women's Soccer World* Alabama March /April 1999 gives the figure as 76,481 spectators.
14 See http://www.mlsnet.com for contrasting views of age and MLS – Dave Dir 'In With the New, Out With the Old' (accessed 20 August 2001) and Bruce Berger 'When Age Is Not An Issue' (accessed 20 August 2001).

15 Adidas promotional leaflet at Women's World Cup 1999. The design depicted 'a colourful representationor [*sic*] icon from each of the seven United States Communities which will host Women's World Cup Games.'
16 The foundation was created with the express intention of supporting projects that will assist soccer in becoming a pre-eminent sport in the United States.
17 See for example M. Penner 'Bare Facts Make These Two Heroes' *Los Angeles Times* 11 July 1999 p. D1.
18 For conflicting opinions about this issue see http://www.womensoccer.com/wwcup99/wwcinterviews.html for the argument by Hank Steinbrecher, the General Secretary of US Soccer, that there was no money to fund the women's programme and www.womenssoccer.com/editorial for the last editorial of 1999 by Roger le groves Rogers, who argues that US Soccer's antipathy to women players is influenced in part by the predominance of British expats in the federation (accessed 24 April 2001).
19 For instance see www.womensoccer.com/letters 'Heinrichs named US Head Team Coach' (accessed 20 August 2001).
20 Mark Zeigler 'Revolutionary Spirit' *The San Diego Union Tribune* 21 April 2001 p. A21. Foudy was famously challenged by US Soccer's Alan Rothberg, 'Show me the money', and in less than a week she had secured sufficient investment to launch the league.
21 For a discussion of the findings see Women's Sports Foundation *Minorities in Sports: The Effect of Varsity Sports Participation on the Social Educational and Career Mobility of Minority Students* New York: Women's Sports Foundation 15 August 1989.
22 See, for example, Birgit Palzkill 'Between Gymshoes and High Heels – The Development of a Lesbian Identity and Existence in Top Class Sport' *International Review for the Sociology of Sport* Vol. 25 No. 3 p. 230 and Pat Griffin *Strong Women, Deep Closets* Champaign, Ill: Human Kinetics 1998 p. xi.
23 For a range of disputes and initiatives see Women's Soccer World *Women's Soccer World* letters to the editor at http://www.womensoccer.com/refs/fans (accessed 28 August 1999).
24 For example, Pauline Yemm *Women's Soccer Trials in Keetmanshoop: Report for the Ministry of Youth and Sport, Republic of Namibia* Unpublished paper 24 June 1997 reports that the team from the Kavango region began to travel on the morning of Friday 20 June to play on the Saturday. Trials began at 6 a.m. and continued under floodlights until late evening.
25 Conrad Angula 'City Win Women's Soccer Final' *The Namibian* 18 July 1995 includes the two schools, Immanuel Shifidi and Dawid Bezuidenhout, in the prizes.
26 I am indebted to Pauline Yemm for the information on Voluntary Service Overseas initiatives in Namibia, her slide collection, scrapbooks and useful contacts.
27 See for example coverage in Conrad Angula 'City Win Women's Soccer Final' *The Namibian* 18 July 1995; Joseph Nekaya 'The Amazons' *The Namibian* 29 March 1996; Conrad Angula 'NAM to meet DR Congo' *The Namibian* 23 September 1997.
28 Nick Barrett *VSO New Services Unit* Issue 3 Sport 1997 p. 13. Football has been used, for example, in response to the Zambian national team crisis following an air crash which caused the death of most of the players and in Eritrea at the end of the thirty-year civil war to help in rebuilding the sports culture.
29 Participant observation at the 2nd World Women and Sport Conference Windhoek 22nd May 1998. At the meeting were women's football administrators from Angola, Botswana, Malawai, Zambia, Zimbabwe, Namibia, Congo, Lesotho, Mozambique, Swaziland, South Africa and Mexico. Also present were

FIFA representative Doris Valasek Dobsa and Donna De Varona in her capacity as Chair of Women's World Cup 1999.

30 See http://rsssf.com for a report of the final and http://wusa.com for Aikide's personal profile (accessed 23 June 2001).

A female future for a man's game?

1 The International Volleyball Federation dictates that, for women, 'tops are to be tight fitting with open back, open upper chest and stomach. Miniscule briefs that measure no more than 6cm high must be worn. No shorts, no T-shirts'.

Bibliography

'1922 Cup Victory for Stoke Ladies' (1968) *Stoke Evening Sentinel* 10 February

Acosta, R.V. and Carpenter, L.J. (1994) *Women in Intercollegiate Sport: Acosta/Carpenter Report* Smith College Massachusetts and Brooklyn College of the City University of New York

Acosta, R.V. and Carpenter, L.J. (2002 edition) *Women in Intercollegiate Sport: Acosta/Carpenter Report* Smith College Massachusetts and Brooklyn College of the City University of New York

Adidas promotional leaflet (1999) FIFA Women's World Cup 1999 Los Angeles

Aldis, C. (2001) *British University Sports Association* files

Allatt, C.S. (1988) *English Schools Football Association Report of 1988: Girls' Football Survey*, 19 September

Allen, R. (1972) *Skinhead Girls* London: New English Library

Allison, L. (1998) *Taking Sport Seriously* Chelsea School Research Centre Edition; Vol. 6, Aachen; Oxford: Meyer and Meyer

Anderson B. (1991) *Imagined Communities*, rev. ed. New York: Verso

Angula, C. (1994) 'Women's Sports Dream Comes to Life' *The Namibian* 4 April

Angula, C. (1995) 'City Win Women's Soccer Final' *The Namibian* 18 July

Angula, C. (1997) 'NAM to meet DR Congo' *The Namibian* 23 September

Anthony, David (1970) 'When to Kick is Unwomanly' *Times Educational Supplement* 10 October

Armstrong, G. and Guilianotti, R. (1997) *Entering the Field: New Perspectives on World Football* Oxford: Berg

Bains, J. (1998) *Corner Flags and Corner Shops: The Asian Football Player's Experience* London: Victor Gollancz

Bale, J. (1979) *The Development of Soccer as a Participant and Spectator Sport: Geographical Aspects* London: Sports Council/Social Science Research Council

Bale, J. (1980) 'Women's Football in England and Wales: A Social-Geographic Perspective' *Physical Education Review* Vol. 3 No. 2 pp. 137–45

Bale, J. (1982) *Sport and Place: A Geography of Sport in England, Scotland and Wales* London: Hurst

Bale, J. (1993) *Sport, Space and the City* London: Routledge

Bale, J. and Moen, O. (1995) *The Stadium and the City* Keele: Keele University Press

Bandy, S. and Darden, A (1999) *Crossing Boundaries* Champaign, Ill: Human Kinetics

Banet-Weiser, S. (1999) 'Hoop Dreams: Professional Basketball and the Politics of Race and Gender' *Journal of Sport and Social* Issue 23 No. 4 pp. 403–21

Batt, P. (1973) 'Dates have the Order of the Boot' *Sun* 17 April

Battersby, K. (1994) 'Mohr earns Germany First Leg Advantage' *Daily Telegraph* 2 December

Begbie, S. (1996) 'The Story So Far: Recent Developments in Women's Football in Scotland' *Scottish Journal of Physical Education* Vol. 24 pp. 302–11

Bender, B. (1993) *Landscape: Politics and Perspectives* Providence, RI; Oxford: Berg Publishers

Bennett, Victoria (2002) 'Women's Sports Journalists in Britain' unpublished Ph.D. thesis, De Montford University

Bergman, M. (1997) *The Globe: Namibia and Eritrea* Windhoek: Abacus

Berry, R. and Wong, G. (1993) *Law and the Business of the Sports Industries: Common Issues in Amateur and Professional Sport* London; Connecticut: Greenwood

Bethell, A. (1983) *Gregory's Girl* (an adaption of Bill Forsyth's original film script by Andrew Bethell) Cambridge: Cambridge University Press

Beveridge, S. (1975) 'Edna – The Sad Soccer Star' *Sunday People* 31 January

Bhattacharya, N. (1992) *Hem and Football* London: Secker and Warburg

Birley, D. (1995) *Playing the Game: Sport and British Society 1910–1945* Manchester: Manchester University Press

Birrell, Susan (1994) 'Achievement Related Motives and the Woman Athlete' in Susan Birrell and Cheryl Cole *Women Sport and Culture* Champaign, Ill; Leeds: Human Kinetics

Birrell, S. and Theberg, N. (1994) 'Feminist Resistance and Transformation in Sport' in D. Margaret Costa and Sharon R. Guthrie *Women and Sport: Interdisciplinary Perspectives* Champaign, Ill: Human Kinetics

Bishop, J. and Hoggett, P. (1986) *Organising Around Enthusiasms: Patterns of Mutual Aid* London: Comedia

Blackstone, T. and Mortimer, J. (1983) *Disadvantage and Education* London: Gower

Blatter, J. (1995) 'The Future is Feminine' *FIFA News* Zurich June/July Editorial

Boaler, J. (1994) 'When do Girls Prefer Football to Fashion? An Analysis of Female Underachievement in Relation to "Realistic" Mathematics Contexts' *British Educational Research Journal* Vol. 20 No. 5 pp. 551–65

Boserup, Ester (1989) *Women's Role in Economic Development* London: Earthscan

Bourdieu, P. (1986) *Distinction: A Social Critique of the Judgement of Taste* London, Routledge

Bourdieu, P. and Passeron, J.C. (1977) trans. Nice, R. *Reproduction in Education, Society and Culture* London: Sage

Bourke, W. (2000) (daughter of Alice Mills Lambert) essays, newspaper cuttings and eulogy provided by personal communication 23 June

Braybon, G. and Summerfield P. (1987) *Out of the Cage: Women's Experiences in Two World Wars* London: Pandora

'Bridgetts United Win Women's FA Cup' (1923) *Stoke Evening Sentinel* July

Bridgwood, Ann *et al.* (2000) *Living in Britain: Results from the 1998 General Household Survey: An Inter-departmental survey carried out by ONS between April 1998 and March 1999* London: Stationery Office

Brumfiel, E. (1989) 'Factional Competition in Complex Society Inequality' in D. Miller, M. Rowlands and C. Tilley (eds) *Domination and Resistance* London: Allen and Unwin

Carter, Michael J. (1981) 'Women's Recent Progress in the Professions or, Women get a Ticket to Ride after the Gravy Train has Left the Station' *Feminist Studies* Vol. 7, No. 3

Caudwell, Jayne (1999) 'Women's Football in the United Kingdom: Theorising Gender and Unpacking the Butch Lesbian Image' *Journal of Sport and Social Issues* Vol. 23 No. 4 pp. 390–403

Cheetham, S. (1994) *Gladys Protheroe . . . Football Genius!* London: Juma

Chitika, E. (1998) 'Opening Address' *Second International World Conference on Women in Sport* Namibia 20 May

Christiansen, Karen, Guttman, Allen and Pfister, Gertrud (eds) (2001) *International Encyclopedia of Women and Sports* New York; London: Macmillan

Commonwealth Games Association of Canada (1998) *Strength Through Sport* Gloucester Ontario: Commonwealth Games Association of Canada

Cook, E. (2000) scrapbook and letters, programme for Mitre Challenge Trophy 1971 and 1972, provided by personal communication

Copeland, T. (1997) 'Coaching Women's Football' *FACA Inaugural Conference Magazine* October

Corinthian versus Bolton Programme (1952) Manchester Athletic Ground, Fallowfield 20 August

Corinthian versus Lancashire Ladies Programme (1951) Festival of Britain, Craven Park 21 July

Cross, G. (1993) *Time and Money – The Making of Consumer Culture* London; New York: Routledge

Crosset, T. (1990) 'Masculinity, Sexuality and the Development of Early Modern Sport' in Michael Messner and Donald Sabo *Sport, Men and the Gender Order* Champaign Ill.: Human Kinetics

Curtis, M. and Grant, C. (2000) *University of Iowa Project on Women's Intercollegiate Sport and Title IX* Iowa

Da Silva, F. and Faught, J. (1982) 'Nostalgia: A Sphere and Process of Contemporary Ideology' *Qualitative Sociology* Vol. 5 No. 1 pp. 125–32

Daunton, M. (1996) 'Payment and Participation: Welfare and State Formation in Britain 1990–1951' *Past and Present* No. 15 February pp. 169–216

Davies, P. (1996) *I Lost My Heart to the Belles* London: Mandarin

De Coubertin, P. (1913) *1913 Olympic Review* September

Denning, Lord (1978) *Theresa Bennet v. The Football Association Limited and the Nottinghamshire Football Association* unreported judgment of 28 July

Denning, Lord A. (1984) *Landmarks in the Law* London: Butterworths

'Dolly Led Stoke (Ladies) to Victory in Cup' (1955) *Stoke Evening Sentinel* 21 January

Donnelly, P. (1993) 'Subcultures in Sport: Resilience and Transformation' in Alan Ingham and John Loy *Sport and Social Development: Traditions, Transitions, Transformations* Champaign, Ill; Leeds: Human Kinetics

Dunning, E. (1999) *Sport Matters: Sociological Studies of Sport, Violence and Civilisation* London: Routledge

East Midlands Women's Football League (1977) Minutes of 2 February

East Midlands Women's League Directory 1998

East Midlands Women's League Directory 1999

Ebbage, J. (2000) scrapbook, letters, programmes, postcards and photographs

Eddie, J. (1993) 'Ladies Soccer' *PACE* Soweto

Elias, N. and Dunning, E. (1986) *Quest for Excitement: Sport and Leisure in the Civilising Process* Oxford: Blackwell

English Schools FA (1986) *Curriculum Time Football Questionnaire* September

English Schools FA (1988a) *Analysis of questionnaire with reference to the interest shown in girls in full time education in the playing of Association Football* Secretary Allatt, C. 19 September

English Schools FA (1988b) *Report: Girls' Football Survey* 19 September

Epstein, C. and Coser, R. (1981) *Access to Power: Cross National Studies of Women and Elites* London: George Allen and Unwin

Equal Opportunities Commission (1978) *The Football Association Limited and Nottinghamshire Football Association v Miss T Bennett* transcript of judgment 28 July

Equal Opportunities Commission (1981) *British Judo Association v Mrs B Petty* transcript of judgment 16 June

Equal Opportunities Commission (1982) *Mrs French v Mr and Mrs Crosby (Links Hotel)* transcript of judgment 7 May

Equal Opportunities Commission (1998) *Gender and Differential Achievement in Education and Training: A Research Review* Manchester: Equal Opportunities Commission

Equal Opportunities Commission (1999) *Hardwick v The FA* Employment Appeal Tribunal Transcript 30 April

Equal Opportunities Commission (2000) *Valuing Women* Available HTTP:<http://www.eoc.org.uk/html> Accessed 23 May

Espelund, K. (1995) *Developing Women's Football* UEFA Youth Conference Paper

European Communities Commission (1996) 'Incorporating Equal Opportunities for Women and Men into all Community Policies and Activities' Section 67

European Communities Commission (1998) 'Incorporating Equal Opportunities for Women and Men into all Community Policies and Activities' Section 122

European Communities Commission Directorate-General for Employment and Social Affairs (2001) 'Towards a Community Strategy on Gender Equality (2001–2005)' Luxembourg: Office for Official Publications of the European Communities

Fasting, K. (1987) 'Sports and Women's Culture' *Women's Studies International Forum* Vol. 10 No. 4 pp. 361–8

Fasting, K., Scraton, S., Pfister, G. and Bunuel, A. (1998) 'Women Playing Soccer – Experiences From Europe' *ICSSPE Bulletin* No. 25 Berlin pp. 25–8

Ferris, E. (2000) 'Promoting Women Sports Leaders: Are Quotas the Way Forward?' *2nd IOC Conference on Women and Sport: New Perspectives for the XXI Century* 6 March

FIFA (1992) *1st FIFA/ M&Ms Symposium on Women's Football* November

FIFA (1997a) *Minutes of meeting no. 10* Committee for Women's Football 18 February

FIFA (1997b) *Survey of Women's Football* Zurich January unpublished paper

FIFA (1998) *Evaluation of the Questionnaire on Women's Football as at 30.7.97*, Zurich 2 March

FIFA (1999a) *2nd Symposium on Women's Football* 8 July

FIFA (1999b) *Women's World Cup Los Angeles 1999 Official Programme* FIFA

FIFA (2000) <www.fifa.com/committees> Accessed 23 June 2000

FIFA (2001) *The Big Count* Available online: <www.fifa.com/survey> Accessed 3 April

Fishwick, N. (1989) *English Football and Society: 1910–1950* Manchester: Manchester University Press

Fletcher, S. (1984) *Women First: The Female Tradition in English Physical Education 1880–1980* London: Athlone

Football Association (1997) *Women's Football Alliance Minutes Appendix D* 21 November

Football Association, The (1998a) 'Growing Up: Youngsters in Football', *FA Coaching Certificate Course Pack Module 6* London: The FA Ltd

Football Association, The (1998b) 'Growing Up: Youngsters in Football', *FA Coaching Licence Course Pack Module 8* London: The FA Ltd

Football Association, The (1998c) *Handbook Season 1998–99* London: The FA Ltd

Football Association, The (1998d) *Women's Football Factsheet 1*, London: The FA Ltd

Football Association, The (1998e) *Women's Football Factsheet 2,* London: The FA Ltd

Football Association, The (1998f) *Women's Football Factsheet 3*, London: The FA Ltd

Football Association, The (1998g) *Women's Football History Factsheet 1* London: The FA Ltd

Football Association, The (2000a) *Coaches Association Membership Details* 18 April

Football Association, The (2000b) Football Association website. Available HTTP <http://www.the-fa.org.womens> Accessed 10 January 2000

Football Association, The (2001a) 'Developing Asian Girls' Football' *On the Ball* May

Football Association, The (2001b) *Women's Football Directory of Leagues and Clubs 1997–1998* London: The FA Ltd

Football Today Cradely Heath:West Midlands May 1985 to June 1986

Foulds, S. and Harris, P. (1979) *America's Soccer Heritage* Manhattan Beach, Calif.: Soccer for Americans

Fredman, S. (1997) *Women and the Law* Oxford: Clarendon Press

Gertze, F. (1997) *Annual Report, Sports Commission, Republic of Namibia* Windhoek

Glanville, B. (1973) 'Goals and Gals Don't Really Mix' *Sunday Times* 24 June

Griffin, P. (1998) *Strong Women, Deep Closets: Lesbians and Homophobia in Sport* Champaign, Ill: Human Kinetics

Goldberg, A. and Wagg, S. (1991) 'It's not a Knockout: English Football and Globalisation' in John Williams and Stephen Wagg (eds) *British Football and Social Change: Getting into Europe* Leicester: Leicester University Press

Goodger and Auden (1988) Letter to English Schools FA, 17 March

Grosz, E. (1994) *Volatile Bodies: Toward a Corporeal Feminism* Bloomington: Indiana University Press

Guttman, A. (1991) *Women's Sports: A History* New York: Columbia University Press

Haliday, J. (1992) 'The Boot's on the Other Foot' *Derby Evening Telegraph* 4 May

Hall, M.A. (1996) *Feminism and Sporting Bodies: Essays on Theory and Practice* Champaign, Ill: Human Kinetics

Hall, S. and du Gay, P. (1996) *Questions of Cultural Identity* London: Sage Publications

Hardcastle, Michael (1990) *Joanna's Goal* (illustrated by Elizabeth Haines) Glasgow: Blackie
Hargreaves, J. (1986) *Sport, Power and Culture* Cambridge: Polity Press
Hargreaves, J. (1994) *Sporting Females: Critical Issues in the History and Sociology of Women's Sport* London: Routledge
Hargreaves, J. (2000) *Heroines of Sport: The Politics of Difference and Identity* London: Routledge
Hennies, R. (1995) 'Firm Bases – Scope at the Summit?' *FIFA Magazine* Zurich May
Highfield Oral History Group and the Sir Norman Chester Centre for Football (1993) *Highfield Rangers: An Oral History* Leicester: Leicester City Council Living History Unit
Hill, J. (1974) 'Take a Tip Revie – It's Time to Follow the Girls!' *News of the World* 12 November
Hill, J. (2002) *Sport, Leisure and Culture in Twentieth-Century Britain* Basingstoke: Palgrave
Hill, J. and Williams, J. (1996) *Sport and Identity in the North of England* Keele: Keele University Press
Hinton, J. (1983) *Labour and Socialism: A History of the British Labour Movement 1867–1974* Brighton: Wheatsheaf Books
HMSO (1975) *The Sex Discrimination Act* 12 November London: HMSO
Hoch, P. (1979) *White Hero, Black Beast: Racism, Sexism and the Mask of Masculinity* London: Pluto Press
Hoey, K. (1997) Keynote speech at the Inaugural FA Coaches Association Coaches Conference Birmingham
Hoggart, Richard (1957) *The Uses of Literacy: Aspects of Working Class Life, with Special Reference to Publications and Entertainments* London: Chatto and Windus
Holmlund, Chris (2001) *Impossible Bodies: Femininity and Masculinity at the Movies* London: Routledge
Holt, R. (1989) *Sport and the British: A Modern History* Oxford: Oxford University Press
Holt, R. and Mason, T. (2000) *Sport in Britain 1945–2000* London: Blackwell
hooks, bell (1994) *Outlaw Culture: Resisting Representations* New York; London: Routledge
Hornby, N. (1992) *Fever Pitch: A Fan's Life* London: Gollancz
Houlihan, B. (1991) *The Government and Politics of Sport* London: Routledge
Howell, M.L. and Howell, R. (1979) 'Physical Activities and Sport in Early Societies' in E. Zeigler *History of Physical Education and Sport* Englewood Cliffs, NJ: Prentice Hall
Howkins, A. and Lowerson, J. (1979) *Trends in Leisure 1919–1939* London: Sports Council; Social Science Research Council
Huizinga, J. (1970) *Homo Ludens: A Study of the Play Element in Culture* London: Paladin
Hulton Getty Picture Collection (2000) *Marks and Spencer's versus Invicta's at Queens Mead in Bromley Kent 8 June 1933*
Hutchins, P.G. (1990) *Football and the North East* Unpublished Ph.D. Thesis University of Sussex June
International Olympic Committee (1998) *Women in the Olympic Movement* Lausanne: IOC

International Olympic Committee (2000a) *2nd IOC Conference on Women and Sport: New Perspectives for the XXI Century* 6 March

International Olympic Committee (2000b) *The Promotion of Women in the Olympic Movement* Lausanne: IOC Department of International Co-operation February

Jardine, C. (1992) 'The Boot's on the Other Foot' *Telegraph Magazine* 23 February

Jarvie, G. (1993) 'Sport, Nationalism and Cultural Identity' in L. Allison *The Changing Politics of Sport* Manchester: Manchester University Press

Johansson, S. (1976) '"Herstory" as History: A New Field or Another Fad?' in B. Carroll *Liberating Women's History* Illinois: Illinois University Press

Johnson, R. (1983) *What is Cultural Studies Anyway?* Birmingham: University of Birmingham Press

Jones, D. (1999) 'The Beautiful, Deadly Game' *Guardian* 6 November

Keating, F. (1977) 'Bridge of Thighs' *Guardian* 16 May

Kerzabi, N. (1998a) 'Muslim Women and Sport' unpublished paper, Institute des Sports Oran, Algeria, 10 May

Kerzabi, N. (1998b) 'Women, Sport and the Veil' unpublished paper *2nd International Women and Sport Conference*, Namibia 23 May

Kgathi, S. (1997) 'Women and Leisure in Botswana', *Proceedings of the 1st African Regional Conference on Physical Education, Recreation and Dance*, Botswana

Kick it Out (1999) promotional material distributed by the Football Supporters' Association

King, Josephine (1999) 'Women Sports Leaders: Issues and Strategies' *2nd FIFA Women's Symposium*, Los Angeles

Klein, A. (1993) *Little Big Men: Bodybuilding Subculture and Gender Construction* Albany: State University of New York Press

Koppelman, A. (1994) 'Why Discrimination against Lesbians and Gay Men is Sex Discrimination' *New York University Law Review* Vol. 69 No. 2 pp. 197–287

Korr, C. (1986) *West Ham United: The Making of a Football Club* London: Duckworth

Kristeva, Julia (1980) *Desire in Language: A Semiotic Approach to Literature and Art* (ed. Leon S. Roudiez, trans. Thomas Gora, Alice Jardine and Leon S. Roudiez) Oxford: Blackwell

'Lambert's Celebrate 50th' (1975) *Pawtucket Times* 18 November

Lanfranchi, P. and Taylor, M. (2001) *Moving with the Ball* Oxford: Berg

Les Mirrior Des Sports Paris weekly editions 1919–21

Leslie, J. and Burgoyne, P. (1998) *FC Football Graphics* London: Thames and Hudson

Lightbown, C. (1990) 'Invincible Belles' *Sunday Times Sport* 29 April

Lomas, J. (1983) 'Skills and Skirts' West Notts and Derbyshire Recorder 29 September

Lopez, S. (1979) 'An Investigation of Reasons for Participation in Women's Football' *Bulletin of Physical Education* 15

Lopez, S. (1997) *Women on the Ball* London: Scarlet

Lorber, J. (1994) *Paradoxes of Gender* Newhaven; London: Yale University Press

Lummis, Trevor (1998) 'Structure and Validity in Oral Evidence' in Robert Perks and Alistair Thomson (eds) *The Oral History Reader* London: Routledge pp. 274–7

Luschen, G. (1970) *Cross Cultural Analysis of Sport and Games* Champaign, Ill: Stipes Publishing

McKibbin, R. (1990) *The Ideologies of Class: Social Relations in Britain, 1880–1950* Oxford: Clarendon Press

Manchester Guardian (1895) Unnamed article *Manchester Guardian* 24 March

Mangan, J.A. (1981) *Athleticism in the Victorian and Edwardian Public School* Cambridge: Cambridge University Press

Mangan, J.A. and Parks, R. (1987) *From 'Fair Sex' to Feminism: Sport and the Socialization of Women in the Industrial and Post-Industrial Eras* London: Frank Cass

Marunda, J. (1998) 'Report of the Midwife and Aerobics Co-ordinator East Region Manicaland' *2nd World Conference on Women and Sport*, Namibia, 23 May

Mason, T. (1981) *Association Football and English Society 1863–1915* Brighton: Harvester

Mason, T. (1988) *Sport in Britain* London: Faber and Faber

Mason, T. (1989) *Sport in Britain: A Social History* Cambridge: Cambridge University Press

Melling, A. (1998a) 'Cultural Differentiation, Shared Aspiration: The Entente Cordirale of International Ladies' Football 1920–45' *The European Sports History Review* Vol. 1 pp. 67–99

Melling, A. (1998b) ' "Ray of the Rovers": The Working Class Heroine in Popular Football Fiction 1915–25' *The International Journal of the History of Sport* Vol. 15 No. 1 pp. 97–122 April

Melling, A. (1999) *Ladies' Football: Gender and the Socialisation of Women Football Players in Lancashire 1926–1960* Unpublished Ph.D. Thesis University of Central Lancashire November

Melling, A. (2001) 'Charging Amazons and Fair Invaders: The Dick Kerr's Ladies Soccer Tour of North America of 1922 – Sowing Seed' *European Sports History Review* Vol. 3 pp. 27–37 Spring

Melling, A. (2002) 'Women and Football' in Cox, R., Russell, D. and Vamplew, W. (eds) *Encyclopaedia of British Football* London; Oregon: Frank Cass

Messing, M. (1999) <http://www.womensoccer.com/wwcup99/wwcinterviews.html> Accessed 9 October

Messner, M. and Sabo, D. (1990) *Sport Men and then Gender Order: Critical Feminist Perspectives* Champaign, Ill: Human Kinetics

Miller, D. (1987) *A Survey of English Women's Football Clubs* Unpublished MA dissertation California State University

Miller Lite (1993) *Report on Sports and Fitness in the Lives of Working Women, in Cupertino with Women's Sports Foundation, East Meadow NJ and Working Woman Magazine*, New York, NY

Morgan, J. (1977) 'You Can Call Me a Ladies' Man' *Daily Express* 16 November

'Mr. Len Bridgett' (1955) *Stoke Evening Sentinel* 22 January

Murphy, P. Williams, J. and Dunning, E. (1990) *Football on Trial: Spectator Violence and Development in the Football World* London: Routledge

Myotin, E. (1996) *Sports Socialisation of 11–20 year old Brazilian Girls in the 1990s: A Social Psychological Study* Unpublished Ph.D. Thesis University of Loughborough

Nandi-Ndaitwah, N. (1998) 'Launch of African Women and Sport' *2nd World Conference on Women and Sport*, Namibia, 23 May

Negra, D. (2001) *Off-White Hollywood: American Culture and Ethnic Female Stardom* London: Routledge

Nekaya, J. (1996) 'The Amazons' *The Namibian* 29 March

Nelson, M.B. (1996) *The Stronger Women Get, The More Men Love Football: Sexism and the Culture of Sport* London: Women's Press

Newsham, G. (1994) *In a League of Their Own!* Chorley: Pride of Place

Newsham, G. (1998) *In a League of Their Own* London: Scarlet
Newsham, G. (2001) scrapbook of Alfred Frankland, the scrapbook and memorabilia of Joan Whalley, Lily Parr's boots, personal memorabilia
O'Neill, J. (1999) 'Awards Night Indicates a Growing Respect' *The Times* 3 December
Office for National Statistics (2001) *Social Trends No. 31* London: ONS
Office for National Statistics (2002) *Social Trends No. 32* London: ONS
Office for National Statistics Social Survey Division (1996) *Living in Britain: Preliminary results from the 1995 General Household Survey* London: Stationery Office
Osterhoudt, R. (1973) *The Philosophy of Sport: A Collection of Original Essays*, Springfield, Ill: Thomas
Palzkill, B. (1992) 'Between Gym Shoes and High Heels – The Development of a Lesbian Identity and Existence in Top Class Sport' *International Review for the Sociology of Sport* Issue 24 No. 3 pp. 221–33
Pannick, D. (1981) 'How the FA Kicks Girl Footballers off the Park' *Guardian* 16 November
Pannick, D. (1983) *Sex Discrimination in Sport* London: Equal Opportunities
Parillo, B. (1999) 'Women's World Cup 1999' *Providence Journal* 10 May
Passerini, L. (1992) *Memory and Totalitarianism: International Yearbook of Oral History and Life Stories* Vol.1 Oxford: Oxford University Press
Perks, R. and Thomson, A. (1998) *The Oral History Reader* London: Routledge
Pauw, V. (1999) 'From Wishful Thinking to Development Policy' *2nd FIFA Women's Symposium* Los Angeles
Penner, M. (1999) 'Bare Facts Make These Two Heroes' *Los Angeles Times* 11 July p. D1
Perriman, A. (1982) 'Girl Not Entitled to Play in Boys' Football Team', *The Times* 18 June
Pfister, G. et al. (1998) 'Women and Football – A Contradiction? The Beginnings of Women's Football in Four European Countries' *The European Sports History Review* Vol. 1 pp. 122–35
Polley, M. (1998) *Moving the Goal Posts: A History of Sport and Society Since 1945* London: Routledge
Portelli, A. (1981) 'The Peculiarities of Oral History' *History Workshop Journal* Vol. 12 Autumn pp. 96–107
Powell, J. (1996) 'Sorry Ladies, You Can't Win a Man's Game' *Daily Mail* 30 January
Pronger, B. (1999) 'Outta My Endzone: Sport and the Territorial Anus' *Journal of Sport and Social Issues* Vol. 3 Issue 4 pp. 373–90
Redhead, S. (1993) *The Passion and The Fashion: Football Fandom in the New Europe* Aldershot: Avebury
Redhead, S. (1997) *Post Fandom and the Millennial Blues: The Transformation of Soccer Attire* London: Routledge
Reilly, T. (2001) 'Physiology and the Female Football Player' *Insight: The FA Coaches Association Journal* Issue 3 Vol. 4 pp. 26–9 Summer
Richards, J. (2001) 'Our Kelly' *Total Football Magazine* July
Richards, J. and Sandland R. (2000) *Feminist Perspectives on Law and Theory* London: Cavendish
Rimati, M. (1999) *Women's Soccer World* Alabama March/April
Roberts, E. (1984) *A Woman's Place: An Oral History of Working Class Women 1890–1940* Oxford: Blackwell

Rollinson S. (2001) scrapbooks from 1978–1992, photographs and newspapers cuttings including Ley's Ladies team, WFA Newsletters 1978–1992

Rossi, A. (1970) *Essays on Sex Equality* Chicago; London: University of Chicago Press

Rothberg, A. (1999) <http://www.womensoccer.com/wwcup99/wwcinterviews.html> 8 October

Rowe, N. and Champion, R. (2000) *Young People and Sport National Survey 1999* London: Sport England Research

Roxxie (1998) *Girljock: The Book* New York: St Martin's Press

Rudd, A. (1998) *Astroturf Blonde (It's a Man's Game – Sometimes)* London: Headline

Rudd, A. (1999) *Astroturf Blonde: Up Front and Onside in a Man's Game* London: Headline

Russell, D. (1997) *Football and the English: A Social History of Association Football in England, 1863–1995* Preston: Carnegie

Scraton, S. (1986) 'Images of Femininity and the Teaching of Girls' Physical Education' in J. Evans (ed.) *Physical Education, Sport and Schooling: Studies in the Sociology of Physical Education* London: Falmer

Scraton, S. (1992) *Shaping up to Womanhood: Gender and Girls' Physical Education* Buckingham: Open University Press

Scraton, S. and Flintoff, A. (2002) *Gender and Sport: A Reader* London: Routledge

Seabrook, J. (1988) *The Leisure Society* Oxford: Basil Blackwell

Sex Discrimination Act (1975) London: HMSO

Silverstone, R. and Ward, A. (1980) *Careers of Professional Women* London: Croom Helm

Smith, R. (1981) 'Women and Occupational Elites: The Case of Newspaper Journalism in England' in C. Fuchs Epstein and R. Laub *Access to Power: Cross-National Studies of Women and Elites* London: Allen and Unwin

Soccer Line (1994) *National Soccer Survey* Florida: Soccer Industry Council of America

Sondheimer, J. and Bodington, P.R. (eds) (1972) *The Girls' Public Day School Trust, 1872–1972: A Centenary Review* London: Girls' Public Day School Trust

Sports Council (England) (1992) *Allied Dunbar National Fitness Survey: Summary of the Major Findings and Messages* London: Sports Council and Health Education Authority

Stearn, T. (1987) 'Report on the Future Development of the WFA and The New Regional Set Up' *WFA News* January

Steffan, M. (2000) 'Financing Women's Sports in Third Millennium' *2nd IOC Conference on Women and Sport: New Perspectives for the XXI Century* 6 March

Stewart, K. (1988) 'Nostalgia – A Polemic' *Cultural Anthropology* Vol. 3 No. 3

Stoke Evening Sentinel (1976) 'They were the champions' *Stoke Evening Sentinel*

Stops, Sue (1992) *Dulci Dando* (illustrated by Gliori Debi) London: Hippo

Sugden, J. and Tomlinson, A. (1998) *FIFA and the Contest for World Football: Who Rules the People's Game?* Cambridge: Polity Press

'Survivor Recalls Famous Team' (1992) *Stoke Evening Sentinel* 18 April

Talbot, M. (1998) 'The Role of Non-Governmental Organisations for Women and Sport' *Proceedings of the 2nd World Conference on Women and Sport*, Namibia 23 May

Talbot, M. (2000) 'Gendering the Sport Agenda in Sport Decision Making' *European Women and Sport Conference* Helsinki 6–8 July

Talbot, Margaret (1998) 'Women and Sport Partnership with Education' *3rd European Conference of Women and Sport* Athens 24 September

Taylor, M. (1997) *'Proud Preston': A History of the Football League 1900–1939* Unpublished Ph.D. Thesis De Montfort University November

Taylor, P. (1990) *The Hillsborough Stadium Disaster (15 April 1989), Final Report* London: HMSO

'Team of the Twenties' (1989) *Coventry Evening Telegraph* 20 November

'The Football Playing Women: A Most Unsuitable Game' (1921) SFA press cutting, 6 December

'They Were The Champions' (1976) *Stoke Evening Sentinel* 12 March

Thom, B. (1981) 'Women in International Organisations: Room at the Top' in Epstein, C.F. and Coser, R.L. (eds) *Access to Power: Cross-National Studies of Women and Elites* London: Allen and Unwin

Thompson, E.P. (1967) 'Time, Work, Discipline and Industrial Capital' *Past and Present* No. 38 Vol. 38 pp. 56–97

Thompson, P. (2000) *The Voice Of The Past: Oral History* 3rd edn Oxford: Oxford University Press

Thomson, Nancy (2000) Transcript of interview provided by kind permission of the Ruth Shuttleworth SFA Archive

Tischler, M. (1981) *Footballers and Businessmen: The Origins of Professional Football in England* New York: Homes and Meyer

Tomlinson, A. (1991) 'North and South: The Rivalry of the Football League and the Football Association' in John Williams and Stephen Wagg (eds) *British Football and Social Change: Getting into Europe* Leicester: Leicester University Press

Tomlinson, A. (1999) *The Game's Up: Essays in the Cultural Analysis of Sport, Leisure and Popular Culture (Arena 15)* Aldershot: Ashgate

Tomlinson, A. and Sugden, J. (1994) *Hosts and Champions: Soccer Cultures, National Identities and the USA World Cup* Aldershot: Arena

Tuan, Y. (1974) *Topophilia* Englewood Cliffs: Prentice Hall

Unknown producer (1960) *Garden Party and Pensioners' Picnic 1960* The North West Film Archive, Manchester: Metropolitan University, accession number 1228

Unknown producer (1950) *Haslingdon Carnival 9 September 1950* The North West Film Archive, Manchester: Metropolitan University, accession number 578

Vienna Declaration of Action (1993) adopted by the World Conference on Human Rights Vienna 25 June

Viner, K. (1997) 'Sidelined' *Guardian* 21 January

Voluntary Service Overseas (1997a) Job description reference NA 99/2 Voluntary Service Overseas

Voluntary Service Overseas (1997b) *New Services Unit* Issue 3, Sport

Wagg, Stephen (1984) *The Football World: A Contemporary Social History* Brighton: Harvester

Walker, Alison *et al.* (*c.* 2001) *Living in Britain: Results from the 2000 General Household Survey* London: HMSO

Walvin, J. (1978) *Leisure and Society 1830–1950* London: Longman

Walvin, J. (1986) *Football and the Decline of Britain* Basingstoke: Macmillan

Walvin, J. (1994) *The People's Game: The History of Football Revisited* 2nd edn Edinburgh; London: Mainstream Publishing Co.

Weber, Chloe (1999) *Mia Hamm Rocks!* Welcome: Rain Publishing

WFA Newsletters 1972–88
WFA of Nepal Leaflet, (2000) Finland, 5 July
Williams, J. and Woodhouse, J. (1991) 'Women and Football in Britain' in John Williams and Stephen Wagg *British Football and Social Change: Getting into Europe* Leicester: Leicester University Press
Williams, R. (1983) *Towards 2000* London: Chatto and Windus
Williamson, D. (1991) *The Belles of the Ball* Devon: R & D Associates
Wilson Report (1988) *Moms, Dads, Daughters, and Sports* New York, NY: Wilson Sporting Goods Co. in cooperation with The Women's Sports Foundation
Wishart, R. (1984) 'Woman on the Wing with a Prayer of Stardom' *Saturday Post* 8 December
'Women's Football' *Goal* May 1968, June 1969 and August 1973
Women's Football Association (1992) *Newsletter*, July
Women's Football Association (*c*. 1992) *WFA News* Action Replay Fusion Creative Products Ltd
Women's Soccer World (1999) *Women's Soccer World* Vol. 3 No. 3 August Editorial and letters page
Women's Sports Foundation (1989) *Minorities in Sports: The Effect of Varsity Sports Participation on the Social, Educational and Career Mobility of Minority Students* New York: WSF
Women's World Cup Los Angeles (1999) *Official Programme* and promotional material
Woodhouse, D. (2001) *The Post War Development of Football for Females: A Cross Cultural and Comparative Study of England, the USA and Norway* Unpublished Ph.D. Thesis University of Leicester October
Woodhouse, J. (1991) *A National Survey of Female Football Fans* Leicester: University of Leicester
X25 Partnership Report (1998) *Top sports programmes week ending March 8*, p. 2
Yemm, P. (1997) *Women's Soccer Trials in Keetmanshoop: Report for the Ministry of Youth and Sport, Republic of Namibia* Unpublished paper 24 June
Zeigler, E. (1990) *Sport and Physical Education: Past, Present, Future* Illinois: Stripes
Zeigler, M. (2001) 'Revolutionary Spirit' *San Diego Union Tribune* 21 April

Useful websites

http://www.eoc.org.uk/html/publications
http://kellysmithsoccer.com
http://www/rsssf.com/women (Recreational Sport Soccer Statistics Foundation)
http://www.womensoccer.com
http://wusaleague.com
www.caaws.com (Canadian Association for the Advancement of Women and Sport)
www.fifa.com/committees
www.wnba.com/basics/uni (Women's National Basketball Association)
www.womensportfoundation.org/issues (US Women's Sports Foundation)
www.womenssoccer.com (*Women's Soccer* magazine)
www.wusa.com/new (Women's United Soccer Association)

Index